THE WINONA LADUKE

Chronicles

THE WINONA LADUKE
Chronicles

STORIES FROM THE FRONT LINES
IN THE BATTLE FOR ENVIRONMENTAL JUSTICE

by Winona LaDuke

Edited by Sean Aaron Cruz

SPOTTED
HORSE
PRESS

Fernwood Publishing
Halifax & Winnipeg

Edited by Sean Aaron Cruz.
Cover Photo by Sean Aaron Cruz:
Heavy Haul equipment meets its fate on its way to the Tar Sands, Niimiipu Territory
Years of work, covering untold thousands of miles of travel in all sorts of weather, all led up to this moment, Winona standing up in front of the Beast, deep in Nez Perce country, an hour or so after meeting with the tribal council, and then she reached out her hands.... Two guards were watching us, but they didn't tell her not to touch the truck....
— Sean Aaron Cruz

I would like to acknowledge the Kindle Project (kindleproject.org) for supporting my writing time for this book. I am grateful. — *Winona*

Book layout and design by Kevin Brown, Smart Set, Inc. [smartset.com]
Photos © 2015 Keri Pickett, Sarah Little Red Feather and John Ratzloff

Published by SPOTTED HORSE PRESS
31446 East Round Lake Road, Ponsford, MN 56575
www.winonaladuke.com
and FERNWOOD PUBLISHING
32 Oceanvista Lane, Black Point, Nova Scotia, B0J 1B0
and 748 Broadway Avenue, Winnipeg, Manitoba, R3G 0X3
www.fernwoodpublishing.ca

Printed in Canada

Fernwood Publishing Company Limited gratefully acknowledges the financial support of the Government of Canada through the Canada Book Fund, the Canada Council for the Arts, the Province of Nova Scotia and the Province of Manitoba for our publishing program.

   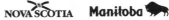

Library and Archives Canada Cataloguing in Publication

LaDuke, Winona, author
The Winona LaDuke chronicles : stories from the front lines in the battle for environmental justice / Winona Laduke.

Co-published by Spotted Horse Press.
Issued in print and electronic formats.
ISBN 978-1-55266-959-4 (softcover).–ISBN 978-1-55266-960-0 (EPUB).–ISBN 978-1-55266-961-7 (Kindle)

1. LaDuke, Winona–Literary collections. 2. LaDuke, Winona–Political activity. 3. Environmental justice–United States. 4. Ojibwa women–Politics and government. 5. Indigenous peoples–Ecology–United States. 6. Indians of North America–Land tenure. 7. Indians of North America–Government relations. I. Title.

E99C6.L236 2017   973.0497'0092   C2016-908069-2
C2016-908070-6

Table of Contents

WRITINGS ON WOMEN, IDLE NO MORE AND CANADIAN COLONIALISM

BLACK SNAKE AND THE PIPELINE CHRONICLES: NORTHERN GATEWAY, KEYSTONE AND THE ENBRIDGE GREAT LAKES LINES

ON FOODS

TRIBUTES AND GRATITUDE
TO THOSE WHO HAVE JOINED THE ANCESTORS

GERONIMO, MILITARIZATION AND THE INDIAN WARS

ECONOMICS FOR THE SEVENTH GENERATION

ACKNOWLEDGEMENTS

I have now more winters behind me than before me. It has been a grand journey. I am grateful for the many miles, rivers, places and people of beauty. Through it all, I have a family which has been with me on many travels and has relinquished me to the larger world at other times. I dedicate this writing to them: my children Waseyabin, Ashley, Jonny, Ajuawak, Will and Gwekaanimad and to my mother Betty LaDuke, who remains a constant inspiration to me. To you, I offer these words and explanation.

Introduction

AFTER THE BURN...

What we know is that, after the fields, the forest floor, and the prairies are burned, new growth comes. There is new life. That is what happens after the burn. That is this book.

In November of 2008, my home burned. This happens. This happened to our family, and our family consisted of myself and eight dependents under 20 years of age. My community, and many people who I did not know and had never seen came to support us. People sent clothing, blankets, books, money, prayers and love. Solar Energy International gave our family a solar photovoltaic system. Many, many people helped us. Women sent me jewelry and old beadwork. People told me that they loved me and respected my family and myself. Someone even sent me a navy blue bra from Victoria's Secret which fit nicely. That was funny. That's what I will say. And I am tremendously grateful. We are all grateful, this family of mine.

It is seven years later. In the interim, many days, I could not write. Many nights I could not sleep. Many days I could not remember what day it was, and amidst it all, I had many losses. I lost those who I loved the most: my father, the father of my children, and my sister. I continued to spin in despair and, frankly, had a hard time breathing and getting a grip. I became a casualty of the PTSD of the modern Indian Wars…. And in my spin, I lost my love, my heart, and some of my closest friends. Sort of the rock-bottom thing.

Yet, amidst all of this, it seems that one must go on. I found solace in writing, when it came back, and found myself more in love with the words, and with the story. In a way I began a new life as a modern day bard... someone who is able to travel across the land and share stories from other lands.

And, then I began to rebuild. I built a home for my family; a home almost completely of salvage and from Craig's List, and I became a bit of a Craig's List junkie. It's worked out pretty well. And one day it will be done, and perfect. Maybe. But through it all, the stories carried me. They became my escape from my depression, from my fears, and they became the way to help others, maybe.

I also began to write for Forum Communications, which is a very large regional news service in our territory, and this opened a new genre, the short story, written for those who, well, let us say, have never had these discussions. This is some of this writing. Other stories are the long form—my favorite form of journalism—and one which is lacking in most media today, but is the only way to tell a story often, moving backwards and forwards between history and present, characters dead, and those yet to come. It is a love of the word. That is this gift to the reader, I hope.

So, having said all of this, I hope you understand and accept my apologies if I cannot remember something, or you. For those who choose to read this writing...is that in the traumatic stress which I have suffered during these past years, I could not remember what I wrote, and sometimes I could not remember what I did , and I sometimes do not remember people. This is not uncommon. So it is that, I decided to look at myself, look at my writing and look through my computers to see if I could remember my journey. That is this book. It is a chronicle of my past years of writing, and it is a thanksgiving to all of those who supported our family. It is a recognition that your mind returns and so does your heart. Love returns. It is also a tribute to our ability to recover and be reborn after the burn.

Winona LaDuke
August 12, 2015

On Place

I have wandered this world. That is what I am able to do. In that, there are many stories to be told and shared. In my favorite form, the long form of writing, I attempt to share these stories. Here are some.

AKIING BIIBOONONG

As I came to write and read these stories (and this I had hoped to do from some other place on this land), yet, my land did not wish to let me go. That is all I know. The deepest of colds had come to *Anishinaabe Akiing*, carried by *Giiwedinong*, the most daunting of winds, that from the North.

A ground blizzard removed the world all around on any road, and to leave would be impossible. So we retreated, back to our lake, to our woods. We retreated and returned to our plans for approaching the world, our plans to approach, and our plans to send back to where they had come from, the forces of the Monsters.

I was trying to leave my land for another world, for another place and all I knew was this, that the land calls us, it calls us home, and it makes us to be the People who our ancestors wish us to be.

We are Thunder Beings, Wolves, Eagles of War, Feathered Heroes, Spirits which Stand in the Middle, Those who Fly Upward, Star Beings, and Those who Shift the Wind.

That is who we are, our Names, our Clans, of Bear, Caribou, Sturgeon and Wolf. All of this ties us to this place and we know only that. We know that because it comes from a Place, it comes from a Story and we tell all of that.

We watched the Others from our place. They came towards us with mining picks in hand, carrying buckets to take our water and saws for our trees. They came singularly, tentatively in ships, and then they came in more and many more. They come, they take and then they retreat. And then they return to take again. We remain. Those who are told of here are those who have remained.

Our world exists only on one plane, for the others are occupied by Beings in the deep, *Ishpeming* the sky world and in worlds unseen. It is readily apparent to us how our worlds would exist in—it is told— eight different worlds.

One must only look at our *Anishinaabe Akiing*, the land to which the People belong, from the eye of a Thunderbeing or an Eagle. There are lakes, rivers and land. The land is surrounded, undulating between the water bodies and the Water Beings. And the sky is endless, full of mystery and—we hope—full of mercy.

This we know. And this is what we live. The stories and people of this book are the People of this land. I have been blessed to know many of them and—to me—in the midst of this, is this question of how it is that we are *Anishinaabeg, Potawatami, Odawa, Ho-Chunk*, in this world of jackhammer noise which surrounds us, the constant din, the loss of Beings and Memories, the ecological, spiritual and cultural amnesia which can be so contagious.

We live as these beings because we are from one of the most powerful places in the world, where Earth, Sky and Water are a constant, underlain with Spirit Beings and copper, food which grows on the water, and a language which places us here and no where else.

We live because our Ancient Beings, the *gete Anishinaabeg* or our ancestral Beings shine in lights in the forest or torches in the lake, and they come to us, in this plane, the one which is in the Middle between the Eight.

This is the plane of Anishinaabeg, and those of us who are indigenous in the present.

This is the plane of the stories of Heroic Beings in this book, stories well told.

MADELINE ISLAND:
RESTORING A MULTICULTURAL SOCIETY IN A SACRED PLACE

"Originally all the inhabitants of the earth (Chippewa Indians) who were to learn the Mide lived on Madeline Island, in Lake Superior, in that portion of the country. They were selected by the divine Manido *to be taught the* Mide *religion…"*

— FROM THE ORIGIN OF THE *MIDE*,
AS DOCUMENTED IN THE 1905 COMPENDIUM
OF ORAL OJIBWE TRADITION: *NAWAJIBIKOKWE*

It was like reading about Atlantis, about the legend of an ancient place. That is my earliest memory of the Island, *Moningwunakauning Minis*— home of the golden-breasted woodpecker—now called Madeline. It is the *Anishinaabe* homeland, and it is a Mecca for the Ojibwe, a sacred place.

This is the place where the Creator and the prophets instructed our people to move to, and to remain. Now, in the 21st century, Madeline Island is a place where the complexity of restoring a multicultural society in a sacred land is being revealed.

The question is, "How do we do so with grace?"

Akawe: In the Beginning

Long ago, during the time of prophecy, the Anishinaabeg were told to follow the *Migis* shell which appeared in the sky, and from our eastern homeland, along the great water, we would stop seven times, ending finally at Moningwunakaauning Minis.

It is here on this island that we flourished and spread our wings as Anishinaabe people. Moningwunakaauning Minis served as the southern capitol of the Anishinaabe nation, which now stretches across what are four American states and three Canadian provinces.

Moningwunakaauning Minis became a center of our *Midewewin* Society, our powerful religion which connects us to the four layers beneath the Earth and the four layers above. It is here on Madeline Island that we refined our lacrosse game, and where the Anishinaabe women perfected our game of *shinny*, a sort of Ojibwe broomball.

It is from here that we launched our fishing boats, collected berries on the many surrounding islands and the Ojibwe became the largest inland naval force in North America, dominating the Great Lakes region with trade, agriculture and fishing.

We lived on the Island unmolested for 300 years before we were "found" by some European immigrants. The French "found" us, and—as European empires do—they built themselves a fort, and a mission. Gotta have a fort and a mission. That was in 1693, and the fort was and is called La Pointe.

Our treaties with the Euro-American immigrants were signed at La Pointe, allowing access to the Great Lakes for miners, loggers and settlement. It was cheaper for the fledgling United States to treaty for land than to fight wars. The western Indian wars were to cost the United States millions of dollars. Treaties were the answer to the uniquely Euro-American problem of how to steal Indian land and displace entire communities at the least cost.

An Indian agent at La Pointe once calculated that millions of acres of Ojibwe territory were acquired through treaties for less than 10 cents an acre. The value of the fisheries, maple syrup, wild rice, agriculture and fur harvested from our treaty lands is incalculable. The copper taken from our homelands alone was worth $5.72 billion based on 1971 markets.

Wanishiniwag: They Disappear

Four treaties were signed by the United States with the Ojibwe, each providing for mining in Anishinaabeg territory. These treaties, signed in 1837, 1842, 1854 and 1855, covered both Michigan's Keweenaw Peninsula and the vast *Mesabi* (Sleeping Giant) iron ore belt in northern Minnesota.

As early as 1849, copper production in the Keweenaw Peninsula of Anishinaabe territory led the world. Similarly—beginning in 1890—mining in the Mesabi Range accounted for 75 percent of all U.S. iron ore production.

Greed is an amazing driving force in the history of America. Not content to steal our wealth, some decided to steal our lives. In 1850 and 1851, four prominent officials of President Zachary Taylor's administration conspired to force the Anishinaabeg onto lands in Minnesota Territory. In 1850, while our ancestors gathered to collect their treaty payments, the Indian agents moved the meeting place from Madeline Island to Sandy Lake, in present day Minnesota.

Four thousand Ojibwe canoed to Sandy Lake that autumn. They arrived on the payment date, fatigued and hungry, only to find no one there to distribute the supplies. Wild game was scarce, fishing was poor and high water had wiped out the wild rice crop. Ill-equipped and confined to a waterlogged area, disease, exposure and starvation ravaged the Ojibwe, killing three to eight people each day.

In early December, with over a foot of snow on the ground and the waterways frozen over, the Ojibwe finally received their annuities. With 170 people already dead, they started on the bitter trail back towards our land here at *Gichi Gummi*, the Great Lake, now known as Superior. Another 230 people died on that frigid journey, later called the Wisconsin Death March or the Sandy Lake Tragedy.

Those who survived returned to our homelands. The sudden death of President Zachary Taylor on July 9, 1850, however, put Vice President Millard Fillmore into the White House, and the public outcry following the Death March forced the suspension of the removal order. The Ojibwe were allowed to remain in portions of our homelands, but President Fillmore opened the territory wide to settlement and exploitation.

Wanishin: Lost

After the Sandy Lake Tragedy, the Ojibwe were forced to moved to reservations throughout the region, but we never forgot our place. The Ojibwe word for reservation is *ishkonjigan*, or "leftovers." It is not a homeland. The reservation era was the beginning of an immense trauma for the Anishinaabeg, and for tribes across North America.

We were forced to move away from our beloved Madeline Island, from our sacred places. Edith Leoso, the Tribal Historic Preservation Officer for the Bad River band of Ojibwe, remembers what is told about Moningwunakaauning Minis:

"We left that island with the understanding that we would never hold lodge there again." Eddie Benton of the Three Fires *Midewiwin* Society said, talking about how the old people who had to leave built this huge bonfire: "...and then we left. They say that when we got to Bad River we could still see the fire. We wanted to remember where our homeland was at, so that when we did ceremonies, we would always know this... that fire, it was also a part of letting go. Yet knowing our connection. Perhaps it was part of the detachment. To try and forget and cope with the trauma of leaving."

Three decades later, most of Madeline Island was privately held and divided into homesteads. The 1854 treaty, however, guaranteed that the Ojibwe would keep some 200 acres at the north end of the Island; that this place would remain for the People, reserved as our fishing grounds.

The Complexity of Wealth

The wealth expropriated and amassed from our territory would also come to the Madeline Island. In the 19th century, it came to the Island in the form of summer homes for some of the most affluent families of the Great Lakes, many from the same families who had originally created the mining and lumber companies that made their fortunes from our lands.

Ironically, some of the poorest residents of Wisconsin live next to one of the state's wealthiest townships, at least during the summer. To be specific, on the Red Cliff reservation on the mainland, only two and a half miles from the Island, unemployment hovers around 50 percent; 65 percent of the population lives below the poverty level; the median household income is about $8,000 and the estimated per capita income is $1,450.

A new casino named Legendary Waters recently opened on the reservation, bringing some new money and probably some more tourists, but, frankly, it does not change the structure of poverty and wealth.

Jobs remain scarce, and mostly involve building or cleaning homes for those who can afford to live on our Anishinaabe homeland.

There are a dozen or so beach homes built on the small amount of land that was reserved for the Ojibwe as our fishing grounds, 200 acres on the North End.

A real estate listing described the Ojibwe land like this: "Amnicon Beach is widely regarded as the most desirable stretch of lakeshore in the Apostle Islands area. The homes in the Amnicon Bay Association share nearly a mile of Caribbean-like sand beach frontage facing Michigan Island in the Apostles. Now you can own and enjoy one of the best properties in this choice development."

The Bureau of Indian Affairs first leased these lands out in 1967 as a tribal moneymaking enterprise. Leaseholders formed the Amnicon Bay Association, a private club consisting of 12 or so families.

Those leases expire in 2017, setting up a test of how far attitudes have come where Indian treaty rights and sacred sites coming into conflict with dominant culture interests are concerned. Historically, the dominant culture would just break the treaty and take what they wanted.

The Bad River Tribe has indicated that they will not renew the leases.

Bad River Ojibwe journalist Mary Annette Pember traveled to the north end of Madeline Island in the summer of 2013 to talk to some of the leaseholders of the Amnicon Bay Association. She was surprised to find that one couple, Amy and Harry Funk, bought a home only seven years before the possible end date of their lease in 2017.

"The people in town said we were crazy to buy a cabin out here, [that] the tribe is taking the land back. But if we did something silly, we did something silly. We love it here. This bay is my spiritual renewal and I'll be sorry to lose it if we have to move. But I'm just happy we've had the time that we've had here." –Harry Funk

The Funks feel a relationship to the Island like all others, Mary noted, "The Funks and other cabin owners expressed gratitude and acceptance, albeit reluctantly, about the land and the possibility of it returning to the tribe."

Madeline Island Culture

Separated by the deepest of waters in a great inland sea, it is very possible to believe you are alone on the Island. The world is distant. That is why people come to Madeline Island—for refuge—and that is how an island culture or subculture emerges.

Summer homes and a tourism economy came to dominate. Farming and fishing subsided and the four remaining farms disappeared one by one, until the Island became an importer of almost every sort of food that would be consumed there.

In 1850, 40 residents of the Madeline Island population were Cadottes, a *Métis*, French Canadian and Ojibwe fur trading family. In 2015, around 40 residents of the Island are Nelsons, relatives of enterprising Swedes who own a stake in the Madeline Island Ferry Line, a construction company, acres of land, Tom's Burned Down Café and other points of interest. The year-round residents, numbering maybe 250, are by and large really nice people.

In some ways there were two classes of people who came to the Island, the very wealthy and those who care for and serve them. This does not mean that the Island is not beloved by both, but it does result in interesting land use policy decisions.

The Yacht People and Historical Amnesia

The USA and Canada both suffer from amnesia, from a massive case of historical amnesia regarding their own histories, and most particularly in how they came to acquire the land.

The Ojibwe were not mythical beings, nor were we Phoenicians. We were and are a living community of 250,000 people. We continue to live in our homeland, just not on our beloved Island.

Many of the yacht people forgot about the Ojibwe. This is made evident by the marina of the Madeline Island Yacht Club that adjoins the cemetery where Chief Buffalo, one of our greatest Chiefs, is buried in a modest grave among about 100 other Ojibwes who were allowed to be buried in the Catholic Indian cemetery.

The initial marina was dredged prior to any regulation or oversight. It was an ambitious moment for the Yacht Club when, in 1984, they decided to expand the berths to allow for more yachts. As it turns out, the entire area surrounding the marina is likely full of Ojibwe remains.

Paul DeMain, from the Lac Courte Orielles reservation, points to a place next to a monument erected by the Ojibwe near the marina, and says:

"That was when they ran into the ancestor, an old man in a dugout canoe, right in the middle of the dig...The ancestor was there, and here is where we remember those who left for Sandy Lake." –Paul DeMain

Portions of the island of been included on the list of National Register of Historic Places, but these include a small fraction of the traditional cultural landscape.

A memorandum requiring the Army Corp of Engineers and La Pointe officials to consult tribal elders prior to development projects has also been proposed by the Advisory Council on Historic Preservation (ACHP). This federal designation, from an Ojibwe perspective, will afford more protection for tribal history on the Island.

All of this is unfortunate if you are an ambitious developer. There has been a number of ongoing proposals to expand the marina, each of which has been turned down for a number of reasons. This is, in part, what happens when one culture decides it wants to build on top of another living culture.

Moningwunakauning Minis 4.0

A couple of summers ago, our family built the first residential summer wigwam on the Island in probably 100 years, maybe more. It's called *Giiwedinong*, or The Place We Come Home To.

There was an interesting meeting with the zoning officials one night— all nice people, many of them Nelsons. "I am not sure this complies with the uniform building code," the zoning director, Jennifer Croonberg, earnestly explained to me. I smiled and said, "I believe it precedes the uniform building code."

The wigwam is not built on the tribal land in the far north of the Island, but on the edge of town within bike-riding distance for young kids. That is because we too are a part of the community.

The tribal presence on Madeline Island is growing stronger, and meetings and ceremonial gatherings have been held with increasing frequency on the Island.

This year, for the first time, an Ashland County commissioner was elected from the Bad River reservation, Joe Rose, an elder statesman and professor at nearby Northland College. Rose represents not only the reservation, but also Madeline Island. Change is slow, but it is one thing that is constant.

There are new community gardens on the Island, and there are signs posted now, finally, in *Anishinaabemowin*, put up by settlers and Ojibwe alike. Nick Nelson, recently elected to the town board, in many ways represents a new generation of settler on the island. He led the project to install bilingual signs on the island, and the first of four dozen such signs appeared in April.

"Language is an introduction, a launching point, for protecting and re-establishing an endangered element of La Pointe's past and present," says Nelson. "This project is essentially about using language as a focal point for revealing the regional importance, the beauty and the depth at the center of the Anishinaabeg culture."

La Pointe's project makes Madeline Island the first place in Wisconsin to have bilingual signs not on a Native American reservation.

"For 400 years *Anishinaabemowin* was the primary language spoken throughout the region," Nelson continued. "It seemed essential to honor this significant element of island history."

Not all things are, by any means, yet resolved. The Madeline Island Museum holds a hefty collection of Ojibwe cultural and ceremonial wealth. Ojibwe who visit the museum often feel very sensitive, as if it is a genetic memory of a great loss.

Edith Leoso explained to me: "When I was in the museum, and saw all those parts of our culture, it evoked historic trauma. It's the heart wrenching sadness—sadness of seeing them, and leaving them, those ceremonial items. But when I go to the Island, I also feel really good. I went to the cemetery with my *migis* shell on. I walked into this gate and this huge wind came by. And I wondered when the last time was that a migis was here with our relatives. When I went over there, I didn't want to leave, I wanted to stay there and reconnect."

Why does it matter that the Ojibwe *giiwewag* [are coming home]? Denied a homeland we are without a compass. Where we were forced to live is not the place the Creator has instructed us to live. And that is why *niwii giiwemin* [we are coming home]. The woodpecker waits. She remains there, watching centuries of humans come and go, and she remains. Each time I am present on the Island, I look up and see the golden-breasted woodpecker and I know I am home.

FULL COST ACCOUNTING: THE CHEYENNE, SPIRIT MOUNTAIN, MINNESOTA POWER AND GLENCORE

There is a case to be made for full-cost accounting. That is where you count the costs of pollution against the future benefits of a project, and this calculation is figured into the project analysis, also known as the triple bottom line.

Although I'm trained as an economist, I am not sure how to do it. That is because I cannot account for the spiritual and cultural impacts of everything. I'm not sure that it can be done. Some economists describe this measure as *unquantifiable*.

What is known is this: the proposed Polymet mine is a big project. It is immense. The EIS on the Polymet mine, however, is limited to look at only local impacts just around the proposed Glencore project. The ripple effect of a mine of this size is much larger; it is larger in a physical sense and it is larger in a spiritual sense. I don't know how to put a price tag on it. I only know that I can try and tell a story about a place, about this place, and here it is:

Where the Spirits Dwell

A long time ago, this place was known as The Place where Spirits Dwell. The *Tsisinstsistots* lived here, and remembered it well. Their name means "The People" in their language, and it always did. They remembered well the Great Lake—the greatest of all—and the mountain on the shore. That mountain they remembered as a Spirit Mountain, as the Place where Spirits Dwell.

It was so; but it was so long ago that they no longer spoke Anishinaabeg. They spoke differently. Almost all of the words were completely different, except one I remember… that was *Nako*, meaning bear or mother. The old word in Anishinaabe is *Noka*, for grandmother as well, almost the same in both languages.

Meet the Northern Cheyenne. In their earliest times, they also came to the Spirit Mountain for their sacred teachings. As Phillip White Man, Jr., Northern Cheyenne Chief, Council of 44, explains, "The band of Cheyenne that came from 'The Place where Spirits Dwell' are named *Suhtai* (pronounced Su-tah) meaning 'Buffalo People'." They are Erect Horn's people. He was the prophet that brought the Sacred Buffalo Hat, which the Cheyenne still have today.

The Suhtai traveled to a place known as "Where the Water comes to an End" (near modern day Duluth) where a White Buffalo came out of the water and instructed them to come to this sacred land. Those instructions moved them away from Spirit Mountain and away from their Algonquin-speaking relatives who remained in the place where the food grows on the water.

That was many generations ago. They traveled far to the west, to a homeland in the heart of the Powder River Basin, Rosebud Creek and eastern Montana. That is their chosen land, and they call themselves *Tsisinstsistots*, or Human Beings. They have a right to continue their existence as such.

Their determination and resilience is well known, and continues today. Despite suffering horrific massacres at Sand Creek in 1864 and on the banks of the Washita in November 1868, they survived, only to be incarcerated and made victims of the worst depredations at the hands of the US military and the volunteer vigilante mobs.

In the so-called Cheyenne Campaigns, a people who numbered thousands, with horses to match, were forced to move away from their home lands because of gold and greed. They were forced to relocate south to the Oklahoma Territory. There, they would die.

They decided to live, however, and a band of Northern Cheyenne fled back north in September 1878, under the leadership of Dull Knife and Little Wolf.

The US Army intercepted part of the Northern Cheyenne and forced nearly 150 Cheyenne men, women and children into confinement at Fort Robinson, Nebraska. This is where the Oglallas had been incarcerated when they had surrendered the previous year under the leadership of Crazy Horse. That was their prison until his assassination in May of 1877.

In January of 1879, after the Cheyenne refused to obey orders to return to the south, the soldiers began to treat them more harshly to force them back. The Cheyenne were confined to a barracks without rations or wood for heat. Most of the band escaped.

On January 9, 1879, in one of the most heroic stories of our times, the Cheyenne, led by Chief Dull Knife, fled the inhumane conditions at Fort Robinson to return to their homeland some four hundred miles away.

As Phillip White Man Junior explains, "When they fled they did not run the entire 400 miles immediately. The majority were killed, but the few that did make it (mostly Dull Knife's family) were hid with Red Cloud's Oglalla band. They eventually made it home to Powder River country. Little Wolf's band also made it home."

That is a land they have fought and died for. That is the center of their identity, along with Spirit Mountain. This past January 9, the Cheyenne remembered this escape. They remembered it as they have since 1996, with a run. It is called the Fort Robinson Run and every year, Phillip White Man Jr. and his wife Lynette Two Bulls sponsor this event. It's a relay, and the Northern Cheyenne youth run the 400 miles in the most biting of winds and challenging of times. They do it for their ancestors, and they do it for those yet to come.

Spirit Mountain

In the meantime, the Anishinaabeg remained at the Place where the Spirits Dwell, at Spirit Mountain. Between 1785 and 1923, the US, England and Canada entered into more than 40 treaties with the Anishinaabeg, the bases for some of the largest land transactions in world history.

Some of the first incursions onto Anishinaabeg land were to secure access to iron and copper deposits. These treaties covered both the Keweenaw Peninsula and the Mesabi "Sleeping Giant" iron-ore belt in northern Minnesota.

By mid-century, more than 100 copper companies had been incor-porated in Michigan, Wisconsin and Minnesota Territories. As early as 1849, copper production at Keweenaw Peninsula led the world. Similarly, beginning in 1890, mining at northern Minnesota's Mesabi accounted for 75% of all US iron ore production. Many of today's US-based transnational mining companies were founded in this era, and on expropriating and exploiting the wealth of the Anishinaabeg lands, including, for instance, Kennecott, Anaconda Copper and 3M. Mercantile capitalism at its best....

All's gone on sort of swimmingly for the mining companies, except the decline and bust on the Iron Range. One could say that the mines of the north went into remission. That was until now.

Enter the Dragon, and Glencore

Enter the Dragon, that is, the dragon of world trade agreements and agreements with China, including the Trans Pacific Partnership (TPP), which is on a contentious fast track with the Obama Administra-tion. That partnership will accelerate all of this trans-Pacific trade. And, here on the shores of Lake Superior and in the shadow of Spirit Mountain, we can watch it happen—or not—to our own land.

Meet Glencore International, the $155 billion multi-national corpo-ration that is PolyMet's primary investor and joint venture partner. Glencore owns the rights to all production from the PolyMet sulfide mine and plant for at least the first five years of operations. As a con-dition of its 2013 merger with the Xstrata mining company, Glencore

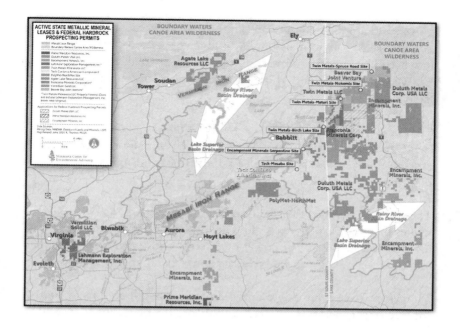

must continue to supply China with copper concentrate for the next eight years.

There is the dragon. In fact, most of what will be produced in the return mining boom to Anishinaabe Akiing, the Great Lakes, will end up in China. And it's going to require a lot of power to get it there, for both transport and extraction. Open pit metals mining, it turns out, is arguably the most energy-intensive and wasteful mining system in the world.

For instance, Polymet estimates the NorthMet Project ore reserve at 694 million tons grading at .074 copper equivalent. This is how that pans out, so to speak. Copper mining is the most inefficient product to produce from a big dig. It takes 1,000,000,000 tons of material to recover 1.6 tons of copper.

That means consuming stupendous amounts of energy. The Department of Energy reports that, "The average copper mine (600-million ton deposit handling 68,493 tons/day) consumes 4,701,000,000 Btu/day in the extraction process. This suggests, according to Colin Cureton at the University of Minnesota, that the NorthMet mine would consume 47.63 trillion btu over the course of its lifetime. That amounts to a lot of power and a lot of coal burned to produce that power, and a polluted landscape left behind, all because Glencore and PolyMet see a way to make money selling copper to China, regardless of what Full Cost Accounting analysis shows the real, true costs to be. We will be stuck with those costs long after PolyMet and Glencore have moved on.

That new energy demand will be met by Minnesota Power, which has the reigning coal–fired monopoly in northern Minnesota, burning coal at its five power plants: Boswell, Laskin, Hibbard, Rapids and Taconite Harbor Energy Center.

These plants installed their first units in the years 1917-1958, which makes them at least 55 years old. One of them is older than my mother, and she's 81. That power goes to the entire region, but the nine largest industrial customers include six mining companies.

Minnesota Power burned up approximately 4.6 million tons of coal for electrical generation in 2012, and there's the matter of some $20 billion spent annually for that coal. Consider the forgone opportunity costs embedded in this system. Consider what could be accomplished if we invested those billions as part of a national strategy to eliminate systemic inefficiencies and build a renewable energy infrastructure.

And that coal comes from the Powder River Basin by train. Minnesota Power will need to move and burn literally mountains of coal to provide btus to the most inefficient mine in Minnesota, plus all the rest of the inefficient mines in or proposed for the system.

This is the story that Full Cost Accounting tells us: Two foreign corporations, however, Polymet—which has never managed a mining project before; and Glencore, whose board chairman is Tony Hayward, the former British Petroleum CEO who was in charge when the Deepwater Horizon oil rig blew up, causing the largest oil spill in history—want us to believe that they know what they are doing and that they can do it well.

So it is that all of this is about to get much worse, that is, if Minnesota Power, Arch Coal, the Tongue River Railroad, Polymet and Glencore get their way.

Last year, Minnesota Power's Vice President, Allen Rudnick Jr wrote a poignant letter to the chairman of the Surface and Transportation Board about a very obscure rail project: the Tongue River Railroad Project. The sole intent is to bring coal to both Minnesota markets and to western ports for export to foreign markets. That project is in Cheyenne territory. So it is that the new residents of the land near Spirit Mountain came back to the Northern Cheyenne.

The Cheyenne Homeland and the Otter Creek Mine

The Northern Cheyenne homeland, a reservation of 225,000 acres, is located in the Powder River Basin, and where there are billions of tons of coal buried under Cheyenne land, and it turns out that the Cheyenne do not want their homeland strip-mined. For the past forty years, the Northern Cheyenne have fought off almost every major coal company in the world to keep their coal.

"Since I was in high school, I've been involved in my tribe's fight to protect our reservation and the environment of southeastern Montana. Gail Small, Director of Native Action tells me. "In the early 1970s, the Cheyenne people heard that our federal trustee, the Bureau of Indian Affairs, had leased over one-half of our reservation to the coal companies for strip mining. The fight was on, and every resource our small tribe had was committed to this battle. I was 21 years old, the youngest on my committee and the only one with a college degree."

That was just the beginning. The Northern Cheyenne fought off the Amax Coal company and led a revolt against illegal mineral leasing by the Bureau of Indian Affairs. It helped, but still, four of the ten largest coal strip mines in the country are on Indian reservations; the Navajo and Crow at the center of it.

The problem is that there is no way back, once the "overburden" of an ecosystem is removed for mining. The National Academy of Sciences reported in 1973, "Surface mining destroys the existing natural communities completely and dramatically. Indeed, the restoration of a landscape disturbed by surface mining...is impossible." This is a big problem if you are on a reservation, as there is no new land.

Tongue River and Arch Coal

Enter Arch Coal. The St. Louis-based company is the second-largest coal supplier in the nation. They want land which is adjacent to the (diminished) Northern Cheyenne reservation, but within their home-lands and allotments. Arch Coal leased the coal from the state of Montana for 86 million dollars up front with future royalties if the mine gets developed. It would be the largest proposed coal mine in the lower 48 states, planned to dig out some 1.3 billion tons of coal.

At hearings, 170 Cheyenne came out to oppose the mine and the railroad.

"We believe our community will bear the brunt of the negative impacts from the Otter Creek mine. Sacrificing the land, water, animal and plant life for mining and money is not worth what our ancestors fought and gave their life," Tom Mexican Cheyenne explained in the testimony. "[We are]...worried about the crime, accidents, drugs and other social issues that come along with boomtowns that our Tribe is not equipped to handle. We are being asked to deal with this so that a transnational corporation can make billions of dollars shipping coal to Asia."

"This destruction you companies call "opportunity" will devastate my homelands that my ancestors fought and died for," Vanessa Braided Hair explained. "I will not stand by and let you Army Corps of En-gineers further destroy and pollute the water, air, land, and future of the Cheyenne people....These coal mines will be built on my family's original homestead. I do not want our country to be the sacrificial lamb for China. Consider alternative energies. Let's go beyond coal, and stop the destruction of Mother Earth," she said.

Arch Coal is pressuring the Cheyenne hard, however, hard, and Min-nesota Power is key in applying the pressure.

In a letter to the Surface and Transportation Board, Allen Rudnick Jr, a Vice President at Minnesota Power, wrote "The Tongue River Rail-road ...is the only viable transportation alternative that would allow access to the significant reserve of Otter Creek.... Minnesota Power urges the Board to seriously consider the positive merits of the Tongue River Rail Road." Rudnick stated that "The rail construction project is the only viable ...alternative ...for the transportation of Otter Creek and Ashland area coal to our facilities."

What is additionally ironic about this is how inefficient and old-school, in the dysfunctional sense, that the whole equation is. Not only is coal the dirtiest of fossil fuels (excepting perhaps tar sands oils), adding significantly to climate change and impacts, but there have been no new coal plants built in the US for three decades.

The Minnesota Power plants are dinosaurs. Coal plant operators are planning to retire 175 coal-fired generators, or 8.5 percent of the total coal-fired capacity in the United States, according to the Energy Information Administration. A record number of 57 generators were shut down in 2012, representing 9 gigawatts of electrical capacity, according to EIA. In 2015, nearly 10 gigawatts of capacity from 61 coal-fired generators will be retired. Massive energy development in PRB coal contributes more than 14% of the total U.S. carbon pollution, and yet, Minnesota Power is still clinging to those plants. The coal from this proposed Otter Creek Mine would release 2.5 billion tons of carbon dioxide into our atmosphere. Basically, they want to blow up a carbon bomb.

So there it is, a story about how a people remember a sacred place, and now are being summoned back, at least their land and homeland, chunk by chunk. None of this will qualify for discussion in a broad Environmental Impact Statement according to federal regulations, but somehow, there is more than meets the eye.

A newly released memorandum in the Environmental Protection Agency where Bob Perciasepe, Deputy Administrator of the EPA, wrote to all regional administrators:

"Treaties are the supreme law of the land, equal in statutes to federal laws under the US Constitution, and the US has the responsibility to honor the rights and resources protected by the treaties. While treaties do not expand the authorities granted by the EPAs underlying statutes, our programs should be implemented to protect treaty covered resources where we have the discretion to do so. "

It would appear that the EPA has a broader scope than it has been taking, with, essentially a very silo like EIS process for the Polymet mine.

In another bureaucracy In early February, the Minnesota Chippewa Tribe admonished the Minnesota Pollution Control Agency for "ecological ignorance", wherein the PCA seems to be trying to re-designate some of the waters where wild rice is found, so that those waters can have diminished water quality.

In short, Chippewa tribal member Norman Deschampe said wrote in a letter to John Linc Stine, Minnesota PCA commissioner: "Waters used for the production of wild rice…must remain on the wild rice waters lists for regulatory purposes. They cannot be pulled off and dropped instead onto the proposed watch list, in effect delisting them as class 4 status of the state with the stroke of a pen."

So it seems like the state of Minnesota might have been trying to pull a fast one on the tribes and it doesn't look like it worked. The MCT leadership has pointed out that this sort of regulatory scheme would violate federal law, namely the Clean Water Act… sort of a big one. Besides, that, wild rice is the only grain specifically protected in treaty.

So the papers move back and forth, between the desks of agencies, assorted bureaucrats and corporate offices. There are a lot of numbers, but there are a lot of stories which do not appear in those numbers. And what happens here will feed or not feed dragons elsewhere, and create even more questions about power choices, efficiency, consumption and economics.

Full Cost Accounting. That is what I have heard it called, where pollution a project creates as well as the foregone opportunities lost are weighed in the analysis.

I prefer the term *Indigenous Economics.* I prefer the idea that not all has a price tag attached to it, and that stories of place stay alive with that place and those people.

Over the course of the past decade, Montana ranchers and the Northern Cheyenne have made a successful resistance to the plans of Arch Coal. Those battles continue on the ground.

This past fall, I was able—with the help of the Fond du Lac Tribe's Department of Natural Resources—to place a sturgeon into the St. Louis River. That is an old fish species, and it will—if allowed to—live a hundred and fifty years. That is far longer than the life span of any mine proposal, although only a fraction of the length of time its damage will endure, and it is older than the EPA or Minnesota Power, for that matter. That is also unquantifiable, the life spans of living beings. All I know is some of the story, and that for sure, the Spirits of that Mountain still watch.

CROW & LUMMI: DIRTY COAL & CLEAN FISHING

"The tide is out and the table is set,"
— JUSTIN FINKBONNER, LUMMI

"Our people had an economy and we were prosperous in what we did. Then with the reservation, everything we had was broken down and we were forced into a welfare state."
— LANE SIMPSON, PROFESSOR, LITTLE BIG HORN COLLEGE

"The tide is out and the table is set," Justin Finkbonner said, gesturing to the straits on the edge of the Lummi reservation. This is the place where the Lummi people have gathered their food for a millennium. It is a fragile and bountiful ecosystem, part of the Salish Sea, newly corrected in its naming by cartographers. When the tide goes out, the Lummi fishing people go to their boats, one of the largest fishing fleets in any Indigenous community. They feed their families from here, and they fish for their economy.

This is also the place where the corporations fill their tankers and ships to travel into the Pacific and beyond. It is one of only a few deep water ports in the region, and there are plans to build a coal terminal here. That plan is being pushed by a consortium of Big Oil corporations, and one American Indian nation.

The Crow Nation needs someplace to sell the coal it would like to mine, in a new deal with Cloud Peak Energy. The deal is a big one: 1.4 billion tons of coal to be sold overseas. There have been no new coal plants built in the United States for 30 years, so Cloud Peak and the Crow hope to find their fortunes in China. The mine is called Big Metal, named after a legendary Crow hero.

The place they want to put a port for huge oil tankers and coal barges is called Cherry Point, or *Xwe Chiexen*. It is sacred to the Lummi. There is a 3,500-year-old village site here. Tsilixw, or Bill James, the Hereditary Chief of the Lummi Nation, describes this place as the "Home of the Ancient Ones." *It was the first site in Washington State to be listed on the Washington Heritage Register.*

Kwel Hoy – 3500 years

Coal interests hope to construct North America's largest coal export terminal on this "home of the Ancient Ones." Once there, millions of tons of coal would be loaded onto some of the largest bulk carriers in the world and exported to China. The Lummi nation is saying *Kwel hoy,* or "We draw the line." The sacred must be protected.

So it is that the Crow Nation needs a friend among the Lummi and is having a hard time finding one. In the meantime, a 40-year old coal mining strategy is being challenged by Crow people, because culture is tied to land, and all of that may change if they starting mining for coal. And, the Crow tribal government is being asked by some tribal members why renewable energy is not an option.

The stakes are high, and the choices made by sovereign Native nations will impact the future of not only two First Nations, but all of us.

How it Happens

It was a long time ago that the Crow People came from Spirit Lake. They emerged to the surface of the Earth from deep in the waters. They were known as the *Hidatsa* people, and lived for a millennia or more on the banks of the Missouri River. They built one of the most complex agriculture and trade systems in the northern hemisphere with their creativity and their diligence. Hundreds of varieties of corn, pumpkins, squash, tobacco, berries—all gifts to a people. And then the buffalo—50 million or so American bison—graced the region. The land was good, as was the life.

Ecosystems, species and cultures collide and change. The horse transformed peoples and cultures, and so it did for the Hidatsa and Crow people. The horse changed how the people were able to hunt—from buffalo jumps, from which a carefully crafted hunt could provide food for months, to the quick and agile movement of a horse culture. The Crow transformed. They left their life on the Missouri, moving west to the Big Horn Mountains. They escaped some of what was to come to the Hidatsas, the plagues of smallpox and later the plagues of agricultural dams which flooded a people and a history.

The *Absaalooka* are the People of the Big-beaked Blackbird—that is how they got their name, the Crow. The River Crow and the Mountain Crow, all of them came to live in the Big Horns, becoming a culture made by the land, made by the horse, and made by the Creator.

A Good Country

"The Crow country is a good country. The Great Spirit has put it exactly in the right place; while you are in it you fare well; whenever you go out of it, whichever way you travel, you will fare worse ... The Crow country is exactly in the right place." –Arapooish, Crow leader, to Robert Campbell, Rocky Mountain Fur Company, c.1830

The Absaalooka were not born coal miners. That's what happens when things are stolen from you—your land, reserved under treaty, more than 30 million acres of the best land in the northern plains, the heart of their territory.

This is what happens with historic trauma, and your people and ancestors disappear.

"1740 was the first contact with the Crow," Sharon Peregoy, a Crow senator in the Montana State legislature, explains. "It was estimated... to be 40,000 Crows, with 100 million acres to defend. Then we had three bouts of smallpox, and by 1900, we were greatly reduced to about 1,750 Crows."

"The 1825 Treaty allowed the settlers to pass through the territory," Senator Peregoy continued. The Crow were pragmatic, she said. "We became an ally with the U.S. government. We did it as a political move, that's for sure."

That didn't work out so well. The 1851 Fort Laramie Treaty identified 38 million acres as reserved, while the 1868 Fort Laramie Treaty greatly reduced the reservation to 8 million acres. A series of unilateral congressional acts further cut down the Crow land base, until only 2.3 million acres remained.

"The 1920 Crow Act's intent was to preserve Crow land to ensure that Crow tribal allottees who were ranchers and farmers have the opportunity to utilize their land," Peregoy explains.

Into the heart of this story came the Yellowtail Dam. That project split the Crow people, and it remains—like so many other dams flooding Indigenous territories—a continuing source of grief. The dam was a source of division, Peregoy said. "We were solid until the vote on the Yellowtail Dam in 1959."

The dam is named after Robert Yellowtail (1889 –1988), chairman of the tribe from 1934 to 1945, and—ironically—one of the main opponents of the dam for not only is it at the center of their ecosystem, but it benefits largely non-Native landowners and agricultural interests, many of whom farm Crow territory. And, the dam provides little financial returns for the tribe.

In economic terms, the Crow are essentially watching as their assets are taken to benefit others, and their ecology and economy declines.

"Even the city of Billings was built on the grass of the Crows," Peregoy says.

Everything we had was Broken Down

"Our people had an economy and we were prosperous in what we did. Then with the reservation, everything we had was broken down and we were forced into a welfare state." –Lane Simpson, Little Big Horn College

One could say the Crow know how to make lemonade out of lemons. They are renowned horse people and ranchers, and the individual landowners whose land now makes up the vast majority of the reservation, have tried hard to continue that lifestyle. Because of history of landloss, the Crow tribe now owns some 10 percent of the reservation.

The Crow have a short history of coal strip mining—maybe 50 years. Not so long in Crow history, but a long time in an inefficient fossil fuel economy. Westmoreland Resource's Absaalooka mine opened in 1974. It produces about 6 million tons of coal a year and employs about 80 people. That deal is for around 17 cents a ton.

Westmoreland has been the Crow Nation's most significant private partner for over 39 years, and the tribe has received almost 50 percent of its general operating income from this mine. Tribal members receive a per-capita payment from the royalties, which, in the hardship of a cash economy, pays many bills.

Then there is Colstrip, the power plant complex on the border of Crow—that produces around 2,800 mw of power for largely west coast utilities and also employs some Crows. Some 50 percent of the adult population is still listed as unemployed, and the Crow need to develop an economy that will support their people and the generations ahead. It is possible that the Crow may have become cornered into an economic future which, it turns out, will affect far more than just them.

Enter Cloud Peak and Big Metal

In 2013, the Crow Nation signed an agreement with Cloud Peak to develop 1.4 billion tons in the Big Metal mine. The company says it could take five years to develop a mine that would produce up to 10 million tons of coal annually, and other mines are possible in the leased areas. Cloud Peak has paid the tribe $3.75 million so far.

The Crow Nation may earn $10 million over those first five years. The Big Metal Mine, however, may not be a big money-maker. Coal is not as lucrative as it once was, largely because it is a dirty fuel. According to the Energy Information Administration, 175 coal plants will be shut down in the next few years in the U.S.

So the target market is in China. Cloud Peak has pending agreements to ship more than 20 million tons of coal annually through two proposed ports on the West Coast.

Back to the Lummi

The Gateway Pacific Coal terminal would be the largest such terminal on Turtle Island's west coast. This is what large means: an 1,100 acre terminal, moving up to 54 million metric tons of coal per year, using cargo ships up to 1,000 feet long. Those ships would weigh maybe 250,000 tons and carry up to 500,000 gallons of oil. Each tanker would take up to six miles to stop.

All of that would cross Lummi shellfish areas, the most productive shellfish territory in the region. "It would significantly degrade an already fragile and vulnerable crab, herring and salmon fishery, dealing a devastating blow to the economy of the fisher community," the tribe said in a statement.

The Lummi community has been outspoken in its opposition, and taken their concerns back to the Powder River basin, although not yet to the Crow Tribe.

Jewell Praying Wolf James is a tribal leader and master carver of the Lummi Nation. "There's gonna be a lot of mercury and arsenic blowing off those coal trains," James says. "That is going to go into a lot of communities and all the rivers between here and the Powder River Basin."

Is there a Way Out?

Is tribal sovereignty a carte blanche to do whatever you want? The Crow Tribe's coal reserves are estimated at around 9 billion tons of coal. If all the Crow coal came onto the market and was sold and burned, according to a paper by Avery Old Coyote, it could produce an equivalent of 44.9 billion metric tons of carbon dioxide.

That's a lot of carbon during a time of climate challenge.

Then there are the coal-fired power plants. They employ another 380 people, some of them Crow, and generating some 2,094 mw of electricity. The plants are the second largest coal generating facilities west of the Mississippi. PSE's coal plant is the dirtiest coal-burning power plant in the Western states, and the eighth dirtiest nationwide. The amount of carbon pollution that spews from Colstrip's smokestacks is almost equal to two eruptions at Mt. St. Helen's every year.

Coal is dirty. That's just the way it is. Coal plant operators are planning to retire175 coal-fired generators, or 8.5 percent of the total coal-fired capacity in the U.S., according to the Energy Information Administration. A record number of generators were shut down in 2012. Massive energy development in PRB contributes more than 14 percent of the total U.S. carbon pollution, and the Powder River Basin ranks among the largest reserves in the world.

According to the United States Energy Information Administration, the world emits 32.5 billion metric tons of carbon dioxide each year. The Crow Tribe will would effectively contribute more than a year and a half of the entire world's production of carbon dioxide, should the project go forward.

There, is, unfortunately, no containment bubble over China, so all of that carbon will end up in the atmosphere.

The Crow Nation chairman, Darrin Old Coyote, says coal was a gift to his community that goes back to the tribe's creation story. "Coal is life," he says. "It feeds families and pays the bills...[We] will continue to work with everyone and respect tribal treaty rights, sacred sights, and local concerns. However, I strongly feel that non-governmental organizations cannot and should not tell me to keep Crow coal in the ground. I was elected to provide basic services and jobs to my citizens and I will steadfastly and responsibly pursue Crow coal development to achieve my vision for the Crow people."

Stranded Assets

In 2009, 1,133 people were employed by the coal industry in Montana. U.S. coal sales have been on the decline in recent years, and plans to export coal to Asia will prop up this industry a while longer. By contrast, Montana had 2,155 "green" jobs in 2007 – nearly twice as many as in the coal industry. Montana ranks fifth in the nation for wind-energy potential. Even China has been dramatically increasing its use of renewables and recently called for the closing of thousands of small coal mines by 2015. Perhaps most telling, Goldman Sachs recently stated that investment in coal infrastructure is "a risky bet and could create stranded assets."

The Answer may be Blowing in the Wind

The Crow nation has possibly 15,000-megawatts of wind power potential, or six times as much power as is presently being generated by Colstrip. Michaelynn Hawk and Peregoy have an idea: a wind project owned by Crow Tribal members that could help diversify Crow income.

Michaelynn says "the price of coal has gone down. It's not going to sustain us. We need to look as landowners at other economic development to sustain us as a tribe. Coal development was way before I was born. From the time I can remember, we got per capita from the mining of coal. Now that I'm older and getting into my elder age, I feel that we need to start gearing towards green energy."

Imagine there were buffalo, wind turbines and revenue from the Yellowtail Dam to feed the growing Crow community. What if the Crow replaced some of that 500 megawatts of Colstrip Power, with some of the 15, 000 possible megawatts of power from wind energy?

And then there is the dam on the Big Horn River. "We have the opportunity right now to take back the Yellowtail Dam," Peragoy says. "Re-licensing and lease negotiations will come up in two years for the Crow Tribe, and that represents a potentially significant source of income – $600 million. That's for 20 years, $30 million a year."

That would be better than dirty coal money for the Crow, for the Lummi, for all of us.

UNDER THE EYE OF SAURON: OIL, GAS, CORRUPTION AND CHANGE IN MANDAN, HIDATSA AND ARIKARA TERRITORY

> *"Every single day there is more than 100 million cubic feet of natural gas, which is flared away. That's enough to heat half a million homes. That's as much carbon dioxide emitted as 300,000 cars. That's crazy."*
>
> —KANDI MOSSETT

I wanted to write a story about strength and resilience. I wanted to write a story about the singers, the horse people and the earth lodge builders of the Mandan, Hidatsa and Arikara peoples; the squash and corn, the heartland of agricultural wealth in the Northern Plains.

That's the story I have been wanting to write. That story is next. The story today is about folly, greed, confusion, unspeakable intergenerational trauma and terrifying consequences, all in a moment in time. That time is now.

For me, this story began at Lake Superior, a place which is sacred to the Anishinaabeg and the source of a fifth of the world's fresh water. I rode my horse with my family, my community and our allies, from that place, Rice Lake Refuge to Rice Lake on my own reservation. Those two lakes are the mother lode of the world's wild rice.

These two lakes and the region are threatened by a newly-proposed Sandpiper pipeline of fracked oil from the Bakken Oil Fields of North Dakota, from the homeland of those Arikara people. We rode, but we did not stop, driven to go to the source, we traveled to North Dakota, accompanied by a new friend from Colorado and an organization called Fractivist. That is this story.

Mandan, Hidatsa and Arikara territory is in the northern Missouri River. A land of gentle rolling hills, immense prairie diversity and the memory of fifty million bison. Today, it's called the Ft. Berthold reservation in North Dakota and it's known as the sweet spot for Bakken crude oil. About 20 percent of the state's oil production is coming from this reservation, in a state with 19,000 wells.

Lynn Helms, ND Director of Mines spoke from a panel, telling us there are 193 drilling rigs in the state, one-sixth of them (28) are on Ft. Berthold, half on trust lands and half on fee lands. There are 1,250 active and producing wells on the reservation, with 2,150 leased and ready to drill. Then, Helms explained, these wells will be in the "harvest phase of production" soon. All of those are fracked oil wells, with gases being burned off in flares that light up the reservation in an eerie way. Everywhere, it is as if the Eye of Sauron (from *The Lord of the Rings* trilogy) is present.

That is what we see. What we also see is that there's a huge change in wealth on the reservation. Things are going so well that the tribal council, which five years ago, was facing a $200 million debt, is now wealthy. The tribal council purchased a yacht, a yacht to take guests like Sen. Heidi Heitkamp and oil company executives on the lake and to enjoy the beauty and opulence many oil rich countries are accustomed to. The yacht sits quietly on a dock by the casino, no fanfare today.

So let us talk about poverty and how North Dakota and the U.S. treated the Mandan, Hidatsa and Arikara people. They were the poorest for many years, an unspeakable poverty of loss, intergenerational trauma and the meanness of America. All that was manifest – not only during the Indian Wars, the small pox epidemics (wiping out 90 percent of their people) – but crowned by the 1954 Garrison Diversion project that drowned a people under Lake Sakakawea, taking 152,000 acres of their best land.

The dams drowned their villages, drowned their agricultural wealth, drowned their history and rewrote it in America's manual of agricultural progress. The sense of despair was, in some ways manifest in the landmark Dana Deegan case, where Deegan abandoned her newborn infant and allowed it to die, an unspeakable horror. For this, she was sentenced to a decade in prison, in a highly controversial federal court decision. Similar cases involving non-Native women resulted in supervised probation and reduced sentences. "The law needs to be changed and Indians need to be treated the same as their non-Indian neighbors," Judge Myron Bright, U.S. Court of Appeals for the Eighth Circuit, wrote in his dissenting opinion.

Bright pointed to the historic trauma and abuse in the Deegan case as the basis for his dissent (See www.FreeDana.com). In the end, there is no grief that I can imagine is deeper; except, perhaps the grief that is to come. That is unimaginable and that grief could be prevented by tribal leaders, or inherited by their children.

That is part of the question to be asked here. How much does the tribal leadership know about what is going on? And how much do the people know?

Kandi Mossett, a Mandan, Hidatsa and Arikara Nation citizen, along with many other community members like Theodora and Joletta Birdbear have been fighting it all. They have been trying to protect their community for a decade from new threats brought by the petroleum reality. This includes the Basin Electric coal facilities, just upwind from their villages, which were rushed through the federal processes. No new oil refineries have been built elsewhere in the U.S. for decades, but tribal sovereignty may exempt this proposed site and expedite its process. The Facebook page "This is Mandaree" contains a wealth of information and stories. They work with the Dakota Resource Council, a non-profit trying hard to turn the tide against extraction industries.

Known and Unknown

In the Anishinaabe universe, there are eight layers of the world – those are the worlds in which we live, those above and below. Most of us live in the present, in the world we can see. What we do, however, may intersect with those other worlds.

Fracking oil is a new technology, despite what oil companies say, it is a big experiment; made possible because of a perfect storm: a lack of federal regulation, a dearth of state and tribal regulation, and unlimited access to water and air, into which everything is dumped.

The 2005 Energy Policy Act had something in it called the Halliburton Amendment. That amendment exempted the oil and gas industry from most major environmental laws. This includes special exemptions from the Comprehensive Environmental Response, Compensation and Liability Act, commonly known as Superfund. That law authorizes the EPA to respond to releases – or threatened releases – of hazardous substances that may endanger public health, welfare or the environment.

Other exemptions for the oil and gas industry in the amendment include:

- **The Resource Conservation and Recovery Act** (Subtitle C establishes a federal program to manage hazardous wastes for its entire existence to ensure that hazardous waste is handled in a manner that protects human health and the environment);

- **The Safe Drinking Water Act** (the main federal law that ensures the quality of Americans' drinking water);

- **The Clean Water Act** (intended to restore and maintain the chemical, physical and biological integrity of the nation's waters by preventing point and non-point pollution sources, providing assistance to publicly-owned treatment works for their improvement);

- **The National Environmental Policy Act** (a law intended to assure that all branches of government give proper consideration to the environment prior to undertaking any major federal action that could significantly affect the environment).

The Clean Air Act is the law that defines EPA's responsibilities for protecting and improving the nation's air quality and the stratospheric ozone layer. Exemptions to the CAA remove the requirement that emissions not be combined with emissions from any oil, gas exploration, production wells and emissions from any pipeline compressor or pump station.

The exemptions have worked out pretty well for industry and one might argue for the short term leaseholder and royalties. Not so for those trying to protect the environment. Edmund Baker, Ft. Berthold Environmental Director, has been challenged in his regulation of the fracking industry.

On July 8, what was known as the Crestwood Spill was discovered. This means about a million gallons of radioactive and highly saline water was leaking from a pipe and headed to a stream and Lake Sakakawea. Industry officials, joined by Chairman Hall, talked about how fortuitously all had been saved by three beaver dams. Let's say leave it to beaver, may be a bit of a simplistic environmental protection plan.

The spill was found. Always a problem, because when something is found, it has usually gone on for quite a while. After all, the 800,000-gallon spill that occurred last year in the Bakken field was discovered about two months after it had started seeping out of a quarter size whole in a pipe. The Crestwood spill is estimated to be well over a million gallons of highly saline and radioactive water. Baker has not been able to review any of the spill data. That data is held by the tribal council.

"My officers had asked if they could get copies of the samples. My officers were denied. I don't have the data, I don't have any solid numbers...I never received anything," Baker said.

His job is already difficult, being as there are 1,200 or so wells on the reservation and twice as many underway, not to mention a pretty substantial waste stream from the fracking industry. Those wastes are not just water, or airborne, they are also solid wastes and some of those are radioactive.

Death by Lethal Injection

Let's start with the problem of water. Fracking involves the use of immense amounts of water – hundreds of millions of gallons per well. One company, Southwest Energy Resources, told reporters that what is involved in fracking is basic chemicals you could find in your house.

That would be – it seems – if you were running a meth lab. Water used by fracking companies is contaminated with over 600 toxins and carcinogens. Those chemicals are considered trade secrets and are not subjected to scrutiny. This has become a bit of a problem. Simply stated: once water has been used in fracking, it is no longer living water. It is dead and it is lethal.

Much of that water is being pumped into deep underground caverns, by the trillions of gallons. In Colorado, there is one injection well alone that is over a trillion gallons. The data from North Dakota is hard to come by but it is emerging. Colorado's data has been probed by a host of concerned citizens.

A report released in June by Abrahm Lustgarten of ProPublica found, "Over the past several decades, U.S. industries have injected more than 30 trillion gallons of toxic liquid deep into the earth, using broad expanses of the nation's geology as an invisible dumping ground."

During its investigation of the EPA's oversight of the nation's injection wells, ProPublica found that the agency was unable to provide basic information to its journalists, such as how many disposal wells fail and how often such failures occur. The investigative news organization also reported that the EPA, "has not counted the number of cases of waste migration or contamination in more than 20 years" and that "the agency often accepts reports from state injection regulators that are partly blank, contain conflicting figures or are missing data."

Shane Davis directs a Colorado organization called Fractivist. Colorado is a few years down the road in fracking. There are 54,000 wells presently in Colorado and in Weld County – where Shane lived – there were 22,000 wells, some 75 within a one mile-radius from his house.

Davis got sick from the wells. He described serious rashes, going blind for a week, gastrointestinal problems and a year-and-a-half of a bloody nose. Then he got angry, "I conducted an investigative study using un-redacted, official COGCC spill/release reports and found that 43 percent of all oil and gas related spills resulted in ground water contamination with chemicals like benzene, toluene, xylene, ethyl-benzene and many more in Weld County, Colorado."

A biologist by training, Davis continued to research and his findings were confirmed by Colorado agencies in 2013. He explained, "Colorado's largest aquifer was also contaminated by thermogenic methane and toluene in 2009. The aquifer was never cleaned, the oil and gas operator was fined $46,200 and the public was never informed by the state about this atrocity.

"Citizens drank benzene contaminated water, people's homes have abandoned oil and gas wells in their back yards and they do not know about them, homes have been built on top of abandoned wells, which leaked gases that subsequently exploded and sent the occupants to the burn center. Billions and billions of gallons of toxic, endocrine disrupting chemicals have been discharged in Colorado's rivers, lands and airways for years with no end in sight."

An interesting question was asked by reporters Joel Dyer and Jefferson Dodge in the Boulder Weekly, "With more than 30 trillion gallons of toxic waste having been injected into the inner earth, what happens if our belief that what goes down can't come up is wrong?"

Flaring: The Eye of Sauron

"Every single day there is more than 100 million cubic feet of natural gas, which is flared away. That's enough to heat half a million homes. That's as much carbon dioxide emitted as 300,000 cars," Kandi Mossett explains. "That's crazy."

There is twice as much flaring on the reservation as off the reservation. That's to say that the lack of infrastructure has been surpassed by the speed of extraction. Natural gas burned in flaring is a byproduct of crude oil. Without enough pipelines to transport the gas at a state level, one-third of what's released each day – worth $1.4 million – goes up in smoke. Tribal citizens say as much as 70 percent of gas from wells on the reservation is flared.

Ironically, last winter – as Debbie Dogskin on the nearby Standing Rock reservation froze to death in the polar vortex and a nationwide propane shortage set in – the Bakken fields flared gas, rich in propane. According to the Bloomberg News, "On a percentage basis, more gas was flared in the state than in any other domestic oil field and at a level equal to Russia and twice that in Nigeria. In Texas, less than 1 percent of natural gas is burned off; in North Dakota, flaring is allowed for six months.

In North Dakota, energy companies can flare for a year without paying taxes or royalties. Oil and gas production is greatest during a well's first three months, exacerbating the problem. Tribal officials are very concerned about the flaring, but the companies have been reluctant to invest in the infrastructure necessary to capture the gases, so flaring continues.

This brings you to what we don't see. "These are called VOCs, or volatile organic compounds," Mossett explains. "They – the companies – have generously put up signs for us, to tell us that the toxins are present in the air. What do we do, just stop breathing when we go by?"

A Colorado School of Public Health study undertaken by Dr. Lisa McKenzie found airborne hydrocarbons near oil and gas facilities. She found a number of carcinogenic chemicals and endocrine-disrupting chemicals being released one-half mile away from the oil and gas facilities, at levels which would increase human cancer rates exponentially.

Dr. Theo Colburn completed an air chemistry study that also found high levels of endocrine-disrupting chemicals (EDCs) being released by the fracking industry. Those make you sterile, among other health concerns. They are not to be trifled with.

Industry has suggested that toxic emissions don't occur, but studies indicate that between 2 and 100 tons per year are emitted into the air per well pad. That includes benzene, toluene, napthene, xylene and more. Those are largely invisible to the eye but they are not invisible to the body, nor an infrared camera.

Davis began using military infrared cameras to document the escaping gases. Those are pretty extensive and can be viewed online, at www.

Fractivist.org. The long term impacts may be more troubling: endocrine disrupters that cause sterility and birth defects.

"A huge portion of the chemicals used in the fracking industry are protected as trademark secrets. This becomes important because when an active oil and gas well pad has an on-site issue, such as a blow out, or spraying chemicals in communities or elsewhere, where there are animals or humans, the victims would not know the nature of the chemical contamination and this puts both the patient and the doctor in jeopardy."

Davis continued: "If there is an issue with a well pad, the emergency response people do not know the chemicals they are responding to and consequently will not have the appropriate equipment for this response. Every operator has a different cocktail which they are using. A huge concern is that the burden of expense has been shifted to the general public to pay for the emergency response and so the oil and gas industry does not have to really get involved."

About the Money

This is – after all – about money, money that provides compensation to tribal citizens for leases and royalties, which makes everyone feel better. There are tribal millionaires, there are oil barons, there are tribal leaders who are oil barons and the state of North Dakota is looking robust in its' economic plan. But not everyone is doing so well because not everyone has mineral rights and those who do may have been cheated out of hundreds of millions of dollars in royalties by complex schemings. "Some of our tribal members leased land for $34 an acre," Mossett said.

Ramona Two Shields and Mary Louise Defender filed a lawsuit in late 2012, which was about the money, alleging that unscrupulous decisions had been made in a complex web entangling casino managers, tribal leaders, BIA and agency representatives, along with oil interests. The legal brief reads like something from the "Pelican Brief."

The case was dismissed on a technicality but has some interesting stories.

Like the story of the 42,500 acres of tribal land that was leased at below market value by the BIA and with approval of the council – worked through some middlemen associated with the casino and Ft. Berthold Development Commission – and Spencer Williams and Rick Woodward as well as other figures in the oil and gas industry.

The Two Shield suit alleges that the BIA, under the influence of various factors, grossly mismanaged the potential revenues from the oil leasing on the reservation, resulting in the loss of millions of dollars to tribal citizens.

More corruption charges were leveled at the tribal council, in particular recently-defeated Chairman Tex Hall. A report released in mid-September included 100 pages of legal analysis and 200 pages of exhibit documents.

"The report," according to the Bismarck Tribune, "lays out a timeline that alleges just days after being elected in 2010, Hall used his office to demand $1.2 million from Spotted Hawk Development, an oil and gas company, before he would sign off on the company's development plan. It also alleges he used his office to secure more than $580,000 in payments for water-hauling to a man who has since been implicated in a separate murder-for-hire scheme. The report further alleges he unfairly competed with other tribal oil service companies."

The problems are deep, however, and more than a little intergenerational as well as multi-jurisdictional. And Tex "Red Tipped Arrow" Hall did not make this whole story, or all the problems. A few years ago he pointed out how the tribe has had to struggle just for a pittance:

"The state has a $1 billion budget surplus and created a $1.2 billon trust fund for infrastructure needs. The MHA Nation has roads that need fixing now. Our tax revenues should not go to a state investment account. In 2011, the State collected more than $60 million in taxes from energy development on the reservation, but spent less than $2 million for infrastructure on the Reservation," Hall testified at a federal hearing.

Flash Forward

It's September 3 at the Great Plains Tribal Chairman's Association and I've had the pleasure of speaking on a panel with four oil and gas guys.

Things are looking pretty good for the industry after all. The BIA has a table, at which they are busy flagging down possible lessees with a bright green pamphlet titled, "Frequently Asked Questions for Indian Mineral Owners," and a price list for what is available and when it might get paid out.

It's sort of an upbeat occasion for the bureau, after all that mismanagement uncovered in the Cobell (Indian Trust) case. This time, the bureau feels it will manage the money well, although that little problem the Two Shield case discusses may remain an issue.

The Ft. Berthold Tribe has celebrated a banner year for oil production, despite a record number of spills, incidents and dirty radioactive frack filter "socks" found in municipal waste, road sides and on an allottees land. "Some kids found some and were playing with them, radioactive frack socks," Mossett said.

Indeed, Hall celebrated tribal sovereignty on Earth Day with a Barrel Oil Sale and Extravaganza in New Town, announced with great pride in the Denver papers and in a full page advertisement in the Denver March Pow Wow program.

"We'll all say it was good while it lasted," is a haunting testimony I heard in northern Alberta from a woman who lives on a small reserve swimming in oil spills today. "It was good while it lasted."

At my friend Jessica and Marty's, we are going into the sweat lodge. I am interested in getting any extra toxins off my body from the oil industry – mental, physical or spiritual. I arrived at their house. Today, an oil rig and flare stares at them, 300 yards from their front door.

The Eye of Sauron looks at us as we leave our car, headed to the shelter of the lodge. I shudder and then cache myself inside. I swear I heard the well breathing.

Marty and Jessica are building an earth lodge and moving their children there, along with their horses and their future. Somehow the oil production projections in the Bakken seem pretty short term in the face of an earth lodge. That is to say, that Bakken oil is about the equivalent to a year's consumption by the U.S. and well capacity is diminishing. That costs money.

On May 27, Bloomberg News reported, "Shale debt has almost doubled over the last four years while revenue has gained just 5.6 percent."

"The list of companies that are financially stressed is considerable," said Benjamin Dell, managing partner of Kimmeridge Energy, a New York-based asset manager. That might be a bit of a problem when it's time to pay up for the damages.

Elsewhere, citizens in Colorado have enacted moratoriums on fracking in seven municipalities, New York and California are deep into battles over fracking, Nova Scotia has just banned fracking; counties in England announced a ban in early September and there are a lot of questions being asked worldwide, and a lot of faucets catching on fire.

North Dakota has not asked many questions. It might be time. It might also be time to ask some questions in Mandan, Hidatsa and Arikara territory.

IN THE TIME OF MONSTER SLAYERS

"In the far back times of the Diné people, Monsters roamed the lands. And in those times, there were great beings who were called upon to slay the Monsters. We need some modern era Monster Slayers."

—ANNA RONDON (DINÉ)

It is perhaps those times again. A battle is raging between major forces: traditional Diné people who seek to maintain a way of life between the six sacred mountains *Sisnajini, Tsoodzil, Dook'o'oosliid, Dibe Nitsaa, Dzil Na'oodilii, Dzil Ch'ool'i'I;* and, the economics of fossil fuels. All of these are the challenges of a tribal government in a difficult position.

So here is the question: What would you do if you were BHP Billiton, the largest mining company in the world and industry analysts told you that "small coal is not financially viable"? And, as you looked out at the US coal market you found that your team of major coal companies had seen their profits and share prices drop 20-30%, including Patriot Coal's bankruptcy with $3.6 billion in assets?

Meanwhile in your boardroom, inside analysts suggested that one mine in particular wouldn't be making the cut on the portfolio? If you were really smart you might start talking to the Navajo Nation about a plan, and maybe a buyout of your thirty-year-old coal strip mine.

This scenario is playing out in the Navajo Nation; high pressure negotiations, and higher stakes. Over 60% of the Navajo general budget comes from fossil fuels royalties, and there are thousands of Navajos employed by the industry; it is the largest employer, after all. Consultants for the Nation reported that up to $80 million in annual revenues were projected to result from the Navajo Mine and the associated coal-fired power plants, including Four Corners Generating Station, and Navajo Generating Station, both of which are scheduled for closure within the next decade due to the need for costly environmental upgrades, and declining coal markets.

At a late March meeting, over 200 miners and their families were bused to the Navajo Tribal Council meeting by the coal companies, to apparently encourage a coal employment responsive vote on a resolution. When the debating and shouting and voting was concluded, here, apparently, is the preliminary plan: the Navajo Nation will take full ownership of the Navajo Mine, continue leases for coal generators at Four Corners Power Plant and the Navajo Generating Station, and remain a fossil fuels powerhouse for the foreseeable future.

On March 30, the Navajo Nation Council passed a resolution approving $2.3 million in supplemental funding for a Due Diligence Investigation into the acquisition of the Navajo Mine. The recent timeline:

Navajo Nation wants to close the transaction by July 1st, 2013. It is a tricky set of decisions in a precarious time.

A Bit of Opposition

Not to be surprised, the plan has generated lawsuits and controversy. "Buying the mine from BHP Billiton means responsibility for millions of tons of coal ash waste with toxic metals leaching into our aquifer and the San Juan River," said Donna House of Diné C.A.R.E. "Navajo people do not want that dirty legacy on our hands, nor the massive costs of cleaning it up. We don't need to pay millions more to high-priced consultants to know this coal deal is a bad deal."

From inside *Diné Bikeyah*—the Navajo territory between those six sacred mountains—a scrappy grassroots organization is suing several parties, including BHP Billiton and the Navajo tribe, hoping to stop the sale of that coal strip-mine.

"Buying Navajo Mine and renewing leases for NGS will only condemn our children to a life-sentence of pollution and a weak economy," says activist Kim Smith. "We should focus on creating a stronger sustainable economy rather than spending thousands to keep these mines and power plants going. If these industries took care of us the way they take care of cities like Phoenix, Navajos would no longer be held economic hostages."

Opposition to mining and coal generation at Navajo is not a new story. It dates back to the 1970s with many protests and arrests, and 10,000 people were relocated from the area that buffers Navajo and Hopi lands and is overlaying coal fields.

Fossil Beings

The BHP Billiton mine expansion is particularly contentious. That expansion will encroach on an area where the last dinosaurs in the world existed.

Arnold Clifford, a Navajo geologist and botanist, is in a race against coal mining. For the past 25 years, he's been researching fossils and rare plants on the Navajo Nation. The geological record in the San Juan Basin ranges in age 50 million to 90 million years old, Spencer

Lucas, curator of geology and paleontology at the New Mexico Museum of Natural History and Science explains, the Basin is "the last age of the dinosaurs up until they went extinct 65 million years ago... This is where you learn about the end of an era."

Clifford says the ancient record is in danger as coal-mining operations continue to advance in unprotected areas. This past fall, a reporter from the Gallup Independent followed Clifford as he worked and took note of a poignant moment:

"Arnold Clifford lay on a pile of rock fragments in the middle of a badland about nine miles north of the Burnham Chapter and took a closer look at what appeared to be a small rounded stone. He put it on his palm and observed it.

'Ain't no pebble. It's a croc's tooth,' he said, adding that the tiny tooth must have belonged to an ancient crocodile that once roamed the San Juan Basin—presumably about 60-65 million years ago."

It is a pivotal time. It is the end of an era of fossil Beings and fossil Water Beings cached away for millions of years are being brought to the surface, and life has been transformed. Now, the terrain is changing. And, indeed, some of those fossils, the last dinosaurs in the Jurassic age are about to be dug up for a coal mine. There are some particularly Diné stories about beings which existed in different Worlds, legends of Monsters and Monster Slayers.

"It's about Spirit Beings who lived on this land long ago, and they are not supposed to come into this time. They were not intended to come into this world." —Navajo spiritual leader

Fossil Water

It is also about water that once existed and may be needed in the future. This fight is about water as well as fuel. Nicole Horseherder, who grew up on Black Mesa, says:

"I have distinct memories of one particular camp, *Tsenitaahotsoh*, which ...means "the green grass at the base of the rock." I would get up before sunrise and take our sheep to a seep there to drink, because right around 4 a.m., pools of water would miraculously appear on the dry arroyo bed. Then when the sun came up a few hours later, the seeps would disappear.

"Our livelihoods depended on those springs, and I remember moving with our herds to follow the water all the way through my high school years, until I left for college in 1987.

"I returned home 10 years later, university degree in hand, ready to take my place as a productive member of my community. But as I began building my home at Tsenitaahotsoh, I discovered that the seeps had vanished, not just with the rising sun each day, but for good. In fact, the springs at all of the camps from my childhood were drying up. Over 20 years, the natural economy of my ancestors had disappeared...."—Nicole Horseherder

There is no shortage of Navajos, just, perhaps the water upon which to nourish them. In 1973, the National Academy of Sciences issued a report suggesting that in arid areas like *Diné Bii Káya*, "a restoration of a landscape disturbed by surface mining, in the sense of re-creating the former conditions, is not possible."

The Academy suggested that if such lands were mined, it was more feasible to deem the land "National Sacrifice Areas" then to attempt reclamation at all.

The Academy's projections from thirty years ago are chilling. Water is scarce, and increasingly so. The Navajo Aquifer underlies the reservation and adjoins the coal bed. It is the only source of drinking water for 50,000 Native people and 14 communities on Black Mesa. It is more than a thousand feet deep, and it provides some of the cleanest water in the Southwest when it emerges as seeps on the surface. The aquifer has provided this life giving water for thousands of years.

As Nicole Horseherder explains, "From 1971 to 2005, the coal industry removed water from the Navajo Aquifer at the rate of 4,000-6,000 acre-feet a year, more than three times the aquifer's known ability to recharge. Since 2005, the Peabody mining company has decreased its use to less than 2,000 acre-feet a year, but that is still more than 13 million gallons a year for an area that gets less than 8 inches of annual rainfall..."

This past year, 2012, saw incredibly heated debate in the Navajo Nation on Diné Water Rights, and the price tag for that water. In the end, despite great pressures from market forces, the Navajo nation did not approve the sale of water rights. To Diné traditional people, water is sacred.

"We've been out of water." Kim Smith, a young Diné artist and community organizer who lives in Window Rock, explains to me. "We've been out of water for two weeks in Window Rock, Crownpoint, Ganado. It's a huge problem. And now, the water that we do have is orange and brown and froze up. The lines froze so bad."

Coal and Air

There are many environmental problems associated with coal generation, and they are not small. The Four Corners Power Plant is the nation's largest source of nitrogen oxides. In the first 10 months of 2010 Four Corners plant emitted 6,690,899 tons of carbon into the air. Add to that, 157 million pounds of sulfur dioxide, 122 million pounds of nitrogen oxides, 8 million pounds of soot and 2,000 pounds of mercury.

The American Lung Association estimates that 16,000 people in the region (15 percent of the population) suffer from lung disease probably caused by plant emissions. Coal combustion waste from the mines supporting the Four Corners and San Juan plants has contaminated local groundwater with sulfates, leading to the death of livestock. According to one source, 70 million tons of coal waste (containing cadmium, selenium, arsenic, and lead) has been dumped in the Navajo Mine, and combined with the San Juan mine, amounts to a total of 150 million tons

Coal's environmental and health impacts, including climate change, have resulted in a transition from coal to natural gas in many utilities, making coal increasingly hard to sell in the US. Coal plant operators are planning to retire 175 coal-fired generators, or 8.5 percent of the total coal-fired capacity in the United States, according to the Energy Information Administration. A record number of 57 generators were shut down in 2012, representing 9 gigawatts of electrical capacity, according to EIA. In 2015, nearly 10 gigawatts of capacity from 61 coal-fired generators will be retired.

Now might be the time for a Plan B.

Green Economics and Diné Fundamental Law:

The Navajo Green Economy Commission was established in 2009, a result of much hard work by its Diné youth organizers. Anna Rondon serves as one of the commissioners and remains frustrated with the lack of progress. "Right now we went through the tribal process of getting the budget approved as we have done for the past three years. And each time, as it gets across the street to Chairman Shelly's office, it gets vetoed." It seems ironic to Anna. "Our water rights are being jeopardized for outside interests. Seems that our leaders never wanted to approve the Commission. They approve the $2.3 million for expertise in coal and some of that money could have gone to that commission."

The commissioners had some high hopes: "We hoped to work with the communities, (and) local chapters to bring in resources, technical assistance with their existing land use plans, and all. Many chapters said they want solar. "Other ideas include solar rooftops on all of tribal buildings.

Rondon seems puzzled by the vetoes by Chairman Shelly, saying "This would not have threatened anyone. Our job as commissioners is to mitigate the impacts of climate change. This is how you do it."

Anna suggests that 110 chapters at Navajo could all have solar farms, pointing to the Moapa Paiute's most recent agreements with Southern California Edison. At Moapa Paiute, a huge solar project is underway on the lands of a tribe faced with similar environmental concerns about coal.

In June, the Interior Department gave the Moapa Paiutes fast-tracked approval to build the first-ever utility-scale solar-energy project on tribal lands—which seems especially suitable in this region of year-round scorching sun. The 350-megawatt plant, to be built on Moapa Paiute trust land, should generate enough power for 100,000 homes, according to the agency, which says the project will mean lease income for the tribe as well as new jobs.

"We should have about 400 jobs at peak construction and 15 to 20 permanent jobs—real career jobs tribal members can look forward to," said Anderson. "Our energy customers will likely be in California, where people have an interest in renewable-energy sources."

Locally, the Shonto Navajo Community is an interesting case study in chapter-based problem solving. Shonto Renewable Energy Division is the first community-owned renewable energy retail and installation company in the Navajo Nation.

Tony Skrelunas, Program Director of Grand Canyon Trust's Native America Program explains, "Shonto community is also creating a business that will create jobs and keep talent on the Navajo Nation, rather than utilizing outside consultants and businesses that are not within the community. They are invested in creating a long-term sustainable model that will adequately address the needs of the community."

"It has been a priority of the Shonto Community to lead by example in embracing renewable energy and sustainable building technology," Brett Isaac, Shonto Economic Development Corporation, (SEDC) Project Manager explains. "It is integrated into the community's plans for new public facilities, and this is the start of a movement by the community to incorporate renewable energy into its facilities in hopes of inspiring other communities to embrace the benefits of alternative energy."

The Shonto model has broad implications. Three years ago, the Diné College was able to install 25 kw of solar on a new building as a result of collaboration between a number of nonprofits using some of the resources from the now-defunct Mohave Generating Station

More ideas are well underway including some forwarded by the Black Mesa communities to turn the infrastructure of coal strip mines and power plants towards utility scale solar generation The long-term vision, according to Waheahlah Johns of the Black Mesa Water Coalition, is to establish a solar manufacturing facility and a series of 20MW - 200MW solar photovoltaic (PV) installations on the abandoned mine land of Black Mesa. In the short-term, the project will begin with a 20MW solar PV installation that includes a community benefits agreement with a small equity ownership stake for the residents, local hire provisions and home solar PV systems for families in the area.

We need a New Era of Monster Slayers

The Navajo Nation is in a pivotal position, and has immense wealth and power. It has the power of a very strong spiritual and cultural tradition, much of which remains intact. A few years ago, for instance, the Navajo General Council passed an affirmation of Diné spiritual teachings in approving Diné Fundamental Law as a part of the Navajo tribal governance:

"Mother Earth and Father Sky is part of us as the Diné and the Diné is part of Mother Earth and Father Sky. The Diné must treat this sacred bond with love and respect without exerting dominance for we do not own our Mother or Father.

"The rights and freedoms of the people to the use of the sacred elements of life as mentioned above and to the use of the land, natural resources, sacred sites and other living beings must be accomplished through the proper protocol of respect and offering and these practices must be protected and preserved for they are the foundation of our spiritual ceremonies and the Diné life way; and...It is the duty and responsibility of the Diné to protect and preserve the beauty of the natural world for future generations..."

This is a challenge in the present scenario and in heated negotiations. This is also a very interesting spotlight under which to view how decisions will be made in this millennium by tribal governments who are both immersed in community wealth and in the wealth of a larger economy. At some level, this debate at Navajo may also be where we learn about the end of an era, perhaps fossil fuels and fossil water. Or, the end of one era and possibly the beginning of another: a solar era.

PHOTO BY TOBY McCLEOD

THE *NUR* AND THE PEOPLE

*"Indian doctors and prophets had been with the
Wintu long ago and prophesized the time when
the salmon would disappear. The prophets told
that the salmon would be hidden behind a river
of ice. "*

—Caleen Sisk, Winnemem Wintu

As the snows cover the mountains and freeze the glacial rivers of
northern California the time of the salmon and people are remembered. Winter is a time of dormancy and rebirth, and so it is for the
Wintu people where perhaps one of the most beautiful and majestic
mountains in the Pacific range, the Ring of Fire as it is called, brings
forth a people and a salmon. That is Mount Shasta, or Boyum Payuk
as the great mountain is called in *Wintu*.

The story of the salmon and the people spans a thousand years of mythology, and in this new millennium the mythology is coming into its
own era. The *Winnemem Wintu* are the Middle Water People, called
so as the McCloud River is one of three rivers which meander through
the foothills of Shasta, filled with spring runoff from the mountain,
and eventually converge into the Sacramento River. The three rivers

are the McCloud, the Middle Fork and the Pitt rivers. Each of those rivers had a two-legged people and a salmon people. It is the salmon people, the *Nur*, who gave voice to the Winnemem Wintu.

Legends speak of a time when the Nur took pity on the Wintu people and gave to them their voice. In return, the salmon only sing as they course the rivers of the Northwest, and only to be heard by the Wintu. The Wintu, in turn, were to care for the Nur always and were to sing. And so they try to fulfill this responsibility a millennium later.

"The people believe that when the last salmon is gone, humans will be gone too." Caleen Sisk explains. Caleen is an Indian Doctor, and a traditional leader of the Winnemem Wintu, a tribe of 200 or so who live in the same place as their ancestors, tenaciously hanging on to a pristine ecosystem hidden between valleys, rivers and mountain passes.

The Winnemem Wintu remember their salmon and their history. Both have faced great loss. A millennium on the river did well for both the people and the salmon. Then came the hard times.

The Winnemem Wintu were cut down to a scant 200 tribal members after the sudden influx of new European diseases, the plagues of small-pox and influenza, wiping out 90% of the people in the region, none of them immune to any of the new European diseases.

Then there were the American bounties on Wintu scalps, and finally the laws which said they no longer existed, despite all of the evidence to the contrary.

The very first legislative act of the new, murderous American government in California was to offer bounties for Indian scalps, sparing only a few of the people, a practice which enabled the Gold Rush and built great fortunes. Although signatories to an 1851 treaty and identified as the tribe who would be drowned in the 1941 federal act which created the Shasta Dam, the Winnemem Wintu ceased to exist as "Indians" under federal law. The Winnemem Wintu, like many other tribes, signed treaties nation-to-nation with the federal government in good faith, even if under duress, but the US Congress never got around to ratifying them.

Termination by Accountant

This strange irony, that the government of settlers and intruders who took your land and killed your people gets to determine if you are still an Indian, remains particularly bitter to many tribes. The Wintu are particularly caught in this quagmire, lacking federal "recognition."

In what Bruce Granville-Miller at the University of British Columbia calls "termination by accountant", a convenient set of legal determinations make the Wintu all but invisible to federal law, and subsequently the protection of a trustee.

Miller, who studies unrecognized indigenous peoples on a worldwide scale, notes, "It's easy for nations to find ways to disqualify them, to make them simply disappear." This is particularly convenient in the case of the Wintu, whose way of life is tied to a river others want, a fish that industry seeks to replace, and who face a small army of agricultural lobbyists. Federal recognition would mean that the federal government would help you protect your way of life. And, in the case of the Wintu, that would be problematic to a lot of powerful, moneyed interests.

So it is that through a gauntlet of 19th century massacres, and another gauntlet of 150 years or so of land theft and legal maneuvering, the US and California governments made the surviving Winnemem Wintu disappear, hid them under that cloak of invisibility of federal Indian law.

It turns out that, however, even if the federal government says you do not exist (as it does for an estimated 250,000 Native people in the US who are part of unrecognized tribes), you still exist in the eyes of the Creator and in the eyes of the salmon. The People—despite all of the injustice that has befallen them—remain on the river, holding their young women's coming of age ceremonies, their doctoring ceremonies at their remaining sacred sites, spanning some 77 miles of the McCloud.

In 1941, the Shasta dam drowned more than 26 miles of the lower McCloud River system, burying sacred sites, villages and history under a deep pool of water destined to benefit cities and Big Ag far away, and tourists who could afford the way of life, a houseboat on Lake Shasta.

The dam blocked the passage of the salmon people, and the McCloud River salmon—the Nur –either interbred with the Sacramento River salmon, or died out in California. The Wintu grieved the loss of their salmon, the Nur who had given them voice, and the loss of the river.

Then came the next round of demands as populations increased, and the greed of American agriculture aggregated itself into California's central valleys. The Shasta Dam would provide the lifeblood for the corporate agriculture, for the farms and the towns and cities growing in the desert, all at the expense of the Wintu and the Nur.

California's biggest dam by a million acre feet is the Shasta dam. In the spectrum of the big dams, it is, to some, a bit of a disappointment, shadowed by Hoover, Glen Canyon, Three Gorges and every other mammoth dam of new. It did in its first round, however, swallow 125 Wintu ceremonial sites, including Salmon Heart Rock, where the Winnemem Wintu gathered to catch and dry salmon. Fish Rock was blown up to make room for a railroad track in 1914, which was, like everything else, drowned by the waters.

What is left of Dekkas Rock, a prayer site, protrudes from the reservoir, as one reporter notes, "a malformed atoll." It was here, next to the river, that the Winnemem held what other tribes in the region call Big Times, where disputes were adjudicated, songs were sung, ceremonies were held and marriages were arranged.

Homecoming

"Our old people said that the salmon would be hidden behind a river of ice. Indian doctors and prophets had been with the Wintu long ago, and prophesized the time when the salmon would disappear."
—Caleen Sisk, Winnemem Wintu

That was almost unimaginable to the Wintu, or to those who "discovered" the salmon of the McCloud and Middle rivers.

Dr. Livingston Stone, a great fish biologist, arrived in Wintu territory noting that the spawning Chinook were so plentiful he could have walked across their backs from one side of the river to the other. In the 1870s, he established the Baird Hatchery on the McCloud, originally as an effort to breed a Pacific salmon to replenish the now dwindling and overfished Atlantic salmon stocks. The Wintu were initially opposed to the fishery, but made peace with the white men of the fisheries on the condition that the salmon would always be able to come home.

In 1890, in a strange turning of events, Stone decided to attempt to transplant the Wintu Nur to another world. This world was *Aotearoa*, or New Zealand. There, in the Rakaia River on the South Island is where the salmon people came to live. The Rakaia River, echoing the prophecy of the Wintu, is a glacial-fed river, a river behind a wall of ice.

The Winnemem Wintu salmon were introduced into Aotearoa's South Island waters between 1901 and 1907, where the fish thrived. The salmon has now established spawning runs in the Rakaia, Waimak-ariri, Hurunui, Waiau, Rangitata, Opihi and Ashburton rivers.

The Vision of Aotearoa

The vision to go to Aotearoa came from a ceremony held at the Shasta Dam. Here in September 2004, the Wintu held a war dance. It is here that Caleen had the vision, where "The Spirits came into the fire area and said we had to get it done, that we needed to mend our relation-ship with the fish in order to heal."

It took a good deal of faith, perseverance and some plane tickets to reunite the Nur and their people, and in the spring of 2010, the Winnemem Wintu and their precious Nur were met again, in a cer-emony on the Rakaia River, where the Maori people now care for the salmon.

The *Nur Chonas Winyupus* ceremony was held on the river, and the people atoned for their failure to stop the Shasta dam, asking forgive-ness from the salmon. 28 members of the Winnemem Wintu—many of whom had never before left their homeland—gathered on the banks of the Rakaia River, accompanied by *Ngai Tahu* elders to commence an intense four-day ceremony which culminated in a dance called the *Nur Chonas Winypus* or Middle Water Salmon Dance.

"We danced very hard for four days; we sang our hearts out. We have so much sadness but we feel relief in reconnecting with our fish. We don't want to leave them." Calleen remembered. And so the salmon people kept their bargain with the Nur. In August of 2011, in an annual gathering to restore the Winnemem Wintu and their salmon, in the shadow of the sacred *Boyum Payuk*, the Winnemem walked up the McCloud River, stopping at each falls in the upper river, diving in for the salmon and putting prayers and songs for their return and recovery.

The story of the Salmon and the People spans a thousand years of mythology, and in this new millennium, the mythology is coming into its own era.

Return to *Boyum Payuk*

That August day, the setting was rather unique. Under the pine trees, a strange gathering of people: the Wintu, the Maori, and representatives from the National Oceanic and Atmospheric Administration (NOAA) and US Fish and Wildlife talked about the fate of the salmon, and their return to the Wintu.

The Wintu have gone over to Aotearoa, they have remembered the songs, and restored their oral history of the movement of the Nur, and they have made peace with their relatives. This is not the same with the US Fish and Wildlife.

The NOAA and US Fish and Wildlife officials are in a sort of labyrinth of laws, politics and genetic confusion. The studies on restoration of the salmon run head on into the plans to enlarge the Shasta Dam. The studies on salmon restoration become confused in DNA structures and genetics, as scientists debate the history of the salmon and propose to introduce new genetically engineered salmon. It is a pandemonium of agendas and confusion.

There is the first question, asked by the NOAA representatives, who apparently do not believe that the salmon remembered by the Wintu and the Maori are the same salmon that came from the river. The NOAA representative refers to "failed attempts" to introduce the salmon, and he is corrected by Pauline Meade of the Maori delegation.

"Five generations ago my great great grandfather met with Caleen's great great grandfather and made an agreement on these salmon. " She remembers an oral history passed down before, apparently, it was recorded for the NOAA scientists.

"We took up a boat up the Raiki River and that is how those salmon got there. Our people packed them in sphagnum moss." Pauline's ancestor was the head of the Maori fisheries at the time the McCloud salmon came to New Zealand.

Caleen talks patiently with the NOAA representatives, "We know where those salmon came from, because we remember. We don't need a DNA test, we just need the salmon returned. I know these are Mc-Cloud river salmon because he's telling me that, I know the salmon came from there."

The NOAA representatives talk about how difficult the situation is, and are unsure of the fish, wishing to do more genetic work, but there are, basically no fish in the McCloud to test. People need to know how the salmon got to the ice wall.

"These two people were paramount chiefs in their own right," Pauline explains to the NOAA representatives, who are really on the side of the Wintu, the Maori and the Nur, but they are engaged in a sort of bureaucratic hand wringing. This consists of a discussion that there is no knowledge on the genetics of the fish, there is a required replumbing of the river to accommodate fish around the dams, and then there are the genetic and political interests which are not on the side of the Wintu, the Maori and the Nur.

In the shade of massive ponderosa pines, they continue their discussions. It is a bit strange and awkward, talking about those who are not present but, the Winnemem would say, wish to come home.

"The salmon were introduced to our country and have done extremely well," Dirk the New Zealand hatchery manager tells the NOAA representatives, Gary Sprague and Brian Elrot.

NOAA is a bit skeptical, "We are behind in terms of working with reclamation to get salmon back to the McCloud," Elrot explains. His delivery seems unconvincing, it would appear to the Maori and the Wintu present, who shake their heads in disbelief. Or maybe, not surprised that the US government is "behind" on any sort of ecological remedy, but bemused by the biologists and the bureaucratic sink hole they are in. Elrot continues, "There is no shortage of issues which need to be addressed. Right now it's you guys and us and not a lot of other support. We need some biological opinions to insure that these are the same salmon genetically, looking at DNA, and then to determine the viability of the return of the salmon."

This seems to outrage the Maori and the Wintu who, instead of DNA testing and studies, have relied on oral history and observation to determine the viability and story of the salmon. "We would say that the strongest have survived, that is these salmon, " says Dirk of the Fisheries. "You guys here get excited about a run of 100,000 fish, we are talking about 2.5 million."

Genetic irony

Whilst the scientists talk about the genetics of the Nur, and if the New Zealand fish are indeed the same fish, new genetically-engineered fish are being proposed for the ecosystem.

"I wish the government would remember why we're so close to a world without salmon," Caleen Sisk wrote in the California Progress Report. "They built dams that destroyed the spawning grounds, dug mines that polluted the rivers and then acted surprised when the salmon disappeared. They've since been trying to replace the salmon they've destroyed with coyote-like machinations, trapping the salmon and hauling them by truck around the dams, building factory-like hatcheries and now the unholy conception of frankenfish."

That fish is the first biotech animal for human consumption being reviewed by the Federal Drug Administration. The fish, called AquaAdvantage by its maker (and Frankenfish by others), takes a fertilized egg of a north American salmon and adds a gene from an eel-like ocean pout fish. This special genetic combination allows the salmon to grow at twice the rate as a conventional salmon. Somewhere between the discussion of the "genetic purity of the Nur" and the industry driven GMO salmon, there has got to be a coyote laughing.

Even though the Wintu continue to be pummeled by federal and state Indian policies, and have ceased to exist as Indians under federal law, they continue to act as if they are unaware of their federal designation. The Wintu remain close to their middle river and to their sacred sites, holding their young women's coming of age ceremonies and their medicine ceremonies.

The discussion becomes long and labored. It is an interesting irony, that to build the Shasta dam which destroyed much of the Wintu homeland and the pathways for the Wintu Nur, little consultation and few studies seem to be required. Now, endless studies, reports on the viability of the salmon, and impact statements on various levels of the Shasta Dam, as well as new proposals to raise the levels of the Shasta Dam continue to mire the return of the salmon. The Wintu are bogged down in White Tape, along with their precious Nur.

The Story of Almonds, Bees and Salmon

The real story is not being discussed by the white men from NOAA this day under the pines with the Wintus. That story is being discussed and plans are made elsewhere. That is the story of the almonds, the bees and the water. That is why the salmon and splittail trout are being killed. Consider this, in May of 2011, federal pumps on the Sacramento River and some state facilities killed 4,400,073 split tail trout and 3600 salmon in just 8 days.

According to Sacramento reporter, Dan Bacher, state and federal water pump projects continued to kill "400,000 to 600,000 imperiled Sacramento split tail and up to 700 threatened spring-run Chinook salmon each day. These fish are being destroyed to divert Delta water to large scale agriculture on the west side of the San Joaquin Valley and southern California water agencies...."

The primary motivation is almonds. As of 2009, California is in the third year of a drought, which is compounded by regulations which are restricting water supplies south of the Delta.

The US leads the world in almond production with a spanking 68% of the world's market. That is where the country's bees winter, incidentally, in the California almond orchards, also a site of much concern with regards to the deadly bee disease, Colony Collapse Disorder. The almond mono-crop orchards have been pushing further and further out and what they need is water. Every almond among millions needs its own gallon of clean water. The primary source of water is Shasta, hundred of miles to the north. That is why the Big Ag interests of California look back to the dam and to the waters of the Wintu to solve their problems.

For the past decade, proposals have been bantered about to raise the water levels at Shasta Dam. An additional 18 feet of lake depth would provide water for a million Californians, and to the almond orchards. That is why the Westlands Water District the nation's largest water and irrigation district (with around 700 farmers and businesses) has purchased seven miles of the McCloud River, just upstream from the Shasta Dam.

That was a very expensive purchase, one Westlands was intent upon securing. That's why the Water District paid around $5 million more than any other bid on the fishing camp owned previously by the Hills Brothers coffee heirs.

Proposals are under consideration to raise the Shasta Dam water levels from 6.5 to 18.5 feet, with corresponding increases of reservoir storage from 256,000 to 634,000 acre feet." "How do they justify flooding the Winnemem Wintu people out twice?" Caleen asks. "They still haven't fulfilled the 1941 Act of Congress that said they are to provide like lands and pay for all the allotment and communal lands…And the Shasta Dam is still not paid for by the public."

Caleen has reviewed the Environmental Impact Statement on the dam and refers to it as a "dehumanizing document – it takes our beautiful culture and summarizes it into a couple of paragraphs, and just names a couple of sites." The Environmental Impact Statement, according to her assessment, is woefully weak. "It doesn't describe the importance of the sites to our people or the heartache and psychological destruction it would cause to us if these places were submerged," Sisk said. "They don't talk about us as the people most impacted, or the fact we have nowhere else to go to practice our religion. We can only teach our distinctive lifeway to be Winnemem here. It will be extremely hard to teach the tribal youth when you can't go to the sacred site, see it and feel it and develop a relationship with it to be Winnemem."

As far as federal interest in the culture and way of life of the Wintu, the EIS is—in Caleen's eyes—a joke. It seems that the Bureau of Reclamation spent a scant $8000 on hiring an archeologist, who found it essential to visit the Wintu just one time.

"How could they possibly know anything about the 'cultural impact,'" she said. "Anthropologists, filmmakers and journalists spend years understanding the vast complexity in the survival of an old living culture. They came out here once when they were introducing the whole idea, and they met with us on the river once. They told us they only had an $8,000 budget to do this archaeological report for the 371 shore miles on the lake and the 200 river miles to the Delta."

In somewhat predictable scientific and government logic, the Bureau of Reclamation has suggested that the Nur will be pleased with a larger dam. The Bureau claims that dam expansion will "increase the survival" of" salmon and steelhead. "A bigger cold water pool IS NOT what's best for salmon," Caleen responds. "It seems as that is one of the first goals in the EIS, but where is the study that shows how just building a water way or fish swim around the dam would benefit and increase the numbers of salmon? A fish swim would be cheaper and produce more salmon spawning grounds in already naturally cold water. It would save millions of dollars in the cost of the cold water pool currently. NOAA has already found that salmon need to go up above Shasta Dam to the McCloud because of climate change. The dam raise would flood more than 7 miles of cold water spawning grounds on the McCloud River, Squaw Creek, and the Sacramento River," said Sisk.

Sisk remains hopeful for a good ear. "If we could describe what a sacred site is, maybe they (the federal government) would understand the connected lines and that all of them have a different purpose, and they all help us in different ways," concluded Sisk. "It's not like a church where you have everything in one place. We could describe how sacred sites are the teachers....We don't want the American dream. We don't want casinos. We want our prayer rocks."

In the shadows of the great mountain, *Boyum Poyu* , and the glacial river, the Wintu remain. Their river changed, the Nur vanquished to far away. The Wintu have suffered, yet there is a hope and a prophecy which is held to. In that hope, there is an understanding that the Nur will return to their river and their people. In this era of fast transportation, they may only need some Fed Ex packaging and a place to go.

IN THE TIME OF THE SACRED PLACES

"It's not like a church where you have everything in one place. We could describe how sacred sites are the teachers.... We don't want the American dream.... We want our prayer rocks."
— CALLEEN SISK, WINNEMEM WINTU

In the time of Thunderbeings and Underwater Serpents, the humans, animals, and plants conversed and carried on lives of mischief, wonder, and mundane tasks. The prophets told of times ahead, explained the causes of the deluge of past, and predicted the two paths of the future: one scorched and one green, one of which the Anishinaabeg would have to choose.

In the time of the Thunderbeings and Underwater Serpents, it was understood that there was a constant balance and a universe beyond this material world that needed to be maintained and to whom we would belong always.

The Anishinaabe people, among other land-based peoples, undulate between these worlds. The light of day, the deepness of night remains; the parallel planes of spirit and material world coexist in perpetuity. All remains despite the jackhammer of industrial civilization, the sound of combustion engines, and the sanitized white of a dioxin-bleached day. That was then, but that is also now.

Teachings, ancient as the people who have lived on a land for five millennia, speak of a set of relationships to all that is around, predicated on respect, recognition of the interdependency of all beings, an understanding of humans' absolute need to be reverent and to manage our behavior, and an understanding that this relationship must be reaffirmed through lifeways and through acknowledgment of the sacred.

Millennia have passed since that time, yet those Beings still emerge: lightning strikes at unexpected times, the seemingly endless fires of climate change, tornadoes that flatten, King tides, deluges of rivers, copper Beings in the midst of industrial society. So it is that we come to face our smallness in a world of mystery, and our responsibilities to the life that surrounds us.

We are a part of everything that is beneath us, above us and around us. Our past is our present, our present is our future, and our future is seven generations past and present. –*Haudenosaunee* teaching

In the midst of this time, land-based peoples work to continue such a lifeway, or to follow simply the original instructions passed on by *Gichi Manidoo,* the Creator, or those who instruct us. This path often is littered with the threats of a fossil-fuel and nuclear economy: a uranium mine, a big dam project, or the Tar Sands. People work to restore or retain their relationship to a sacred place and to a world. In many places, peoples hold Earth renewal ceremonies, for example, or water healing ceremonies. In an Indigenous philosophical view, these ceremonies are how we are able to continue. This essay tells some of those stories.

The Notion of *Frontier*

This essay also tells a story of a society based on the notion of *frontier.* Born of a doctrine of discovery, *terra nullius,* and a papal-driven entitlement to vanquish and destroy all that which was Indigenous, America was framed in the mantra of Manifest Destiny.

This settler-focused relationship to this North American continent has been historically one of conquest, of utilitarian relationship, of an anthropocentric taking of wealth to make more things for Empire. That society has named and claimed things, one mountain after another (Mt. Rainier, Harney Peak, Mt. McKinley, Mt. Lassen, Pikes Peak, Mt. Hood), all named, and claimed, for empire.

Naming and claiming with a flag does not mean *relationship;* it means only naming and claiming. Americans have developed a sense of place related to empire, with no understanding that the Holy Land is also here. To name sacred mountain spirits after mortal men who blow through for just a few decades is to denude relationship.

Americans are also transient, taught an American dream of greener pastures elsewhere. This too belittles relationship to Place. It holds no responsibility, only a sense of entitlement—to mineral rights, water rights, and private property—enshrined in the Constitution.

In the times we find ourselves, with the crashing of ecosystems, dying out of fish and trees, change and destabilization of climate, our relationship to place and to relatives—whether they have fins or roots—merits reconsideration.

On Sacred Places

Since the beginning of times, the Creator and Mother Earth have given our peoples places to learn the teachings that will allow us to continue and reaffirm our responsibilities and ways on the lands from which we have come. Indigenous peoples are place-based societies, and at the center of those places are the most sacred of our sites, where we reaffirm our relationships.

Everywhere there are Indigenous people, there are sacred sites, there are ways of knowing, there are *relationships*. The people, the rivers, the mountains, the lakes, the animals, and the fish are all related. In recent years, US courts have challenged our ability to be in these places, and indeed to protect them. In many cases, we are asked to quantify "how sacred it is, or how often it is sacred." Baffling concepts in the spiritual realm. Yet we do not relent, we are not capable of becoming subsumed.

Copper and Iron, Wild Rice and Water, and Wolves

"Sometimes it seems like people aren't interested in sticking around for another thousand years." —Mike Wiggins, Bad River Anishinaabe Tribal Chairman

To the East, on the shore of *Gichi Gummi* (Lake Superior), the Anishinaabeg *Akiing* ("the Land to which the Anishinaabe people belong") stretches throughout the Great Lakes region in a territory of lakes and rivers, wild rice, and wolves.

On this land the Underwater *Manidoowag*, the *Miskwaabik* and *Biwaabik* spirits of copper and iron ore, have lived, *omaa akiing*, since the time of the Thunderbeings.

As one early European explorer recorded, "Copper was said to belong to the Underwater *Manitouk*.... One often finds at the bottom of the water, pieces of pure copper.... I have several times seen such pieces in the Savages' hand, and since they are superstitious, they keep to them as so many divinities, or as presents which the gods dwelling beneath the water have given them and on which their welfare is to depend."

The Underwater *Manidoowag, Miskwaabik* and *Biwaabik*, were viewed not as spirits by the American government, but as objects of empire. Some of the first incursions by the US government onto Anishinaabeg land, in the early 1800s, were to secure access to iron and copper deposits. Within a very short period, four treaties were signed by the United States, each providing for mining in Anishinaabeg territory. By mid-century, more than 100 copper companies had been incorporated in the *Anishinaabeg Akiing*. Many of today's US-based transnational mining companies, including Kennecott, Anaconda Copper, and 3M, were founded in this era on the wealth of the Anishinaabeg.

The wild rice has also been here since the time of Thunderbeings. Indeed, it was a part of the Anishinaabeg migration story and of a set of prophecies instructing the people to "Go to the Place where the Food Grows upon the Water."

Called *manoomin* ("a seed of the Creator") by the Anishinaabe, wild rice is the only grain endemic to North America and is one of the greatest gifts imaginable to the land and waters. There are few other places in the world where such a bountiful gift is delivered to those who live there, whether they have wings or hands.

Owing to the unique nature and adaptability of the manoomin, the lakes and rivers each year offer a wild rice crop at some place in the region. That is an amazing food security for a people and for the waterfowl that nest and eat in these same waters. It is because of this bounty that where there is wild rice there are Ojibwe or Anishinaabeg people, and where there are Anishinaabeg, there is wild rice. This is a sacred food and a keystone of the ecosystem of the Great Lakes region, or Anishinaabe Akiing. As copper and iron mining despoiled the waters of the lakes and rivers, so it devastated both the manoomin and those whose life and ways depended upon it.

The decimation of the Anishinaabeg by plagues, starvation, and federal policies closely mirrored the destruction of the *ma'iingan*, the wolf. The Anishinaabeg relationship to the ma'iingan is deeply sacred in the traditions and history of the people. It is said that the first friend of the half spirit/half human being *Naanaaboozhoo*, a central figure in Anishinaabeg culture and teachings, was the ma'iingan. In Anishinaabeg prophecies, that which befalls the wolf will befall the Anishinaabeg. The limiting of territories—to reservations for the Anishinaabeg and to a few refuges and a few sparse patches of the north woods for the wolves—occurred for both. Like the people, the wolves were brought to near-extinction.

Yet both wolves and Anishinaabeg have returned to the northland. Today, nineteen Anishinaabeg reservations span the North Country, from Michigan into Montana. This same territory is today the home of the largest wolf population in the lower forty-eight states. Where there are 60,000 Anishinaabeg, there are 5,000 wolves—both relatives, one with two legs and one with four, rebounding after catastrophic losses.

The Predator Returns

The companies forged of empire in the 1850s are also returning home now, having ravaged the world, fortified their empires, and left memorials to the copper that once was in the form of huge pits. New mines are proposed throughout the Anishinaabe Akiing. Thus far they have been fended off by citizens and tribal opposition, but the region is incredibly challenged, as Ojibwes note in a letter to the United Nations requesting assistance: "Currently, an aggressive mining boom throughout Anishinaabeg territory, of present-day Michigan, Wisconsin, Minnesota, and Ontario, threatens the water quality and ecosystem of almost every sub-watershed of Lake Superior."

Eagle Rock, known as "the Home of the White Wolf," is a sacred site and prehistoric navigation site on the Keewenaw. It is considered sacred to not only the Anishinaabeg, but also the Ho-Chunk and Cheyenne peoples. The tribes living today in this territory, as well as the National Congress of American Indians, have requested that the rock be protected as a site of religious worship.

Underneath the rock, in a world below, is *Miskwaabik Aabinoojiins*, or the Copper Child. This copper ore body, appearing in GIS imaging as a baby, awaits its scheduled end like a convict on death row: Rio Tinto Zinc, a UK-based mining company, through its subsidiary Kennecott, plans to mine the copper deposit adjacent to the sacred place.

It has been a seven-year battle for the sacred site, marked by arrests and legal actions, and now by a petition to the United Nations for intervention under the Declaration on the Rights of Indigenous Peoples not only to protect their sacred sites, but to be protected from minerals exploitation, which will destroy the aquatic ecosystems of wild rice and a rich land upon which the Anishinaabeg have lived for five millennia.

The Michigan regulatory authorities, who have taken jurisdiction over the area, have ruled against the tribes, the water, and the sacred site, stating essentially that the site could not be sacred or did not have spiritual significance because a place of worship must be a building. On these grounds, the state approved the mining permit.

Proposals in both Wisconsin and Minnesota would eviscerate water quality laws, with severe impacts on the wild rice or manoomin of the North. In turn, the recent delisting of the wolf by the US Fish and Wildlife seems synchronized exactly with the interests of new mining companies in the region.

But it is a time when relationships are changing. It is ironic that the two largest challenges to the wholesale mining of the North may be manoomin, or wild rice, and the ma'iingan. Tribal communities, joined increasingly by northern residents, have opposed the threats to water and wild rice throughout the North Country, and regulatory battles are underway in Minnesota.

And, while the wolf has been delisted by federal agencies under the Endangered Species Act, tribal communities are opposing the delisting in their territories. This is significant, as the wolf territories coincide with reservations and the areas surrounding tribal reservations still within tribal jurisdiction due to treaties and court decisions.

In this time, tribal governments and intergovernmental agencies in the North pledge to retain their relationship and responsibility to the ma'iingan, and our communities remain vigilant in working to protect the sacred beings from the mines of the predator.

Doko'oo'slid: The Mountain of *Kachinas* and Recycled Ski Areas

To the far south, in the realm of the sacred mountains of the Diné or Navajo people, *Diné Bii Kaya,* the four sacred mountains, are again facing threats. Mt. Taylor is once again proposed for uranium mining, and *Doko'oo'sliid*, the Sacred Mountain of the West to the Navajo, is being desecrated for the pleasure of skiers.

This volcanic highland area of Arizona began forming over 6 million years ago with the eruption of nearly 600 volcanoes. The most dramatic of those eruptions created a place sacred to thirteen tribes, a cluster of three 12,000-foot mountain peaks known as the Sacred Mountain of the West, one of four cornerstones marking the borders of *Diné Bii Kaya*, the land of the Diné or Navajo. The Diné know it as a place where the *Kachina* spirits emerge. In the proud vernacular of American empire, the sacred mountain is called San Francisco Peaks.

The highest point in Arizona, the only arctic-alpine vegetation in the state, which grows here in a fragile two-square-mile zone and Arizona's best examples of Ice Age glaciations, can all be found here. It has been a place for the gathering of sacred herbs and the practice of religious ceremonies since the dawn of time.

In 1984, the United States Congress recognized the fragile ecosystems and cultural significance of the area and designated the Kachina Peaks Wilderness. Yet here, in this unlikely place, in an ostensibly protected Wilderness in the desert, a ski resort has been proposed, with a plan to pipe treated sewage water from Flagstaff to spray artificial snow on the sacred mountain. There is no water source on the mountain other than what falls from the sky.

Despite the known ecosystem, archeological and cultural issues, and determined opposition from Native nations and conservation organizations, the Ninth US Circuit Court of Appeals recently allowed the Arizona Snowbowl Recreation project to proceed with its plan.

Flagstaff-treated sewer water will be trucked to Snowbowl until a 14.8-mile pipeline is complete, and then some 180 million gallons a year of treated effluent from the city of Flagstaff will be pumped up the sacred mountain to the ski area for snowmaking. The treated sewage has been proven to contain contaminants such as pharmaceuticals and hormones. Snowbowl hopes to attract ski-starved desert dwellers to its resort with clever marketing, but it remains to be seen how enticing a mouthful of Snowbowl effluent cocktail might be.

The Snowbowl owners have already clear-cut some 74 acres of rare alpine forest for new ski runs. A 10-million-gallon retention pond and another 12 miles of pipeline will be built to distribute reclaimed sewer water along the ski runs, all desecrations in the eyes of the Diné people. In the summer of 2012, protests continued in defense of a sacred place, in a call for access to water for people and the land, and ultimately in a questioning of priorities.

This is the difference between worldviews, one that views a land as a rich ore body, or a playground, and another that views it as a source of great spiritual and cultural wealth.... This is the story of the time in which we find ourselves.

The Auction of the Sacred

As the wind breathes out of Wind Cave, I am reminded of the creation of humans and my own small place in this magnificent world. Wind Cave National Park in the Black Hills is named for the cave itself, called *Washun Niya,* ("the Breathing Hole of Mother Earth") by the Lakota People. In the Lakota creation story, it is from here that they emerged to this world.

It is a complex cave system. According to scientists, we may only have a sense of five percent of the cave's volume and breadth, and likely even less of its power. Some might call this the "known unknown." Most Indigenous peoples would understand it as the Great Mystery— that which is much larger than our own anthropocentric understanding of the world—reflecting the understanding that, indeed, there is more than one world surrounding people.

So it is that in 2012, a time of change and transformation signaled in an American election year and predicted in the Mayan Calendar, we find the smallness and the greatness of humans in the much larger world around us coming face-to-face in the Black Hills. A most sacred place, *Pe'Sla*, in the center of the Lakota Universe, came up for sale, and values and worldviews clashed.

Pe'Sla, to the Lakota, is "*Center of the Heart of Everything that is*, one of a small number of highly revered and geographically-cosmologically integral places on the entire planet," according to Lakota scholar Chase Iron Eyes. It is "the place where Morning Star, manifested as a meteor, fell to earth to help the Lakota by killing a great bird that had taken the lives of seven women; Morning Star's descent having created the wide open uncharacteristic bald spot in the middle of the forested Black Hills (on American maps, this is called Old Baldy). The Morning Star placed the spirits of those seven women in the sky as the constellation 'Pleiades' or 'The Seven Sisters.'"

On August 25, 2012, the Center of the Heart of Everything was to be placed on the auction block, destined to be diced into a set of 300-acre tracts proposed for ranchettes, with a possible road through the heart of what has been, until now, a relatively un-desecrated sacred site.

"We didn't even know it was going to be sold," Debra White Plume, an Oglala Lakota activist from Manderson told me. "We heard nothing about it until we saw the auction announcement."

America is a country where private property is enshrined as a constitutional right, but the rights of nature, of the natural world, or of unborn generations are not. In the time of the crashing of ecosystems and worlds, it may be worth not making a commodity out of all that is revered.

A 2005 editorial in the generally very conservative Rapid City Journal points out that protecting Lakota sacred sites is of interest to all: "Non-Indians have little to fear if familiar sites are designated as sacred; visitors are still allowed at Bear Butte, Devil's Tower, and Rainbow Bridge, even though they are being managed as Indian sacred sites. And in fact, expanding non-Indians' knowledge and appreciation of the Indian lore surrounding such sites could lead to greater cultural understanding."

With less than two weeks remaining before *Pe'Sla* was to be auctioned off, word spread through Lakota communities (three of which—all Lakota reservations—are in the economically poorest counties in the country), through the use of Facebook, the Internet, and the media, from the Huffington Post to the Seattle Times.

The story of the Lakota people, their sacred site, and the proposed auction was repeated in whispers, and then in rallies and in outrage. Using the Internet, the communities raised over half a million dollars, which was then matched by tribal money originating with the Rosebud Sioux Tribe, and other donations. The auction was cancelled, and the Lakota people have begun to negotiate for the purchase of their sacred site.

It is incredibly ironic, however, in many ways, particularly considering that the *Paha Sapa*, the Black Hills, was never purchased from the Lakota but illegally taken by the United States with the advent of gold mining (the Hearst empire).

Though over $105 million was allocated for the Black Hills by Congress to pay Lakota people for the illegal taking, that money has never been accepted. Hence the irony: the people must buy back land they have never considered owned by anyone else.

On a Return to Sacred Lifeways

There is always hope, and for those of us who remain involved in our ceremonies, there is also faith. That faith is reaffirmed when small miracles of spirit occur, and the world changes.

On the banks of the McCloud River in Northern California, the Wintu gather, despite citations and legal opposition by the state of California, to hold their sacred coming-of-age ceremonies for their young women. This is how life continues.

And, one day, not too far away, those salmon will return home from Aotearoa. And there will be a celebration of the Nur and the Wintu.

In the north woods, the Anishinaabeg celebrate one round of opposing the Beast. In 2012, the huge GTAC mine in the Penokee Mountains of Wisconsin—the headwaters to the Bad River, the centerpiece of the Bad River tribal community of Anishinaabeg—was defeated, like another four before it in Wisconsin. The defeat may be temporary, but it is breathing room for Mother Earth, and in 2012, it seems that *Pe'Sla* will be protected from becoming a set of luxury ranchettes, and may continue as a place where a people pray and reaffirm their relationship to Creation.

The Recovery of Names

And then there is the renaming, or the recovery of names. Several decades ago, Mt. McKinley became Mt. *Denali*. On the other side of the world, Australia's Ayers Rock became *Uluru*, in the name of the people who live there, not the white man who found it.

In 2010, in Canada, the *Haida* homeland was formally renamed *Haida Gwaii*, eclipsing Queen Charlotte Island, named for a Queen who had likely never seen that land nor understood Haida traditions. And further south, the Salish Sea is emerging in what was Puget Sound, and more reaffirmations of place and history are reframing our understanding of the holy land that is here. These stories join with the stories of a people and their allies who have come to live on this land.

On a larger scale, the New Zealand Courts have recently affirmed the rights of a River to exist, in a court system that emerged from colonial and church authorities. The Whanganui River became a legal entity under the name *Te Awa Tupua* ("an integrated, living whole") and was given the same status as a person under New Zealand law in 2012.

The industrial predator, however, is unrelenting. Voracious in appetite, greed, and lacking any heart, all that is becomes prey ...

If 57 percent of the energy produced in the US is wasted through inefficiencies, one might want to become less wasteful to survive. And if two-thirds of our material-based economy ends up in waste dumps relatively quickly, we may want to cut our consumption. These are economic choices, political choices, and personal choices. And they ultimately have to do with empire, the need for new frontiers, and making peace, *Omaa Akiing*, here on this land.

In the din of crashing worlds, it is possible to watch and breathe. In the 2012 deluge of the city of Duluth, rain fell constantly for two days onto the streets of a city with aging infrastructure. The Anishinaabeg remember a Great Flood from the earliest of memories, after which the world was made anew. The Anishinaabeg watched the flood from our reservations, an island safely away from this deluge and crash.

The tally in economic terms of the 2012 flood is somewhere around $100 million. That figure represents just the beginning of climate-change-related expenses in this year. By March of 2012, there had been over 129,000 recorded weather records on a worldwide scale. World insurance agencies project that we will be spending 20 percent of our GDP on a worldwide scale on climate change-related disasters.

The polar bear is freed by the Duluth deluge from the zoo, escaping his pen. As the bear headed north from the Duluth Zoo, we Anishinaabeg knew that the time was changing. We watched and we understood that we, as sacred beings in this millennium, have an opportunity to do a righteous and *pono* thing—to take a good path.

In the time of Thunderbeings and Underwater Serpents, the humans, animals, and plants conversed and carried on lives of mischief, wonder, and mundane tasks. The prophets told of times ahead, explained the deluge of past and predicted the two paths of the future: one scorched and one green, one of which the Anishinaabeg would have to choose.

All of us have the same choice, and somewhere in this time, there is the potential to take a right path.

Postscript: In the winter of 2014, four tribes of the Oceti Sakowin (Great Sioux) *nation purchased 437 acres of* Pe'Sla, *the "heart of everything" .. a place central to the Oceti Sakowin star knowledge and understanding of our place in the universe. The purchase was a collaborative with the Indian Land Tenure Foundation.*

In the Time of the Sacred Places *is Winona LaDuke's contribution to the anthology,* Spiritual Ecology: The Cry of the Earth, *edited by Llewellyn Vaughan-Lee*

THE HEAVY HAUL COMES TO TOWN

"We will be here forever"

— Niimiipuu woman

When 750 Nez Perce, accompanied by 1,000 horses, fled the U.S. Cavalry on a 1,200 mile route through the mountains, valleys and rivers of Oregon, Idaho and Montana in1877, their path took them past the Heart of the Monster, from whence the Nez Perce, or *Niimiipuu* people, had originated, and through their precious Bitterroot Mountains. Their route was treacherous but their determination to survive was unshakeable.

Some 140 years later, the black heart of industrial society has come to torment the Nimiipuu, using that same route. Exxon Mobil and some other large oil traffickers want to run massive trucks and machinery (imagine the Statue of Liberty on its side, with wheels) through Oregon, Idaho and Montana, headed for the Athabascan tar sands in Alberta, Canada.

Those gigantic specialized trucks will carry monstrous pieces of mining equipment imported from Korea up to the Tar Sands project, where oil is being extracted from a mammoth pit by blasting saturated sand with steam. It is already the largest and most destructive industrial project in history, and those trucks could be shuttling supplies up there for the next 50 years. No trucks have made the entire run to Alberta thus far, but Exxon hopes to get the green light for the Heavy Haul soon.

The supply route begins at the port in Lewiston, Oregon and runs along the Columbia River, over Highway 12 in Idaho, and up through Lolo Pass into Montana and then north into Alberta. Those behemoth trucks would traverse through the territory of the *Nimiipuu*, the Blackfeet and other Native peoples. If approved, this project—dubbed the Heavy Haul—would create a permanent industrial corridor in the heart of Nez Perce territory and that of the Blackfeet, and would pass by the homes of thousands of people. The Alberta tar sands industry, which is served by , the Heavy Haul will destroy 10% of Canada's boreal forest, and the lives of thousands of Native people. Which is why the people are rising up against it, from Lewiston to Alberta.

At a well-attended community meeting in Lapwai, Idaho on February 27, tribal members expressed safety concerns about the proposed deliveries, and larger concerns about what the Heavy Haul will mean for the *Nimiipuu* and for Mother Earth. They were thinking big-picture, long-term, but having Highway 12 clogged with massive trucks for the next 50 years might seem pretty close to forever, particularly if you're in a traffic accident on that road, which is already adorned with crosses honoring the many *Nimiipuu* who have died on its treacherous turns.

The website for The Rural People of Highway 12 Fighting Goliath lists a few of the reasons that road is special for Natives, and for all Americans. It crosses or runs parallel to more than 80 miles of the Lewis and Clark National and Nez Perce National Historic Trails; runs along 70 miles of two nationally designated Wild and Scenic Rivers and—in perhaps the most telling appraisal of the natural beauty here—was named by *Motorcycle* Magazine as the #1 recreational motorcycle route in the nation for its many curves and magnificent vistas (Big, big trucks love curves).

On an overcast and icy day in early March, one of those massive trucks got stuck on the road near Lolo Hot Springs, not far from where those citizens had gathered a few weeks earlier to voice their concerns. It was a test run to a refinery in Billings, Montana that turned into a portentous preview of what the Heavy Haul will be like. One giant load made it into Montana only two minutes before its Idaho permit expired, and this truck was stuck for days before the driver was finally able to inch it down the highway. A run that had been scheduled for four days had taken two weeks.

The stranded truck stopped after it scraped a rock outcropping on the side of the road and the driver now faced even more treacherous passes ahead. Then came the snow and ice, which changed driving conditions from dicey to dangerous. With armed guards keeping a wary eye on the truck, the driver waited, occasionally looking at the highway's scenic—and potentially deadly—overlook. When a Nimiipuu woman stopped to take a picture of the load with her young son, the driver asked how long they would be there, and she told him, *"We will be here forever."*

For the past two years, oil companies have been courting transportation and state authorities in Idaho and Montana, promising road expansion and a boom of economic development in jobs all along the route. A closer look suggests, however, that this "boom" may not be audible. The trucks will not be stopping at the usual tourist designations on the heritage road, and the drivers will be not be local people. Road expansions will undoubtedly create jobs for some Nimiipuu people (a few were hired this past year for the first expansion), but Tribal Employment Rights Office quotas may have already been fulfilled, and the loss of income from tourism will outweigh the benefits to the community. It is also worth noting that tourists—who pump $500 million into the area each year—are unlikely to care for the change in scenery the Heavy Haul trucks will bring to Highway 12.

Nevertheless, the Idaho Department of Transportation hearing processes have been fast-tracked in an effort to screen the project from public scrutiny. In those hearings, industry executives have often represented the project as merely a small, interim excursion through this road and that, rather than the massive and long-lasting movement of industrial oil machinery that the project actually calls for. The companies have repeatedly said that these trucks and this route are the only reasonable option. Exxon's Ken Johnson said in one hearing with the Idaho DOT that the colossal and precarious project was "safe and efficient." Another Exxon representative, Harry Lilo, said he expects the novelty of the huge loads to wear off quickly: "We're hoping about the time the fourth or fifth [truck] goes by, people are going to say, Oh, there goes another one."

That is unlikely, especially since people who live along Highway 12 will not able to drive that lifeline when the trucks travel through their neighborhood. The trucks chug along at around 12 miles an hour, and hog the road on either side because of how wide the loads are. That's why the road is blocked by a set of flaggers for a truck's entire journey. Alleviating the inevitable traffic jams is a laborious affair—the trucks inch to the nearest pullout and wait while a batch of cars pass.

The DOT estimates that whenever a Heavy Haul truck is on Highway 12, commuters can expect delays of at least an hour. Longer, of course, if there's a mishap. "I remember an accident last summer," Patricia Carter says. "There was no cell phone service, and people had to run a quarter-mile on each side of the accident to stop the cars from coming." Many of the loads will be moved during basketball season, when teenagers are on the road, driving over icy roads that have been the culprit in many fatal car accidents.

As a point of comparison, consider this: As of 2009, there had been only four trucks allowed on American highways of comparable size to those that will be used in the Heavy Haul. Those four trucks averaged 65 tons and traveled less than 80 miles total. The Heavy Haul loads are more than twice as heavy (150 tons), and will travel almost 1,000 miles. The highways in the proposed route, most of which have just two lanes, were not engineered to sustain such large loads—the maximum load discussed in most state DOT regulations is 15 tons; the Federal DOT allows for loads up to 40 tons on the interstate highway system. Do the math: 15 tons, 40 tons, 65 tons, 150 tons.

The project has been criticized by the citizens of Oregon, Idaho and Montana, and by many of the tribal communities that lie in the path of this impending trucking armada. The Nez Perce Council passed a resolution stating, "The project would establish a dangerous and unacceptable precedent in one of the most beautiful and pristine federally protected corridors in the US." It also noted that the Tar Sands project utilized "an environmentally destructive method that will have proposed negative impacts on the First Nations of Alberta."

The Tar Sands Project may seem to be an unrelated issue here, but ignoring it would require one to adopt an extremely narrow view of the world we live in, and the world we hope to live in. The Athabascan tar sands are the largest oil reserve outside of Saudi Arabia. The catch is that this isn't a "drill a hole and watch the oil spurt out" project. Extracting the oil from the sands is an expensive, toxic process requiring massive amounts of money, energy and infrastructure.

Thus far, the US has invested some $100 billion in this project. An area the size of Lake Superior is slated to be strip-mined. Picture an ugly hole in the earth—a scar—the size of one of the Great Lakes. Environmental regulations in Alberta are very lax. The province of Alberta and Canada (considered to be a "Climate Criminal" by WHO TK because of this project) has leased over 65,000 square kilometers of land for tar sands development.

Tar sands production is licensed to use more water than Alberta's two major cities—Calgary and Edmonton—combined. That water is turned into poison, laced with chemical sludge, and is polluting the entire Athabascan River system. The project burns 600 million cubic feet of natural gas to produce tar sands oil, enough natural gas to heat three million homes. The carbon emissions from the project surpass those of 97 nations combined. The forest and all that lives in it is being killed. Geese, ducks and other wild life land on the sludge ponds perish.

Alberta grizzly bears are now listed as threatened (numbers dropping by over 100 animals during the past decade) largely because of the loss of and contamination of their habitat as a result of the massive industrialization in the area. Dene, Cree and other communities near the pit now have elevated levels of bile cancer and other rare diseases, contaminated ecosystems, and oil rig workers from across the continent littering their communities.

At every link in the tar sands production chain, communities are rising up against the project. The oil is being sent through pipelines to American consumers and those pipelines are being opposed, spurred in part by safety issues raised by the recent oil disasters in Michigan and the Gulf of Mexico.

No one agrees on what the real potential for disaster is with the Heavy Haul, but Idaho Governor C.L. "Butch" Otter has mandated that both Exxon Mobil and ConocoPhillips post $10 million bonds in the event that either company has a 'mishap' on the road.

Others affected by the tar sands have already had their mishaps. For example, the people in Michigan who live on the Kalamazoo River, where Enbridge (one of the largest pipeline contractors for the tar sands) recently spilled over 1 million gallons of oil, forcing families to evacuate their homes. The spill contaminated water over 30 miles away in a matter of days. Enbridge has had 23 spills in Michigan and Minnesota since 1999, many of which still have not been cleaned up. But Enbridge continues to make huge profits, and their CEO, Patrick Daniel pulled down a salary of over $6 million in 2009. That would go a long way toward covering one of those $10-million "oops!" bonds.

Whether it be pipeline spills, a toxic pit as big as Lake Superior or the hauling of mammoth machinery over roads that could collapse under the weight, the Tar Sands project is dangerous. The reality is that some oil comes at too high a price, and whether that is the oil from the deep wells of the Gulf or that from the Boreal Forest of Cree and Dene people, this oil is dirty, and will always be dirty. The history of this region—one filled with courage, horses and the Nimiipuu people—demands that we be vigilant.

In August, 2013 a number of Nez Perce tribal members, including several member of the Tribal Council, were arrested while blockading the movement of a Heavy Haul load on Highway 12.

Nez Perce opposition forced Exxon/Mobil to dismantle their giant machines and take alternate routes on Interstates 90 and 15 to the Tar Sands.

TREATIES IN THE NEW MILLENNIUM
BINAAKWE'O GIIZIS 5, MOON OF THE FALLING LEAVES

"Individually, each tribe may have limited resources and influence to achieve this grand vision of buffalo restoration. However, our combined voice and expressed political unity will help us achieve broader support for ecological restoration and the enrichment of tribal cultures."
—LEROY LITTLEBEAR, BLACKFEET

This past month, three treaties were signed, each spanning international political boundaries, and covering vast geographic expanses. The treaties exhibit diametrically opposed views of the direction of our societies and economies.

Some may say that one view brings the economy and countries forward, the other backwards, but I have a feeling that not all are equal for the continent. And, I think it's time that Canada takes some advice from Indigenous peoples.

The Northern Tribes Buffalo Treaty was signed between eleven First Nations, crossing an international border in the northern plains, the first treaty among them in more than 150 years. The second treaty—between Canada and China—is essentially the Canadian version of the Trans-Pacific Trade Agreement, and grants legal rights to China that threaten First Nations lands under veils of secret proceedings. The third treaty, regarding the protection of the Salish Sea, includes nine First Nations and also straddles the U.S.—Canadian border.

The Northern Tribes Buffalo Treaty

Signed September 23, the Buffalo Treaty encompasses 6.3 million acres of land held by the Blackfeet Nation in the US and Canada, Blood Tribe, Siksika Nation, Piikani Nation, Assiniboine and Gros Ventre Tribes of Fort Belknap Reservation, the Assiniboine and Sioux Tribes of Fort Peck Reservation, the Confederated Salish and Kootenai Tribes, and the Tsuu T'ina Nation. Those First Nations are largely in the Montana and Alberta region.

The Nations have come together to restore the buffalo, or *"iiniwaa"* the Blackfeet word, to its natural territory.

The North American buffalo herd was once the largest migratory herd in the world, surpassing the African wildebeest herds in size. The large herds bio-engineered the prairie, and were able to support themselves through harsh winters without any fossil fuel inputs, unlike present day cattle. Last September's freak blizzard killed l00,000 cattle in South Dakota, but not a single buffalo was reported lost.

Leroy Littlebear, Blackfeet scholar at the University of Lethbridge, explains: "Tribes and First Nations in Canada and the United States own and manage a vast amount of intact prairie habitat across the Great Plains and mountain foothills…These intact grasslands provide suitable habitat for…buffalo if they remain intact, un-fragmented and in their natural state. Native peoples of the northern Great Plains are culturally disposed to protecting their homelands, connecting with free-roaming buffalo, and have expressed considerable interest in their repatriation to native landscapes."

Littlebear continues, "Individually, each tribe may have limited resources and influence to achieve this grand vision of buffalo restoration. However, our combined voice and expressed political unity will help us achieve broader support for ecological restoration and the enrichment of tribal cultures."

The tribes are calling on federal, state and private parties to support the restoration of the buffalo, Littlebear said in a formal announcement.

The Canada – China Protection-of-Investment Treaty

In contrast, Canadian Premier Stephen Harper ratified an "Agreement Between the Government of Canada and the Government of the People's Republic of China for the Promotion and Reciprocal Protection of Investments."

The treaty went into effect on October 1 and will last for 31 years, until 2045. According to Canadian Newsweek, the treaty "allows China to challenge Canadian laws it deems harmful to Chinese assets, and only requires the lawsuit be made public once an award is issued by a tribunal."

Treaty law expert Gus Van Harten warns this could be problematic: "The treaty makes no limits on the damages that can be awarded."

Other critics point out that the treaty also threatens treaty obligations between Canada and First Nations. "Paired with the terms allowing Chinese entities to buy anything they wish without foreign investment review, China will have access to—and potentially be able to gain control of—Canadian resources, including resources on First Nations' lands, which Canada does not own." Newsweek Canada reported.

The treaty allows China to sue Canada in secret tribunals for Canadian laws that interfere with Chinese investments. Those investments are substantial. Chinese companies have a hefty $30 billion invested into the Canadian tar sands and even more into mining industries in the Ring of Fire, with similar interests growing in the US. Canadian investment in all sectors of the Chinese economy totaled $4.2 billion in 2012. In short, it's not exactly an equal interest.

We'll see how it all pans out, but Canadian investors are considering the agreement incredibly one-sided in favor of China. And, I just want to point out that China has the third largest military in the world, and you, Canada have no military, if things go poorly. Native people have a lot of experience with this.

The International Treaty to Protect the Salish Sea

Nine First Nations whose territories lie in between the Alberta Tar Sands and the foreign fossil fuel markets that Steven Harper's government craves, declared the proposed oil tankers and the pipelines and other infrastructure that would feed them illegal "...as a matter of our ancestral laws, Canadian constitutional law, and international law on the rights of indigenous peoples and all human beings", and vowed to "take collective action, if necessary, to enforce the protection of the Salish Sea...."

"By signing this treaty, we have agreed to mutually and collectively use all lawful means to stop this project", said Rueben George, of Tsleil-Waututh Nation Sacred Trust Initiative. "Kinder Morgan's expansion project will never get built."

The Salish Sea treaty lays out the First Nations perspective: "We, the proud Coast Salish people stand united by our ancestral ties to each other and to the Salish Sea. We are obligated by our spiritual traditions and laws to ensure the integrity of the waters and lands that sustain our peoples."

"The spiritual leaders *(Siems)*, are our highest authority", said Chief Maureen Thomas of Tsleil-Waututh Nation. "Their wisdom has guided our people for millennia, and this treaty is an expression of our unextinguished and constitutional protected indigenous laws."

Native people have over 370 treaties signed with foreign countries, and most of those have not worked out too well for us; particularly those signed with aggressive military powers with huge economic interests.

Canada, you might learn a thing or two.

Short Stories and
Fargo Forum Communications

The short form stories, written for various publications in our region, including *The Circle, Fargo Forum Communications, News from Indian Country, Indian Country Today, Duluth Tribune, Duluth Reader, Lakota Sun Times,* and *High Plains Reader. Miigwech* to these editors.

IN THE MOON OF THE FALLING LEAVES

I've just returned from New York City, where I attended the Climate rally, 400,000 people walked the streets of New York demanding that government takes action on the climate. It was the largest such rally in US history. I was joined by my two 14-year old sons, there to witness history in the making.

Since we were in town, we also went to the United Nations to see the Indigenous peoples. This is to say, the *Tadadaho*—the leader of the Iroquois Confederacy—opened the General Assembly of the United Nations (He's sort of like the Dalai Lama of the Iroquois confederacy in my mind).

This is the first time that an Indigenous spiritual leader has spoken his language at the United Nations, and opened the General Assembly, representing in this case the oldest North American democracy, and a People much older than the United Nations.

Let us say that history is often made in such moments; those moments are part of a force which changes the course of history. That we know. What that means now, here today, is what I am pondering.

History, after all, teaches that there are moments when a paradigm shift takes place, sometimes ignited by a speech. Those transformational moments are often a result of many a civil or public action, whether by lawsuit, police-and-civil-society conflict or by any sort of demonstration or symbolic event.

One such historic moment took place on August 28, 1963, the March on the Lincoln Memorial in Washington, where Reverend Martin Luther King delivered his immortal *I Have a Dream* speech.

"I have a dream that my four children will one day live in a nation where they will not be judged by the color of their skin, but by the content of their character."

That was a defining moment in the American Civil Rights Movement and in the history of the nation, leading to the passage of the Civil Rights Act one year later. That law guaranteed to all people the right to desegregated schools and motels, restaurants and almost all public facilities.

In 1964, Martin Luther King, Jr. was awarded the Nobel Peace Prize. In his acceptance speech—another defining moment--he said:

"I refuse to accept the view that mankind is so tragically bound to the starless midnight of racism and war that the bright daybreak of peace and brotherhood can never become a reality."

When the 1970 Kent State University anti-war protests resulted in four students being shot to death by the National Guard, our country took a moment to pause. After all, the guardsmen fired 67 rounds over a period of 13 seconds, killing four students and wounding nine others. *Not all defining moments are welcome.*

The Vietnam War did not end until 1973, but that was a moment I clearly remember as a child, that Kent State time. We questioned what we were doing in our own country as well as abroad. We began to step up as a nation to stop an immoral war. Wars, however, I think we all know, take a while to stop.

In 1993, the people of South Africa held their first free elections, after suffering decades of extreme repression, violence and the 28-year jailing of Nelson Mandela under apartheid. All South African people now had a right to vote, and what had been a modern slavery system was abolished.

It took time, consciousness and many forces to bring about change, many defining moments. I don't know, but maybe we will learn something from Ferguson, Missouri as well. Like, perhaps military weapons should not be used to equip civilian forces. Perhaps we will think about whether US citizens who engage in protest or other civil action should be tear-gassed or shot by their own police, even if they are not white college students.

So, here is to say, that it is time to be aware, that we must be conscious of this time and opportunity to take action to make our world better. It's time to change the course of our collective history. After all, governments have been negotiating on climate for about half of my life.

Carbon dioxide levels are 63% higher than they were in 1990. North Dakota has some of the dirtiest coal plants in the country, along with neighboring Montana and Wyoming, all Big Sky states, with aging and obsolete coal generation equipment and practices.

Flaring off all that fracked oil and gas is not helping much either. On a percentage basis, more gas is flared in the state than in any other domestic oil field and at a level equal to Russia and twice that in Nigeria. It's about the equivalent to 300,000 cars on the road. Might want to look into that, if we want to hang out for a bit longer, and not end up in catastrophe.

Change happens in different ways. The day after the climate rally, Rockefeller Brothers Fund, an $800 million foundation which made its money on fossil fuels, announced that it would divest its fossil fuel holdings, because holding them when the planet combusts is a bad idea. It's called a *stranded asset,* and even the Rockefellers see the need to change. That's a different form of change, but it is a shift.

I witnessed history being made this past week. Native leaders—after forty years of asking the United Nations to recognize the rights of Indigenous peoples—were present in all their glory, conscious of the significance of this moment.

There's a US Justice Department investigation into the police use of force in Ferguson, which I hope will result in some rethinking of police behavior and weaponry. And who knows what else.

In this moon of the falling leaves, we were all present for some remarkable moments. We all should be that change.

New York City, September 24, 2014

ON THE IRISH, THE POTATO AND THE CHOCTAW

Let me just say that I am a fan of the Irish. Not a lick Irish, however I do love the Irish, their music, their tragic sense of humor, their resilience and their food. Well, maybe not the food and I'm not much of a drinker, so not even a Guinness.

But what I will tell you is that I've found many a kindred spirit in Ireland, I traveled there in 1981 at the height of the Hunger Strikes. There men were dying on the infamous H Block, a notorious prison for political prisoners, including Bobby Sands, who had been elected as a Member of Parliament while on the hunger strike.

Sands—as a member of the Irish Republican Army—was not seated, and instead died in this prison, the first of seventeen to die in that horrible time.

That was my first visit to Ireland, and it was the first time I ever saw razor wire and armored personnel carriers patrolling residential neighborhoods; and, it was my first riot. Leave it to the Irish to mess up my idea of what First World democracy looks like. And then write songs about it.

So, in honor of St. Patrick's Day, which has always been a bizarre holiday to me, I write this story about the Irish, the potato and the Choctaw:

The potato is one of the great gifts from the Western Hemisphere; a gift which would be given by Indigenous peoples to the world, who have provided about two thirds of the major food crops in the world (corn, tomatoes, potatoes, chocolate, just a few of the contributions).

The lesson of potatoes, however, did not go with those tubers. That is to say the 3,000 or so varieties of potatoes perfected in South America demonstrated immense agro-biodiversity, yielding variations in nutritional contents, pest resistance and agility to become the food that would feed the world.

Potatoes provided 7.5 million calories per hectare of land (compared to wheat offering 4.2 million calories), provided a source of vitamin C and improved nutrition immensely.

It's argued that the potato liberated Europe from famine. After all, historian Jack Weatherford would write that there were 111 famines in France from1371 to 1791, leaving a lean country indeed.

The simple elegance of the potato--something which is cultivated below ground, yet is poisonous above ground, meant that nutrition and, subsequently, population would flourish. These characteristics, arguably, did not work out so well for those of us in the Western Hemisphere, but definitely helped secure the world power status of Europe.

Not so for the Irish. But that fact is—as we all now know—a result of British colonialism, which forced the Irish to rely upon a potato monocrop, until the blights killed off the harvests. The result: a million Irish perished and another million were forced to emigrate in order to survive.

This was an enforced famine, the result of British policy. Wheat harvests flourished in Ireland during the famine, but the British harvested and exported these crops to feed their people in their colonial conquests worldwide. Had the Irish been able to access this food source, the numbers who died from hunger would have been far fewer.

Mono crops are dangerous and the fact is that the Irish potato famine should have taught us that. Today the potato mono crop is plaguing western Minnesota, where fifty thousand acres of potato mono crop now demand extensive water and a cocktail of chemicals, contaminating groundwater in the region.

That story is still unfolding as the RDO Offutt Company seeks to turn pine lands into potato fields, adding up to 27,000 acres more. The Minnesota Department of Natural Resources has a very short comment period, open now.

But, back to St. Patrick's Day: Let us recognize the fine relationship between Native people of the Americas and the Irish. In the city of Cork in southern Ireland, a sculpture is being erected to honor the Choctaw Nation.

The Choctaw Nation sent $710 to the Irish for famine relief in 1845. The equivalent of that would be close to $1 million today in foreign aid. "These gentle folk were at their most downtrodden, yet they raised $710 and sent it across the Atlantic to Ireland to ease our famine woes," Sculptor Alex Pentek tells a reporter from the Irish Examiner.

Pentek is finishing 'Kindred Spirits', a giant, stainless steel sculpture in praise of the Choctaw people. The sculpture is a metal set of eagle feathers in a bowl form; $100,000 worth of homage.

"These people were still recovering from their own injustice. They put their hands in their pockets and raised $1 million in today's money", Pentek said. "They helped strangers. It's rare to see such generosity. It had to be acknowledged."

Just 13 years before the Famine, the Choctaws were forced to march 1200 miles on the Trail of Tears. The Choctaw, Cherokee, Muskogee, Chickasaw and Seminole (the five Civilized Tribes) were forced to abandon their fertile lands and driven at gunpoint, and exiled to Oklahoma territory. At least 6000 perished on the way.

"It was a slowly unfolding horror story. To see members of your family drop to the side of the road and to be powerless. To change that course of history. That stirred my imagination," said Pentek.

So it is, far away, that there is a tribute to this little-known page in history.

On this St. Patrick's Day, I want to remember the dignity of the human spirit from the Choctaw to Bobby Sands, and celebrate the diversity and beauty of the potato, one of the great gifts to us all.

DESMOND TUTU AND ME

"Climate change is the moral struggle that will define humanity this century. I hope you will find yourself on the right side of this struggle, the one which will say 'no' to the pipelines and the carbon."
— Archbishop Desmond Tutu, June 1, 2014

I may never wash my hands. Just a few days ago, I held hands with Archbishop Desmond Tutu, the great South African religious leader, partner to Nelson Mandela, and leader of the Peace and Reconciliation Commission of South Africa. This was one of those breathtaking moments in life. I sat within feet of him and listened to him giggle at his own stories, express great love for all of us, and call upon us to do better.

The place was Ft. McMurray, Canada, a city about the size of Fargo, but lacking in infrastructure. That's because it is the boom town for the Alberta Tar Sands, where rent is $4600 a month for a house, men are bused out for their 12-hour shifts, or live in the notorious Man Camps.

It is perhaps the most international small city in Canada, and it is a very challenging place. Perhaps the future of Williston, but I think not. It is also the home of the Athabasca Chipewyan First Nation. That is who invited both Tutu and me.

It was an unusual setting. The conference, themed "As Long as the River Flows", took place in the only LEEDS gold-certified building in Alberta, a center owned by the Athabasca Chipewyan (complete with solar panels) and brought together a former director of Syncrude Canada, a former Premier of Alberta, Desmond Tutu, many First Nation leaders, doctors, scientists and myself.

What did I learn?

"You have to have a sense of humor. Otherwise, you will end up crying into your grave. You will die of a broken heart," Tutu told us. Then he told stories, and giggled a lot. "I am old, and sometimes I repeat stories," he said and then launched into a fabulous story of himself and Nelson Mandela.

"You are all Africans" he would say, referring to the origins of mankind, and then he giggled a bit more. He was about five feet two tall, from what I can figure, and one of the funniest cool guys I have ever met. Really.

He taught lessons, well-learned in a country like South Africa, which until 1993 had essentially legalized slavery. He reminded us that we must be strong of moral character: "You must have the willingness to acknowledge the damage done, and ...the willingness to forgive."

In the broader philosophical world view, he also said, "The ability to be magnanimous is essential...putting ourselves in the shoes of the other. If Nelson Mandela stunned the world after he walked free from prison after 27 years, it was due to his almost other-worldly magnanimity; he set an example."

Archbishop Tutu spoke in the broad context, but he came to the Athabasca River to speak about climate change and the tar sands. Now, it's really hard to criticize someone like Tutu, but I have to say that the Alberta media did try and make it appear that the Archbishop was misinformed.

Tutu himself, however, could not have been clearer: "The urgency of our responsibility to take action has never been clearer. Every day hundreds of millions of lives and livelihoods are effected by global warming," Tutu told us.

"The struggle of individuals against the pipelines and oil sands put them at the front of the most important struggle today. Oil sands not only devastate our shared climates, but are also stripping away the rights of First Nations to protect their land from being poisoned. The oil companies have benefited from everything. They have taken the food out of our plates, and water from our cups."

Then he asked that rhetorical question which puts the onus of responsibility squarely on each of us: "Who can stop this? We can stop this... We can. You, you, and I can stop this (this is when he reached out and held my hand, and I almost fainted), and it is not just that we can stop it. We have a responsibility to do so. "

"Those countries and companies responsible are not going to give up on fossil fuels. They are too beholden to short sighted profits. We need to push them to do the right thing. Just as Canadians reached out to help Africans rid themselves of the scourge of apartheid, we can work together again to rid our shared planet of the threat of climate change."

Then he said: "If we do not learn to live together as brothers, we will perish together as fools."

Amen.

MONEY CORRUPTS ELECTIONS

What do pipelines, boobs and elections have in common? They're all homes for dirty corporate money.

Politics should involve principles, and the health of women should not be a publicity blitz for polluters. Elections and Breast Cancer Awareness Month (October) are in danger of becoming tainted.

Corporate money in politics is out of control. Most people who say this have not run for office, but I have a bit of street credibility and scars to prove it. I've run twice for U.S. vice president as the Green Party candidate. I've been vilified by Republicans and sued in 13 states by Democrats, and had Al Gore's loss in the election blamed on my running mate, Ralph Nader, and me. I've seen how deep pockets decide elections.

Here's our challenge: It's a mid-term election year, the one with lower turnout, which means every vote counts. There is a lot of money involved. A Supreme Court decision called Citizen's United made that all the more possible. The case basically declared that corporations are people and therefore have the right to fund election campaigns without limits.

Citizen's United v. Federal Election Commission spawned the creation of so-called "Super PACs", which can accept unlimited contributions from corporate and union treasuries, and from individuals. These groups spent more than $600 million in the 2012 election cycle. It also triggered a boom in political activity by tax-exempt "Dark Money" organizations that don't have to disclose their donors.

One of the largest financing machines of the Republican Party is a couple of billionaires, the Koch brothers. (Together they are the richest guys in the world, leaving even Bill Gates in the dust). The Koch brothers are spending about $480 million on midterm elections for a lot of reasons. Take the Alberta Tar Sands. The brothers Koch stand to make billions of dollars on the extraction of oil from the tar sands because they are among the largest leaseholders there. To sell that oil, they really could use a pipeline, any pipeline, or let's say, maybe the Keystone XL or the Alberta Clipper.

Koch has billions of dollars worth of assets in Minnesota and North Dakota they might want to protect. They gave money to Mike McFadden, the banker who is challenging Sen. Al Franken, D-Minn. (The Kochs' oil refinery in Rosemount released nearly 740,000 pounds of toxic chemicals into Minnesota watersheds in 2012).

My other pet peeve is about money that should not be on my boobs. An ethical question: Should companies that contribute to breast cancer and at the same time release cancer-causing chemicals into the environment sponsor Breast Cancer Awareness Month and benefit from the publicity? Or, conversely, should organizations fighting breast cancer accept donations from corporations that put carcinogenic chemicals into the water?

Here's the story: Baker Hughes, a manufacturer of equipment used in hydraulic fracturing, has painted 1,000 of its drill bits breast-cancer pink (the usual color is gold) and also donated $100,000 to Susan G. Komen *Race for the Cure,* a leading breast-cancer charity. As Bill Debo, director of operations for U.S. land drill bits at Baker Hughes told the blog *Fuel Fix*, "Our hope is from the water cooler to the rig site to the coffee shop to everywhere, someone gets this information to their spouses, their girlfriends, their daughters so we can create awareness and end this disease forever."

Fair enough.

But, since oil and gas fracking involves breast cancer-causing chemicals and airborne emissions (toluene, benzene, et al.), I am concerned. Although the pink drill bits are pretty and the signage is good, the sponsoring is hypocritical.

I've never won an election, and I'm not the best fundraiser in the world; so maybe I'm a failure at that. But I'd like to keep my principles. A democratic society and public interest work best without money from Big Oil in the middle of it. My advice: Get out and vote, challenge illicit money and keep your principles. They are worth everything.

INDIGENOUS PEOPLES DAY

"This has been a long day coming and people are going to feel really good about how we're moving forward and advancing a racial equity agenda that really elevates the voice and contributions of American Indian people."
—ALONDRA CANO, MINNEAPOLIS CITY COUNCIL

I was proud to be there on that day in October when Minneapolis became the second major city in the US to replace a commemoration of a villain with the celebration of a People. It was a great day for all of us. More than a thousand people showed up at the American Indian Center to celebrate and honor Native peoples.

Alondra Cano, wearing a traditional huipil, an exquisitely embroidered blouse from Mexico, exemplifies the complexity and the beauty of our times. Born in Chihuahua, Mexico, she is the first Mexican

American woman to be elected to the Minneapolis City Council. She was joined by Peggy Flanagan, a White Earth Tribal member and Minneapolis school board chair, representing some of the leadership of Indigenous women in modern politics.

The fact is that we are a multi-cultural society, and—in Indigenous Peoples Day—that fact is celebrated and our place in the history of this nation acknowledged, with beauty. The event was well attended. Minneapolis Mayor Betsy Hodges proudly came out; Senator Al Franken told of his work on the Violence Against Women Act; state representatives Karen Clark, Keith Ellison, Susan Allen and others spoke, along with the mayor.

This was not an apologetic, half-way celebration. The day was full of vitality, dignity, fanfare and pride, and it ended with a fabulous *Pre-Colonization Feast*, provided and executed by The Sioux Chef, consisting of foods that were originally cultivated by the indigenous peoples of the Americas over thousands of years. Chocolate, tomatoes, potatoes and avocados as well as corn are all western hemispheric in their origins, and let's be honest, those are some central foods in world cuisine.

As a child, I remember having to choke down the Columbus Day holiday, as if a history of millions of people who existed prior to the arrival of Columbus did not happen. As if Columbus and those who followed him did not murder millions of Native people, hanging them at times thirteen at a time in honor of their twelve apostles and their Savior. As if the European colonizers did not have Native children torn apart by trained dogs in front of their parents and families.

It was egregious, to be honest. The fact is that when Columbus Day was recognized as a federal holiday in 1934, Native American nations and communities had little voice to protest the celebration of the onset of colonization and genocide in the Western Hemisphere.

After all, the Indian Reorganization Act had just been passed, where the federal government forced a foreign government system into national Indigenous governance in the tribal government era. Long-term federal policy goals were always directed at seizing Indian lands and breaking up Indian communities, one way or another. Inflicting loss and suffering on the "vanishing" race was considered "progress", and there was a lot of money to be made in the act, regardless of which political party was in power at the time.

Land seizures under the General Allotment Act's fallout were minimally stopped, but First Nations peoples remained burdened and traumatized from the effects of the long history of Indian Wars; from the systematic infliction of residential and boarding school atrocities on generations of children and families; from the countless epidemics of imported infectious diseases that decimated the continent, killing tens of millions of people; from the unfathomable greed and inhumanity that extinguished entire species of animals and plants; from the "social" epidemics brought on by the newly dominant culture that plague our communities today, bringing diabetes, heart disease, alcoholism, depression and PTSD to the People; and, from the contamination and poisoning of the Land itself, and of the Water.

The federal Termination Act was passed in 1958, sort of an American "Final Solution" to tribal political power. And police brutality against Native people (now forced by the hundreds of thousands into urban areas by the Relocation Act) was at an all-time high. Native religions were outlawed and persecuted in this country until 1978.

In reality, Columbus Day is both a metaphor and painful symbol of that traumatic past and of the ongoing legal injustices that permeate American society today.

The deliberate undermining of Indigenous cultures, languages, economic and political systems and religions has been a predominate, defining mission of the expanding, imperial United States from its infancy all the way into the 21st century, to be factually accurate.

Roxanne Dunbar Ortiz explains in her new book, *An Indigenous History of the United States:* "None of Columbus's voyages touched the continental territory now claimed by the US. Yet, the United States soon affirmed that a 15th century Papal Bull, known as the 'Doctrine of Discovery', applied to the Indigenous nations of North America."

This Doctrine of Discovery remains rooted in US law, the basis for claiming that Native nations are "domestic, dependent nations" with no inherent rights to the land. The legal legacy of Columbus survives in American and Canadian law, and despite some 370 treaties. The federal court systems generally continue in the colonization framework and trajectory of denying the rights and existence of First Nations that began with the arrival of Cristobal Colón.

As evidenced by the current debate surrounding the Washington, D.C. football team's name, words are profoundly important.

Indigenous Peoples Day recognizes the self-determination of indigenous peoples in the Americas despite hundreds of years of colonization, oppression and denial of rights.

Indigenous Peoples Day was first officially marked in Berkeley in 1992, five hundred years after that fateful arrival. For twenty two years, the steps forward in the transition were slow, meeting with deeply-rooted opposition. Denver, for example, has had major conflicts for two decades on the verge of riots on Columbus Day, as Indigenous peoples and those who oppose the transition clashed over the holiday.

As in the case of the "Nameless" Washington football team, or of the former Fighting Sioux teams of the University of North Dakota, words mean something, and imagery is held onto for generations.

That is, until this year, when Minneapolis took the first step—followed by Seattle—to become cities that made a break from the Columbus mythology and now celebrate Indigenous Peoples instead. Duluth and Red Wing joined them, as well as cities like Sebastapol and Santa Cruz in California. It is a nice evolution for all of us.

Now, I'm going to keep enjoying Italian food, and I will remember that lullaby my mother used to sing to me fondly (*Avante Populo*, an Italian political anthem), because letting go of Columbus Day just means releasing our minds, schools, institutions and American society from a false story, and the truth is more painful, but far more beautiful.

IRON EYES AND OBAMA: PUTTING OUR MINDS TOGETHER

The United States agrees that "(land)...is set apart for the absolute and undisturbed use and occupation of the Indians herein named..."
— 1868 TREATY BETWEEN
THE UNITED STATES AND THE LAKOTA NATION

I like that President Obama traveled to see Sitting Bull's people at the Standing Rock Reservation. He is the third sitting president to visit a reservation. After all, our ancestors signed treaties with your ancestors, and great nations should reaffirm these relationships for our common good, as should we as people.

There were some strong words said by many. Those words were in Lakota as well as English. Eyapaha Chase Iron Eyes of Standing Rock had some very interesting things to say. An attorney as well as a traditional representative, Iron Eyes talked with depth about many issues which are skirted in the media.

Iron Eyes talked about the 1868 peace treaty between the Lakota Nation and the US, nation to nation, which reserved large parts of the Dakotas for the Lakotas. The treaty has been violated, and the US Courts have upheld that the land was illegally taken. The Lakota have turned down the settlement offer, now amounting to around a billion dollars. It sits in the bank, because the Lakota still believe in their treaty and in their land.

"We have a Creator-given right to live, die and be buried in our sacred Black Hills," Chase told Obama, reflecting the continuing position of the Lakota people that the Black Hills must be returned. He suggests that "a practical solution" can be found.

For instance, co-management transitioning to Lakota management of the millions of acres of national and state parks in the Black Hills region would be a good step. (Remember that Lakota and Mandans like Gerard Butler, former superintendent of Mount Rushmore National Park, and now supervisor at the Badlands National Park, have some experience).

Also remember that the Lakota have thousands of years of management experience in the area. "The US did not give the Sioux nation any rights," Iron Eyes said, "*We reserved to ourselves specific rights. We never gave up the right to govern ourselves and to exist under our spiritual instructions in our territory.*"

The 1868 treaty also included the so-called "Bad Man clause" of Article One; "If bad men among the whites...shall commit any wrong upon the person or property of the Indians, the United States will... proceed at once to cause the offender to be arrested and punished according to the laws of the United States, and also reimburse the injured person for the loss sustained."

This clause is reflected in the recently approved Violence Against Women Act. The law allows the prosecution of non-Indian perpetrators who commit sex crimes on the reservation.

The 1868 treaty could also be applied to polluters in Lakota territory, like those companies discharging fracking fluid onto the roadways.

The United States agrees that "(land)...is set apart for the absolute and undisturbed use and occupation of the Indians herein named..."

In turn, the Lakota "...withdraw all opposition to the construction of the railroads...not attack any persons at home, or traveling, nor molest or disturb any wagon trains, coaches, mules, or cattle belonging to the people of the United States, or to persons friendly therewith.." The Lakota also agreed to, "Never capture, or carry off from the settlements, white women or children."

Ironically, it turns out the opposite is true, as the state of South Dakota has removed perhaps 10,000 Native children from their Indian homes, despite the Indian Child Welfare Act. In short, not abiding by agreements has put us all in a bad situation, morally and legally.

Iron Eyes talked about President Obama, hoping that Native people can be part "...of the American Dream." He suggested, "We have our own America Dream that is different than the consumption and procurement of material wealth ... without regard for Mother Earth and the resources which sustain us. *It is the original Indigenous dream.* And we want you to be part of it. That is, if we recognize the common humanity that we share with every other ... being that shares a spiritual relationship with the cosmos."

Iron Eyes talks about this economy to "...provide food security for our nations, national security and renewable energy." And, in the larger sense, talks about how "There is enough to provide for all of us...But not enough to provide for all of us in the global consumerism and neo classical economics."

I think that there is some very good wisdom on Standing Rock, and that President Obama knew where to go to hear something perhaps a bit outside of the Washington paradigm. It reminds me of the words of one of the world's greatest military leaders and philosophers, Sitting Bull, who said, "Let us put our minds together to see what kind of future we can make for our children." He was right.

THE TEAM WITH NO NAME

Riding across the desert on a horse with no name ... Entering football and hockey season with a team with no name. That's gonna be a challenge.

I am not much of a football fan. That I will totally admit. I am, however, not a fan of racist mascots. So it is that I joined 4,000 or so other people at the University of Minnesota stadium on Sunday November 2, to challenge the Washington Football Team and its mascot. I was in good company.

"The choice the Washington NFL team is making to use a racial epithet for its name is an offense to the values of the people of Minneapolis," Mayor Betsy Hodges told the crowd. "It is baffling that in 2014 a company would retain the use of a racist logo for its product. From a human standpoint it is reprehensible and from a business standpoint the brand becomes more tainted every day." She chastised the team for being "last millennium" in its behavior.

Almost thirty speakers and performers spoke on a beautiful Sunday to a jubilant crowd. The Change the Name rally was multi-cultural and upbeat. Spike Moss, representing the NAACP, said that if this was a problem for Native people, it was a problem for African Americans. Former governor Jesse Ventura stepped up to the microphone to support the cause, and Amanda Blackhorse, the Diné woman who filed a lawsuit against the Washington Redskins spoke eloquently. Everyone did.

The "Red Skins" name refers to the skins of Native people, which were sought by bounty hunters and openly traded and sold in the United States throughout the 17th, 18th and 19th centuries. Federal, state and local policies did not discriminate between murdering Native men, women and children in the bounty department.

Susanne Shown Harjo, the original plaintiff in the 1993 lawsuit, *Harjo et al vs. NFL*, as well as a leading advocate on this case, explains the meaning of the R-word and why it is a slur against Native Peoples:

"The use of that name harkens back to a time when we were actually skinned by bounty hunters who turned in our skins for payment. So, you had companies, colonies and states that issued bounty proclamations for dead Indians. And what were presented as proof of Indian kill were the bloody redskins.

"Those who close their eyes to the origin of this word are simply not dealing with the reality of the practice of skinning our people. But even if you don't know that and don't care about what happened then, the use of a description of someone's skin color is wrong. And when it occurs solely in a particular area, you're talking about invidious discrimination. You would not see a day where its corollary would be used to describe any other races or ethnicities of people. "

The Minneapolis Civil Rights Commission notes that the American Psychological Association and the National Congress of American

Indians strongly oppose the use of derogatory and disparaging Native American sports names and mascots. Studies link the mascots to lower self esteem and a feeling of being marginalized by Native people, with longer-term emotional impacts.

It's a bit ironic how long the Washington football team has held fast to that name.

Hundreds of colleges and high schools have changed their names since the National Congress of American Indians (NCAI) first made the appeal in 1968, most of my lifetime ago.

The University of Oklahoma retired its "Little Red" mascot in 1970; Marquette University abandoned its "Willie Wampum" mascot in 1971; Stanford University and Dartmouth College changed their mascot names in 1972.

I know that the University of North Dakota is having some problems with this, and is between nicknames since it ended use of "Fighting Sioux" in 2012. That's been a battle, to say the least, and they've got this "cooling off period" before they choose one. That will hopefully be in 2015.

So for all of you wondering, I'm often asked if I can give an Indian name to someone. Now, I haven't been asked to give sports teams' names yet, but there may be some options on this.

I'm thinking that the North Dakota team might be, well, the Sandbaggers, which is what you get when you build your city in a flood plain, and you get good at it. Or the Frackers. That may be a short term solution, but could be bitter sweet. I admit. OK, I know that won't fly, but thought I'd offer it.

And for the Washington team, maybe the Washington Drones. I think that sounds promising and accurate. After all, someone might actually refer to you in the paper if you get a name people like. Right now, most major newspapers and much of the media won't even call the Washington team anything besides the Washington team. Bummer to be the team with no name.

HOW DO WE TREAT IMILS
(INDIAN MASCOT IDENTITY LOSS SYNDROME)?

In early April, the University of North Dakota dropped a vilified mascot name "the Fighting Sioux." That is, after a decade of litigation (including an NCAA lawsuit against the school for the racially offensive logo) and around 20 years of protests. The Frozen Four hockey powerhouse (with a $100 million Ralph Engelstad Arena full of 1,200 logos inset in arena seats) will have to undergo changes.

The day after the announcement, hundreds of pro-mascot protesters flocked to the university's grounds to show their dismay. It's gonna be a tough year. Probably a lot of counseling will be required for those suffering from "Indian Mascot Identity Loss Syndrome" (IMILS), and generally a challenge for the university. I applaud the North Dakota Board of Higher Education for taking a decisive and healing move.

Things change; we need to be grown-ups and address the change. Despite an80-year attachment to a mascot, it is just a mascot. It's not like you had your homeland buried under a dam project, or had your village burned by the military. And, the Lakota people and other native people deserve to be recognized as more than mascots.

Consider that despite how "proud" some folks might feel about the mascot, they might not feel so proud about the economics of the Sioux. It is 120 years after the Wounded Knee Massacre of 1890, and 10 of the 20 poorest counties in the country are native reservations. The majority of them are Lakota and Dakota reservations.

The poorest people in the country should not be native people, and I believe that rich people and families like the Engelstads (who received some front- page coverage in The Forum about their concerns) should do better things with their money - like maybe invest in the environment, culture and restoring local food systems. Trustee Kris Engelstad McGarry said in a news release that the family felt "deceived" and was so concerned about the status of the logo that they financed much of the legal fight against the National College Athletic Association.

Let me explain a bit about being deceived: How about some 470 broken treaties. How about promises like *"as long as the grass shall grow and rivers flow."* How about promises to not dig up people and put them in museums for everyone to see. How about treaty guaranteed rights of hunting, fishing and wild ricing being ignored by state authorities. And, how about those 23 Congressional Medals of Honor awarded to soldiers who committed the Wounded Knee Massacre, or the fact that Congress has never issued a formal apology for the devastation wrought.

I would like to feel sorry for the Engelstads family and UND mascot supporters, but I can't muster up that sympathy. I could suggest counselors who have experience in the American Indian community's ongoing historic trauma. I would be happy to work on helping the Engelstad family and university move to a just relationship with Native people. Just let me know.

THE QUIET TIME: TAOS PUEBLO

When our family went to visit friends at Taos Pueblo, we were told of the Quiet Time.

Taos Pueblo in northern New Mexico is a World Heritage site; a 1000-year-old village, all off-grid, no running water, old school. Classic, North American style. The traditional people at that village go into the Pueblo for about a month in December and January, and go off the grid, so to speak. They heat and cook with wood, use their outhouses, and haul water from the springs. They live with no cell phones, no television, and then they remember who they are.

I try the Quiet Time. I look at the fire in my house. I rankle at the amount of energy I consume in my own house, albeit solar and wood are two components of my energy scheme. I know that each gadget uses power, that leaving all that stuff plugged in means that there's a "ghost load" in the outlet, and that someone—probably out in North

Dakota—is living next to a big, dirty coal-fired generator just so that I keep it all going.

I dislike how complicit I have become in the whole scheme, how entitled. No one in the world consumes more than a North American. And it's pricey: contaminated water, global warming, oil pipelines and nuclear waste. I am grateful that my water from the Sand Point pump at my house is clean.

So in this time I think about the link between energy, consumption and happiness. After all that Holiday season, and in a time of deep cold, it seems appropriate.

This is what I find: *The average American consumes more than his own weight daily in stuff.* We buy clothes, electronics, games and products at a rate where today, some 70% of the US economy is based on consumption. Since we are importing these goods from China and elsewhere, we do not have an economy based on production, we have a pretty high debt of exchange to China, and we use a lot of fossil fuels.

We are not necessarily happier for it. On a worldwide scale, new indicators of happiness and well-being are being forwarded by some of "least developed countries" in the world, who indeed, say that they are happier than Americans. Bhutan (a Himalayan nation of around 750,000... think North Dakota), instituted something called a Gross National Happiness Index, instead of Gross Domestic Product.

Another set of indicators, the Happy Planet Index of some 178 nations, listed Costa Rica and Vanuatu as two of the happiest countries in the world. One is an island with an 80% local economy and the other does not even have a military.

How did the US rank on the Happy Planet Index? Of the larger First World economies, Germany ranked 81 on this index, Japan 95th and the US 150th.

Consumption does not make us happier. North America and Western Europe comprise 12% of the world's population, but account for 60% of global private consumer spending. The disparity of wealth is high.

One percent of the American population controls some 34% of the wealth, while the bottom 90% of the population shares a much leaner 26.9% of the wealth.

In turn, social relationships are challenged by a number of factors: transience, job instability, and the fact that more Americans actually watch television and movies in the isolation of their home than go out and "socialize" (Americans spend an average four hours and 49 minutes a day in front of the television).

Americans consume more psychotropic drugs than any country in the world (anti-depressants and sleeping pills for instance) and—in general—we also consume too much food. Around a third of our population is overweight. Finally, we shop. Some say we shop to appease our pain, or in order to create that momentary bliss of "retail therapy."

Four decades ago, the linking of Gross National Product and happiness was questioned by Robert Kennedy in a speech delivered at the University of Kansas. "Too much and for too long, we seemed to have surrendered personal excellence and community values in the mere accumulation of material things," he said.

"Our Gross National Product is now over $800 billion dollars a year, but that GNP measurement counts air pollution and cigarette advertising, and ambulances to clear our highways of carnage. It counts special locks for our doors and the jails for the people who break them. It counts the destruction of the redwood and the loss of our natural wonder in chaotic sprawl. It counts napalm and counts nuclear warheads and armored cars for the police to fight the riots in our cities.

"The Gross National Product (of a country) does not allow for the health of our children, the quality of their education or the joy of their play. It does not include the beauty of our poetry or the strength of our marriages, the intelligence of our public debate or the integrity of our public officials.

"The (GNP) measures neither our wit nor our courage, neither our wisdom nor our learning, neither our compassion nor our devotion to our country. It measures everything, in short, except that which makes life worthwhile."

He could have been from Taos Pueblo, really.

I have put myself on a fossil fuels diet. And in this Quiet Time, I pledge to happiness in 2015.

MY RECOMMENDED DAILY ALLOWANCE OF RADIATION

"Technically Enhanced Naturally Occurring Radioactive Material." To be honest, I haven't heard such an Orwellian phrase used by public health officials for years. I got to hand it to you, North Dakota Department of Health. "I think enhanced generally implies improvement," Dean Hulse told the Health Department at a Fargo Hearing. I think Dean is probably right.

This past week I stumbled on some hearings, announced at Christmas, held in Williston, Bismarck and Fargo in short succession February 20-22.

What's up? The North Dakota Department of Health is considering increasing the amount of radioactive materials put in landfills by a factor of 1000% or from 5 pico curies per liter to 50. That would help the fracking industry out tremendously, because most of those fracking wastes and other cool stuff – 27 tons of it a day are coming in at 47 pico curies per litre, and we've an illegal dumping problem. So, let's just make it a non problem?

Now to be fair, these are "special landfills" for the oil and gas fracking business (whose wastes are supposed to be called "special" not "hazardous"), but the idea of a set of low level nuclear waste dumps might concern folks. Particularly since North Dakota has set a limit of 5 picocuries — the standard measure for the intensity of radioactivity — of radium per gram of soil in order to be considered not radioactive.

The new proposal would be ten times that much. Timing of the hearings, a quickly-put-together pro-industry study and the lack of public notice and participation, all make me a bit nervous. So to be clear about it, the North Dakota Department of Health is thinking that instead of reducing risk to the general population, they will just magically change the math equation and give us a new recommended daily allowance of radiation.

Wow.

Let's review radiation. There is no safe level of radiation exposure. It's all risky. Not just Fukishima, or Chernobyl. In 1972, Dr Abram Petkau discovered that low levels of radiation exposure accrued over a longer period of time were more damaging than higher doses over a short period of time.

Once you ingest or inhale even very low levels of radioactive particles, the Petkau Effect immediately starts creating potentially lethal tissue ionization. That fact hasn't changed, no matter what industry says.

It doesn't take much common sense to understand this, or much research, either. It all says the same thing: Background rates are increasing unnaturally. That is because we are taking stuff out of the ground we should not mess with, and we are having accidents with it—big ones, like Fukashima and Chernobyl, and small ones (relatively) like that 3 million gallon spill of radioactive brine, and toxic filled dangerous water spill.

The U.S. Environmental Protection Agency notes problems for workers: "They may inhale radon gas which is released during drilling and produced by the decay of radium, raising their risk of lung cancer. In addition, they are exposed to alpha and gamma radiation released during the decay of radium-226 and the low-energy gamma radiation and beta particles released by the decay of radium-228.

"Gamma radiation can also penetrate the skin and raise the risk of cancer." I am thinking that most of those oil workers are going to be there for a year or two, but the Mandan, Arikara and Hidatsa people have been here 10,000 years or so, and probably plan on hanging around, as do a lot of North Dakotans.

So, long term exposure is going to be a big problem. Once radio nuclides are released into the environment they circulate and are carried with the winds until they become part of the soil and food chain.

They land in our drinking water, are on the pastures that our livestock graze on, are on our vegetables and in our fruit trees, pastures, and then—of course—in us. We've got a big problem because we're like the apex or the T Rexes of the ecosystem, the top of the food chain, and all this stuff bio accumulates. In us.

Diseases from the low level exposure include, leukemia, lymphoma, solid tumors, endocrine disruptions, reproductive abnormalities and the like. All rotten stuff that you would hope your health department would try and avoid. But maybe I am mistaken.

All sorts of a slippery slope, if you ask me. I did hear something pretty comical from a female representative of the North Dakota Oil and Gas Industry. That was, "Nuclear radiation isn't so bad; it's not like Godzilla or anything. It's more like Norm from Cheers, just there sitting at the bar."

I want more of whatever psychedelic drug she's taking. Well, maybe not. And I really think that North Dakotans deserve better, and the Department of Health should protect the people, not endanger them, and maybe hold hearings when people can get to them. But, maybe I am just old fashioned.

Postscript: North Dakota regulatory authorities approved the increase in radiation exposure.

ON SOMALI PIRATES AND THE JOY OF FIXING THINGS

I recently took an almost completely trashed iphone to the I Care repair shop in Fargo, North Dakota. I arrived somewhat embarrassed at the state of the phone, its face in 100 pieces, and was reassured that it could be fixed. It was so, and I was grateful. I was grateful because I like seeing things fixed, and I hate seeing things thrown away.

I grew up in a household which was somewhat minimalist in the things department. We used whisks to mix, and cooked from scratch;

when Gramma came to visit, torn and buttonless shirts were mended. My grandfather—a house painter and carpenter—fixed things at the house for a busy family, and made small items for delighted children.

I am happiest when things can be fixed, or when I choose something which can be fixed by an ordinary person, like my sewing machines. I take them to Janke's, and the vacuum cleaners, too. After all, I built an entire house off of Craigslist and the Reuse and Restore centers. Yup, that is me. I know that I am not alone. It's a bit of a generational thing I'm sure, but I'm going to argue that might be throwback time on this one.

A lot of us have moved away from being handy and it's hurting us. We fix less, buy more. I could say it hurts the planet, the environment, and charismatic mega fauna like, well, gorillas in the Congo (think Blood Coltan for cell phones, smart bombs and consumer electronics).

Coltan is a "conflict" mineral ore that is mostly found in the Congo, where it is mined and sold by militia groups and criminal gangs, who use a lot forced labor, including as much as 30% of area school children, to dig it out of the ground.

I think it hurts us. We have become a people who lack agency, who buy more things that we know will go to the dump, who have people take care of us, and that's getting to be a problem in terms of our society.

Our Linear Society

We have created a linear society in which one of our largest industries is waste. And seventy percent of our economy is based on consumption. Not on production, not on services, but on *consumption*. And—within about three months—a lot of what we've bought is at a landfill, out of sight and out of mind.

Most of that stuff we bought came from China, and we owe them a lot, it seems. And then we put in more mines to sell them copper and other minerals to make more stuff. We generate about 3 trillion pounds of waste annually, or about 1,242 pounds per person, and this doesn't count the "waste water" we make in the process.

"Waste water"

"Waste water." That's a strange construct on a planet with only so much water, and what is drinkable is far less. We are making a lot of waste water these days in western North Dakota for sure, like there's a water fairy coming to see us in twenty years.

And then there's the social production of waste: prisons. We've got more prisoners per capita than any country in the world. Of the 9 million prisoners in the world some 2.2 million are in the US and that's a huge growth industry as well. And that's a bad idea in my humble opinion.

Throwing People Away

When someone says "throw it away," *what does that mean?* In 1987, the Mobro 4000 barge (known famously as the Gar-barge) got our attention. With a New York landfill at capacity, the barge was filled with 3,100 tons of garbage, hooked up to the tugboat Break of Dawn, and first towed to North Carolina, where it was hoped that it could be turned into methane, though not by North Carolina officials, who refused permission and ordered it to leave.

The floating landfill was towed more than 5,000 miles in 112 days, its operators looking for a place to dump their load. The barge was refused entry at Key West and other ports. The Governor of Louisiana threatened to take military action if it approached; the Mexican Navy ordered it out of their waters; and, Belize authorities turned it away.

Unsuccessful, the Mobro returned to New York with the same load of garbage, where it was incinerated. The barge became a symbol of our own stupidity, and helped create pressure for major changes in recycling programs nationwide and the passage of the 1990 Clean Air/ Clean Water Act.

But not all landfill stories end like that, however. A lot of ships and barges like the Mobro 4000 have illegally dumped their toxic loads in Somalian coastal waters, for example, and many of those have been carrying radioactive waste.

Somalia, that country of political instability, with a long and unguarded coastline, became a victim of international dumping. Then came the barges of toxic waste that dump on their shores. Then came the fishing of their waters illegally by international fleets, and then came the pirates that we saw in Captain Phillips. Pirates came from circumstance; they did not come from Never Never land.

So, what's the antidote? Quit dumping stuff, and get handy; get stuff fixed if you can't do it yourself. Buy stuff which you don't need to throw out, just to fix when needed, and buy used. After all, I met a lot of people building this house off Craigslist and everything has a story.

And I hate feeling helpless. I also like doing cool stuff with other countries, not trying to dump my garbage there.

I still like to fix clothes up, patch pants, sew buttons, and all. I like the idea that I don't have to buy everything and that some of us are still handy. In fact, I still go to see the cobbler - I think the name is still used, for something besides a berry cake. I'm a bit handy, but you don't want me to fix a car or a mechanical thing. That's why I was so happy when the cell phone got fixed. Thank you, handy guys, may there be more of you...

RECOVERING FROM DRAMA OF ELECTION

We just saw some $6 billion spent on the most expensive election in history. I've recovered from the drama, and I am trying to get my head straight. I thought I'd take this time to share some thoughts. After all, I certainly know what losing a national election is like ... maybe Mitt Romney and Paul Ryan might be interested in my opinion.

What have we Learned?

People want to be heard. Florida, the state with hanging chads that cost Al Gore the 2000 election (often blamed on Ralph Nader and me) still has problems. People stood in line for up to seven hours to vote. It was harder to vote if you were dark. According to the Hart Research

Project and the AFL-CIO, voting lines were twice as long for African-Americans than for white voters. In general, 15 percent of Barack Obama supporters spent more than a half-hour waiting to vote, while only 9 percent of Romney supporters had to wait.

Restrictions not Popular

In Minnesota, the measure to require additional voter identification was defeated. In general, tribal members in Minnesota voted "no" on this measure, 10 percent more than the non-Native population. In one precinct with a very high Native population, 86 percent of the voters rejected the voter ID amendment. LaPrairie Township on White Earth (Rice Lake) voted two-thirds against voter ID, Twin Lakes (including Naytauwash), almost three-fourths. Similar voter registration laws in Alaska, Florida, Michigan, South Dakota and Wisconsin were defeated.

Race Matters

Romney won the white male vote. But, it turns out that that is not the only vote in this country. Slightly more women than men voted Democratic, 93 percent of African-Americans, 73 percent of Asian Americans and 71 percent of Latinos voted for Obama, with similar statistics in the native vote. In Naytauwash, in the heart of the White Earth reservation, Obama won resoundingly. And, some 60 percent of youth and some 69 percent of the Jewish community voted for Obama.

Money Can't Buy Love

It was a $6 billion election. All was legal because the U.S. Supreme Court decided in the 2010 Citizens United case that the First Amendment prohibits government from restricting independent political expenditures by corporations and unions.

Consider:
• Massachusetts: Scott Brown spent around $27 million, and lost to Elizabeth Warren, a Harvard professor and consumer advocate.

• Montana: It was the most expensive race in the history of the state. Sen. Jon Tester acknowledged that the Native vote was key to his re-election.

- North Dakota: Heidi Heitkamp took the Senate seat. Her net vote gain in counties with Native communities was high: 4,282 votes. It seems the Native vote and moderate politics carried the election.

- Minnesota: There was one place where money did buy votes, or love. Rep. Michele Bachmann held onto her seat by a narrow margin. She spent 12 times more than her opponent, Jim Graves.

Moving On

Romney and the Republican Party were dealt a pretty resounding defeat, despite huge expenditures of money and a good deal of posturing. Richard Mourdock (Indiana) declared during a debate that he opposed abortion, even in the case of rape. And Missouri Rep. Todd Akin told us that pregnancy as a result of "legitimate rape is rare because the female body has ways to try and shut that whole thing down." Both lost.

It is time to talk about the real issues of America, not get dragged into the right-wing politics of "trade wars with China," cutting student loans, cutting social services, outlawing gay marriage and banning abortion. Post-election is an opportunity to challenge ourselves to be better, and to consider that American politics should be defined by the diversity that is America, not by those who have the most money or the loudest advertising.

REMORSE AND GRATITUDE

These are two fundamental and essential emotions which allow us to live well (I could say "function in society", but that seems too clinical): Remorse: to feel sorry, to express regret (*minjinawezid* - he is regretful). And, gratitude: to be grateful (*migwechiwendam*, to be thankful). Remorse and gratitude.

We need these feelings and emotions, and we need to be able to express them. Then we are able to have empathy for other beings, and we are able to live with more joy. I have realized that my own children at times lack these emotions. I have witnessed my own teenage sons—and some of my other children at times—being unable to say they are sorry, or not accepting or realizing that their own self-centered or mean behavior effects many other people, and when questioned or confronted, the discussion is rejected.

Similarly, I have witnessed more than once a lack of gratitude, an inability to say "thank you" for a gift. I have always believed that I was raised by gracious parents, and that these are essential expressions, despite the difficulty at times.

I make mistakes, and I sometimes forget to be thankful. I do not wish to be a bad parent, yet know that somehow if a generation of children is raised without these emotional skills, things will not go well. And, I think that's what may be going on at the societal level here in the USA.

On remorse: I have a grandson who sometimes has had a very difficult time saying he is sorry. He is now seven years old. When he is asked to express some remorse, there is sometimes a good deal of pouting which occurs first, and then there's a time out until the magic words "I'm sorry" come forth from that little pouty guy.

Now, what does this mean in the larger context? It is a societal problem. From an Indigenous perspective, we are keenly aware of it. The 1890 massacre in the snow and ice at Wounded Knee was egregious. Three hundred people were slaughtered, many of them stripped of their clothing, which was to end up in museum displays and private "collections."

There were 18 Congressional Medals of Honor awarded to the military for this horrific massacre, in which four Hotchkiss guns were used by 500 members of the Seventh Cavalry on defenseless men, women and children. The Army casualties that day were mostly from what they call "friendly fire."

Just as a point of reference, only nine Medals of Honor have been issued to date for the nation's long war in Afghanistan.

When the descendants of the survivors of the Wounded Knee massacre asked South Dakota Senator Tom Daschle to issue a Congressional apology, he replied "We really can't do that. If we did that we'd have to apologize to a lot of other people too."

In fact, the U.S. Army has awarded an astonishing 425 Congressional Medals of Honor over the years for killing American Indians on American soil. The citations do not specify whether the Indians killed were men, women or children sleeping in their mothers' arms, as all were eligible for the same treatment.

So, in 1990, the US Congress issued a joint resolution which "expressed regrets" if not actual remorse about the slaughter. Essentially the same thing happened with U.S. Senator John McCain in Arizona in 1996. South Dakota has since had a Year of Reconciliation or so, but really, this remorse thing has not worked out well in America. The US is still in the pouty-guy phase.

Then, there is the example of the Chevron Corporation in Ecuador. It is a bit confusing, but let's say that Chevron bought Texaco's assets in the country after Texaco has left a large mess behind itself in the Amazon rain forest, including some 30,000 plaintiffs who live there.

Texaco left behind rivers reeking of oil, toxins in holding ponds, piles of oil garbage and a lot of Ecuadorian people who are not able to safely eat fish from their rivers and lakes any more. There are a lot of people who are sick from this destruction (This sounds, unfortunately a bit like North Dakota could look, perhaps, in twenty years), and they are looking for some expression of remorse.

Anyway, Texaco is bought up and the 30,000 villagers now have to go after Chevron instead of Texaco. After a long legal battle (which Chevron wanted to occur in Ecuadorian courts), the court ruled that Chevron is liable for $9.5 billion in damages.

Chevron continued to fight and the Court then doubled the fine (about half the BP settlement, just for reference), suggesting that the lack of remorse by the company, essentially, is causing additional hardship to the plaintiffs.

Then, as the New York Times notes: "Chevron said …that it had no intention of apologizing for the environmental damage to the Amazon rain forest for which an Ecuadorean court ruled it responsible.

Attorneys for both sides have said that if Chevron apologized, its legal liability of $18 billion would have been cut to $9.5 billion."

The company's position: "Chevron does not believe that the Ecuador ruling is enforceable in any court that observes the rule of law." Corporations do not feel remorse.

And, according to business journals, "Investors seem not to believe that the award, the second-largest environmental damages award ever imposed on an oil company (after the $20 billion compensation for victims of the Gulf of Mexico spill agreed by BP)—will (ever) be paid." Nice to know.

There we go. That's what is happening in Ecuador now; but after watching a number of US corporations declare bankruptcy and then re-organize rather than pay these fines, I might be a bit concerned. I might be really concerned if I lived in North Dakota. Take a look at the track record, I'd say.

On gratitude: Well, we are a First World country of the premiere kind. This means that we get food from all over the world; we get resources from all over the world. We have health care, lots of shopping malls, lots of gadgets and lots of stuff. And we usually want more. We shop pretty consistently; in fact, 71% of our economy is based on consumption.

But are we grateful? That's what I'm worried about. My sons have a room full of clothes on the floor, which they will leave there if I'm not after them. And shoot, I actually worked to buy those clothes, and it looked like they needed them.

But, that's sort of America, right now. We have a lot of stuff and we throw out a lot of stuff, and as a society, we make a lot of garbage. I, for one think it's a nice planet and I'm grateful to be here. So there ya go, remorse and gratitude, two special words that we need to remember from Sesame Street, church, or maybe just learn.

THE GIFT: THE IROQUOIS NATIONALS
AT THE WORLD LACROSSE CHAMPIONSHIPS

"Lacrosse is our gift to the world...The game is a microcosm of the big game of life. We are in that arena right now."

—Oren Lyons, Onondaga

The Gift and the Legacy

Oren Lyons has never given up faith in the Creator, his people or the game. The 84-year-old Onondaga statesman is a 47-year member of the Iroquois Council of Chiefs, and a still-active lacrosse player of world renown.

"There are two times of the year that stir the blood. In the fall, for the hunt, and now for lacrosse." —Oren Lyons

I met Oren in July at the World Lacrosse Championships in Denver with the Iroquois Nationals, a team he founded in 1983.

Some of my friends were puzzled as to why I drove, with two 14-year-old boys, the 1,200 miles from the White Earth Indian Reservation in Minnesota to attend the games. But for me and for other Native people, lacrosse is not only a game. It is an epic journey through centuries.

According to my people, the Ojibwe, the first game of lacrosse was played between the mammals and the birds. The bat, that creature which spans two worlds, won that game for the mammals. So today, birds fly south in the winter while the mammals stay put. Later, the Creator gifted the sport to the two-legged. Since then, it has been "the Creator's game."

"Lacrosse was traditionally used as a means of healing between parties when hurtful conflicts were imminent," says Faith Spotted Eagle of the Yankton Indian Reservation in South Dakota. "History tells of a Yankton Chief, Waanatan, who oversaw a game that lasted several days, eventually leading to the settling of a conflict between camps. Many of our communities plagued by violence would benefit from this ancient way of resolving conflicts and pursuing healing."

Sid Jamieson, a Mohawk (of the Iroquois Nation), is a former Bucknell University lacrosse coach. "In the sport's earliest days, players would only step on the field if the clan mothers deemed they were pure in spirit enough to earn the honor," says Sid. "The game was played ferociously. There wasn't any ill feeling about that, because the game was meant to be played rigorously, with fairness and all-out effort."

Lacrosse is the preeminent, fundamental indigenous sport of North America, played from the Great Plains to the Atlantic Ocean. *Tewaaraton* (Little Brother of War) is the Mohawk word for "lacrosse"—a French word. The Ojibwe word for lacrosse is *baaga'adowewin* (The Stick) and in Eastern Cherokee it is *da-nahwah'uwsdi* (Little War).

Today, lacrosse is the fastest-growing sport in the United States. This year, Uganda, Belgium, China, Colombia, Costa Rica, Israel, Russia, Thailand and Turkey competed in the World Championships. Of the 38 countries to send teams to the games, the Iroquois Nation was the only indigenous nation.

Oren tells me that prior to the 2014 games, the members of the Iroquois Nationals had only practiced five times together.

"I asked the U.S. coach," Oren told me, "'What was your player pool?' He said, '200,000. What's yours?' I replied, '100.' That's where we were this year. With Indians, the odds have always been out there."

The lack of practice doesn't show. The team is young and gifted, and on the field their play is seamless, as if they are communicating with the Creator.

The history of lacrosse is also the history of attempts by the Iroquois Nation—the longest-standing democracy in North America—to gain recognition under international law.

In the last half of the 19th century, the East Coast, European-American elite adopted lacrosse as a collegiate sport. But the Native teams remained dominant. In the late 19th century and for much of the 20th, the Iroquois teams were so strong that the government of Canada excluded them from international competition on the pretext that— because they played exhibition matches to fund their travel expenses— they were professional athletes and therefore ineligible.

During this time, when the teams representing the Iroquois Nation were not permitted to play their own game at international events, the Iroquois Nation itself was being denied political participation as a sovereign nation at the UN.

Then, in 1977, Iroquois chiefs attended the first formal UN meeting on the rights of the indigenous people in the Americas. That meeting resulted in the *Declaration of Principles for the Defense of the Indigenous Nations and Peoples of the Western Hemisphere.* That same year, the Iroquois Confederacy issued *Haudenosaunee* (Iroquois) passports for international travel.

Haudenosaunee passports

Six years later, in 1983, the Iroquois Nationals played their first game, and in 1984, the team was invited to tour England, where they won every game but one.

Significantly, the team traveled using their Haudenosaunee passports.

In 1987, the Federation of International Lacrosse accepted the Iroquois Confederacy as a member nation, and in 1990, the Iroquois Nationals played in their first World Lacrosse Championships. Only the United States, Canada, England and Australia have played in all 12 world tournaments.

For the next 20 years, the Iroquois Nationals played around the world. In 2010, however, the UK refused to recognize their Haudenosaunee passports, and denied the Iroquois Nationals entry into Great Britain to compete in the championships.

"It was heartbreaking," Denise Waterman said. Denise is the Iroquois Nationals executive director and the mother of Iroquois Nationals general manager Gewas Schindler. "I remember thinking, 'What will the children who are holding sticks think of us? Of all our dreams for sovereignty? Maybe they will think this is a tribe but they didn't make it.'"

But, she says, when the team came home, "It was the total opposite. *They were heroes.* Little kids said, 'I want to be an Iroquois National'" (This is where Denise and I both get sort of teary).

Victory in Denver

In the stands I meet Brian Miller, whose grandson Zach is a 19-year-old Seneca and a rising sophomore at Denver University. In the past year, Brian has driven his Ford F-150 pickup truck more than a dozen times from the Allegheny Indian Reservation in upstate New York to Denver—more than 3,200 miles round trip—to watch his grandson play home games.

On the edge of our seats on July 19, we watched the Iroquois Nationals as they—having lost to Canada and the United States—battled Australia for third place. They won 16 to 5 and took home the bronze medal, their first in the sport their ancestors originated centuries before.

So there it is. An epic story, which represents far more than a game for Indian country. It is a sport that nourishes traditions and, in many cases, education and leadership. More and more Native lacrosse players are getting recruited for colleges with scholarships. It inspires our youth.

Lyle Thompson, who this year received the NCAA's *Tewaaraton* Trophy for best college lacrosse player (along with his brother, Miles), explains, "When I go back to the rez and talk to kids, the first thing I ask is, 'How are your grades? Get your grades up no matter how hard it is.' Second, 'Keep loving the game.'"

"It's almost a spiritual happening, these games today," says Oren. "We used to settle wars that way, with a game. *The game represents principles of equity and peace. The ball is a medicine.* Somebody always loses, but we've lost a lot of games and we won't be defeated. We won't ever be."

Like Oren, I too have faith, *faith in the Gift.*

MAORI WARRIOR HONE HARAWIRA

"We did not get anything without a fight,"
—HONE HARAWIRA

In the past 30 years, Maori activists have accomplished much in New Zealand, gaining a prominent place in the national government. Of the 120 members currently in Parliament, 20 are Maori, and several Maori have been appointed to various political positions in the federal government.

"We did not get anything without a fight," Hone Harawira, one of the most prominent Maori activists, reminds me. *Hone Pani Tamati Waka Nene Harawira, Member of Parliament, Maori Party.* "You always have to fight to gain."

His electorate is in the far north of New Zealand, and includes his home community of Kaitaia. Some weeks, Hone hitchhikes the 200 miles to his office in the Capitol, rather unusual for an MP.

I first met Hone in 1983, when he came to the International Indian Treaty Council in Okmulgee, Oklahoma. We became fast friends, largely because I was his most reliable ride. I took him on a road trip through a couple of thousand miles of Indian Country.

In 2011, many years, children, grandchildren, battles and political campaigns later (for both of us), he took me on a road trip through his Aotearoa. It was an honor and a pleasure.

There have been many other achievements as well. Maori language knowledge has risen from around 3% to almost 100%, and it's estimated that at least 30% of Maoris are fluent speakers. There are over 100 language immersion schools, and some 50 tribal communities of Maoris, with various community development corporations, and a huge Maori media empire (radio, print and television).

There are around 700,000 Maori in New Zealand (representing maybe one fifth of the population). Of the 66 million acres in the country, the Maori have 3 million acres of communally-held land.

The Maori Party was founded in 2004 with this mission:

"The Māori Party is born of the dreams and aspirations of *tangata whenua* to achieve self-determination for *whānau, hapū* and *iwi* within their own land; to speak with a strong, independent and united voice; and to live according to kaupapa handed down by our ancestors.

"The vision for the Māori Party will be based on these aspirations, for they speak to us of whānau whose wairua is strong and vibrant; who have fully developed their spiritual, intellectual, emotional and physical well-being; and who are confident, secure and pro-active in all aspects of the environmental, social, cultural, economic and political life of this great country of ours."

He is still a passionate activist, one of the few members of Parliament with a long arrest record, which he compiled while protesting for the land rights of Maoris and for environmental rights.

He also faced a long legal battle because of his support for the South African Anti-Apartheid Movement, but at least he got to meet Bishop Desmond Tutu.

"That was the freakiest experience of my life," Hone tells me. This was back in 1983. Hone had been arrested while protesting the visit of the South African Springboks, that country's national rugby team (See the recent movie *Invictus*, starring Matt Damon and Morgan Freeman, for a dramatized version of this story).

Hone was charged with 96 years' worth of felonies, including participating in a riot and assault with intent to create grievous bodily harm.

"The case went on for a couple of years, from 1981 to 1983. In those two years, my defense lasted maybe 45 minutes," he said.

When the date for his trial was finally set, Hone had an epiphany: *South African Bishop Desmond Tutu has come to New Zealand at the invitation of the Anglican Church to talk about apartheid. Hone would request Bishop Tutu testify at his trial as an expert witness.* Hone's mother was active in the Anglican Church, and she spoke to Bishop Tutu.

The trial starts. There are 10 defendants, but Hone elected to defend himself. He delivers his testimony to the jury. As he is winding down, he recalls, "There is a head poking up in the back of the court room; it is one of my colleagues. He nods to me as I am sitting on the witness stand, completing my testimony."

At that point, the judge asked Hone if he had any witnesses to bring forward. Hone says he does, and calls Bishop Desmond Tutu to the stand.

Hone and his nine co-defendants were acquitted of all charges.

It is now 27 years later, and Hone Harawira is still an uncompromising leader. Here are some of his candid thoughts on political activism, on working within the system and on meeting the challenges of representing rednecks:

On compromise: "Compromise your strategies, not your principles. Be bold in your positions. When governments say, 'Maori need to be realistic'. What they are really saying is 'No'. But that shouldn't make us afraid to say what our people want, and commit ourselves to doing our best to achieve that. If we are not successful, don't let it be because we let somebody else stop us from daring to succeed."

On the importance of dedicated Indigenous seats in Parliament or Congress: "At that level it's about learning the skills of macro management, rather than bullshitting yourself that you're part of government, because the white boys will kick you out."

On literacy: "The Maori people drafted a declaration of independence in 1835. Five years later, the Treaty of Waitangi was signed, recognizing Maori sovereignty rights to natural resources and land. At that time, the Maori were more literate than the *Pakeha*, the non-native settlers. The treaties were written in Maori, and interpreted in Maori for the people. Today, 100% of the Maori is largely bilingual, while perhaps 10% of the rest of the New Zealand population is bilingual.

Maori is one of two official languages of New Zealand—it's Maori and sign language."

On representing his constituents: "I don't really care about what the rest of my constituents think, I care about what the Maori say. There are another 100 or so members of Parliament who can represent their interests, and they will definitely not represent the Maori interests."

On Indigenous People working in mainstream politics: "You can get knowledge anywhere, even from the enemy. If we're talking about sovereignty and we want to run a country, we have to know how to manage a country. *There are concessions to be made, but substantive change doesn't come through national politics. Not unless your leadership is courageous.*"

Comparing Native Americans in political office with Maori politicians: "Your energy is spent trying to placate people you don't like, like rednecks in South Dakota. I'd rather represent my tumultuous relations in the five reservations. I'd be happier to represent them than the people of Rapid City. I see that Maori people who hold office with white parties are basically ignored. They are trotted out to do a speech or a performance, and then kicked out of the room when the decisions are made. I think we should spend more time building capacity within, rather than externalizing that."

On the people who have inspired him: "Muhammed Ali, Nelson Mandela, Huey Newton and the Maori people—Sid Jackson, Maori Marsden, my mom and my wife, Hilda. When I was young, the heroes—in terms of change for people of color—were Black. And they were so far off the planet because of what they were saying, you couldn't help say, 'That was cool!' Ali had that going for him—he was really articulate and if anyone didn't agree, he could smash them."

On the future battles: "Maori politics remains an uphill battle to gain more political power at all levels, from grassroots to Parliament. The politics of poverty remains significant in Aotearoa, as well as in the U.S., as increasing numbers of people fall into more desperate economic situations."

Writings on Women, Idle No More and Canadian Colonialism

REMEMBERING JANCITA EAGLE DEER

*"She worked for that one governor, you know,
He did all those bad things. Nothing stuck to
him."*

—LOUISE ERDRICH, *The Round House* (A NOVEL)

This morning I awoke thinking of Jancita Eagle Deer. *I am sure she is
watching us, from the other side, the side of the Spirits.* She is watching as Congress debates the Violence Against Women Act, and hoping someone remembers her.

Jancita was a Lakota woman from the Rosebud reservation. In 1974, she testified that William Janklow (her legal guardian as a child) had raped her on a ride home from babysitting for the Janklow family. The incident had occurred in 1967, when she was 15 years old.

Rosebud Tribal Judge Mario Gonzalez wrote that Ms Jancita Eagle Deer testified under obvious emotional difficulty that she had been raped by William Janklow, and that he had threatened her life with a gun. Portions of her testimony were corroborated by her high school guidance counselor, her foster parents, a rape examination, and a BIA investigator.

The evidence was enough to disbar William Janklow, but he was never convicted of the crime. *The Rosebud Tribal Court had no jurisdiction.* Janklow was elected South Dakota State Attorney General on November 2, 1974.

Jancita Eagle Deer was killed by a hit-and-run driver near Aurora, Nebraska while outside of a vehicle on April 4, 1975. She had been apparently walking in the middle of the highway when she was hit. The circumstances were mysterious. She was killed only a few months after she had testified against William Janklow in Rosebud Tribal Court, over 200 miles away from her home.

Janklow's star continued to rise, and he was elected governor twice, becoming known for turning South Dakota into the "Mississippi of the North." Under Janklows' political leadership, South Dakota was renowned for its poor treatment of Native people and seizure of Native lands and jurisdiction.

After serving additional time in the House of Representatives and in jail for vehicular homicide, Janklow passed away in 2003. At every turn in his career, Native people rankled at his rise in power, and at the lack of justice for Jancita.

In the least, Jancita's story reminds us why the Violence Against Women Act deserves passage.

The House of Representatives continues to debate the question of tribal government jurisdiction over non-Native perpetrators of violence against Native women if the crime occurs in Indian Country.

It's an interesting case of the un-equal protection under the law, as Senate Select Committee on Indian Affairs Chair Maria Cantwell remarked:

"We cannot vote for an amendment...that basically strips the rights of Native American women and treats them like second-class citizens. Nor can we just go silent on what is an epidemic problem in our country." –Senator Maria Cantwell

The bill passed through the Senate after a lengthy debate, and now these issues remain a high concern to many Republican representatives.

To the Native community, the debate remains a clear example of a discriminatory legal system. Indeed, since the Supreme Court's 1978 decision in *Oliphant vs Suquamish Indian Tribe* stripped tribal communities of much jurisdiction over non-tribal members, many reservations are now the residence to large non-Native populations.

The Oliphant decision amounted to providing free *Get Out of Jail* cards to any non-Native criminal or sexual predator operating on tribal lands.

In contrast, Native people are prosecuted under both tribal and non-tribal law, and often constitute a disproportionately high percentage of the prison population. In short, Native people are subject to the laws of a different political entity, but non-Native criminals find themselves without legal repercussions in Indian Country. Tribal courts can't reach them, and they know it.

Take a North Dakota reliving of history, in fiction and in law: Fiction writer Louise Erdrich's latest magnificent book *The Round House* speaks to a similar case and the entanglements of laws and lack of justice in the case of rape of tribal women.

In one facet of the book, Jancita Eagle Deer bears an uncanny resemblance to fictional murder victim Mayla Wolfskin. *"She worked for that one governor, you know, He did all those bad things. Nothing stuck to him."* Erdrich writes fiction, and issued a disclaimer. The truth, however, is often a mirror to fiction.

Presently, 34% of American Indian and Alaska Native women will be raped in their lifetimes; 39% will be subjected to domestic violence in their lifetimes; 67% of Native women victims of rape and sexual assault report their assailants as non-Native individuals and—on some reservations—Native women are murdered at more than ten times the national average.

Not good. This set of facts is paired with unfortunately high declination rates: U.S. Attorneys declined to prosecute nearly 52% of violent crimes that occur in Indian country; and 67% of cases declined were sexual abuse related cases. *Pretty much the luck of William Janklow.*

I asked Lisa Brunner, Executive Director of Sacred Spirits, a national tribal organization working on these issues, to comment:

Brunner explained that some of the concern stems from a lack of understanding of tribal jurisdiction. In some cases, tribes will, in fact, not have criminal codes which allow this legal process. Brunner suggests that the answer was to fund the tribal process, and educate the non-Native population. The answer was not to put more funding in non-Indian jurisdictions, as declination rates for prosecution remain at over 62% in rape and sexual assault cases.

As well, there are safeguards built into the provision which ensure that all rights guaranteed under the Constitution are given to non-Native defendants in tribal court. Further, the special domestic violence jurisdiction is narrowly restricted to apply only to instances of domestic or dating violence where: 1) the victim is an Indian, 2) the conduct occurs on tribal lands; and 3) where the defendant either lives or works on the reservation, i.e., where the defendant has significant ties to the community.

In their letter to Congress, the National Council of American Indians patiently explained that Indian tribes are not a racial class, but are *"...a political body – so the question is not whether non-Indians are subject to Indian court – the question is whether tribal governments, political entities, have the necessary jurisdiction to provide their citizens with the public safety protections every government has the inherent duty to provide."*

As Senator Cantwell testified, "The notion that this is somehow abrogating individual rights just because the crime takes place on a tribal reservation is incorrect. So I ask my colleagues, do you want to continue to have this unbelievable growth and petri dish of crime evolving? Because criminals know (that) when you have a porous border that is where they are going to go."

Jancita Eagle Deer deserved justice that she did not receive. It is almost forty years later and there should be no statute of limitations on justice. The Violence Against Women Act would provide a process for justice and serve as a deterrent providing legal protections for all women.

I remember Jancita and hope her story from the next world is heard.

Postscript: The Violence Against Women Authorization Act eventually passed Congress and was signed into law by President Obama on March 7, 2013.

IN PRAISE OF THE LEADERSHIP OF INDIGENOUS WOMEN
(FOR VANDANA SHIVA)

"A nation is not conquered until the hearts of its women are on the ground. Then, it is finished no matter how brave its warriors or how strong their weapons."

—CHEYENNE PROVERB

"There is a powerful metaphor between the economic policies of this country Canada and the USA and their treatment of our Indigenous woman and girls....I have learned that our movement is very much led by women, this is something I am very comfortable....the sacredness of Mother Earth in the tar sands for example and the fact that this represents the greatest driver of both Canadian and US economies, then you look at the lack of action being taken on the thousands of First Nations women and girls who have been murdered or just disappeared, it all begins to all make sense. It's also why our women have been rising up and taking power back from the smothering forces of patriarchy dominating our economic, political and (other spheres)....

"When you look at the extreme violence taking place against social and—I would say—spiritual institutions. When we turn things around as a peoples, it will be the women who lead us, and it will be the creative feminine principle they carry that will give us the tools we need to build another world. Indigenous peoples have been keeping a tab on what has been stolen from our lands, which the Creator put us on to protect, and there is a day coming soon where we will collect. Until then, we will keep our eyes on the prize, organize and live our lives in a good way and we welcome you to join us on this journey."
—Clayton Thomas Muller, Cree, 2013

Resistance Emerges in the Place where the
First World meets the Third World in the North

In the winter of 2012, Chief Theresa Spence of the *Attawapiskat* First Nation in northern Ontario drew the world's attention when she went on a hunger strike in front of the Canadian capital in Ottawa, Ontario. Spence, a modest woman, helped inspire an international movement called *Idle No More*, which drew attention to Canada's hyper-aggressive resource extraction era, and to the Harper Administration's aggressive violations of the human rights of Indigenous peoples, and the destruction of the Earth.

Chief Theresa Spence is the leader of Attawapiskat First Nation—a very remote Cree community from James Bay, Ontario, which lies at the southern end of Hudson Bay.

The communities on reserve number 1,549 residents (a third of whom are under 19) and they have weathered quite a bit: the fur trade, residential schools, a status as non-treaty Indians, and limited access to modern conveniences like a toilet or electricity. Conditions like this are, unfortunately, commonplace in the North, but the advent of a massive diamond mine has exacerbated the suffering of many in the past five years.

Enter DeBeers, the largest diamond-mining enterprise in the world. The company moved into northern Ontario in 2006, where the Victor Mine reached commercial production in 2008 and was voted "Mine of the Year" by the readers of the international trade publication Mining Magazine. The company states that it is "committed to sustainable development in local communities."

This is good to know, because—as Canadian MP Bob Rae discovered in 2012 on his tour of the rather destitute conditions of the village—this is also the place where the First World meets the Third World in the far North.

Infrastructure in the subarctic is in short supply. There is no road into the village eight months of the year. Four months a year, during freeze up, there's an ice road. A diamond mine needs a lot of infrastructure, and all of this equipment has to be shipped in, so the trucks launch out of Moosonee, Ontario (another rather remote outpost) connected to the south by a railroad. Then, they build a better road. The problem is that the road won't work when the climate changes, and already stretched infrastructure gets tapped out.

There is some money flowing in, that's sure. A 2010 report from DeBeers states that payments to eight communities associated with its two mines in Canada totaled $5,231,000 that year. Forbes Magazine reports record diamond sales by the world's largest diamond company "...increased 33 percent, year-over-year, to $3.5 billion...The mining giant, which produces more than a third of the world's rough diamonds, also reported record EBITDA of almost $1.2 billion, a 55 percent increase over the first the first half of 2010."

As the Canadian Mining Watch group notes: "Whatever Attawapiskat's share of that $5-million is, given the chronic under-funding of the community, the need for expensive responses to deal with recurring crises, including one that DeBeers themselves may have precipitated by **overloading the community's sewage system,** it's not surprising that the community hasn't been able to translate its...income into improvements in physical infrastructure."

Last year, Attawapiskat drew international attention when many families in the Cree community were living in tents in the dead of winter. The neighboring Kashachewan Village is in similar disarray. They have been boiling and importing water. The village almost had a complete evacuation due to health conditions, including a scabies and impetigo epidemic.

And, on top of all of this: "...fuel shortages are becoming more common among remote northern Ontario communities right now," Alvin Fiddler, Deputy Grand Chief of the Nishnawbe Aski Nation (a regional advocacy network) explained to a reporter. That's because the ice road used to truck in a year's supply of diesel last winter did not last as long as usual. "Everybody is running out now. We're looking at a two-month gap until this winter's ice road is solid enough to truck in fresh supplies", Mr. Fiddler said in an interview.

Kashechewan's chief and council are poised to shut down the band office, two schools, the power generation centre, the health clinic and the fire halls because the buildings were not heated and could no longer operate safely.

According to Chief Derek Stephen "In addition, some 21 homes had become uninhabitable due to flooding." (Just as a side note, in 2007, some 21 Cree youth from Kashechewan attempted to commit suicide, and the Canadian aboriginal youth suicide rate is five times the national average.) Both communities are beneficiaries of an agreement with DeBeers. Sort of a third world situation, eh? In one of the richest countries in the world.

Now that story could be a story from India, Pakistan, Papua New Guinea, or the Congo–but it's a story of the North. It is a story of the Indigenous communities of the North, and a story of the reality of a resource extraction state which is cannibalizing the land from which it sprang legislatively, economically and with a new onslaught of militarization.

With our communities living in these conditions, how can there be consent given to fossil fuel extraction and mineral mining contracts? Indigenous women have resisted the dominating and coercive spirit of the predator economy, which devastates the land and our bodies, since our land was first colonized. That colonialism continues.

The Colonization Model and the Manufacturing of Consent

"The intent is hyper-acceleration of resource extraction and development, and these are on Indigenous territories, and the way to accelerate that process is to create legislation, and to have that legislation part of the instrument through which poverty is utilized. This is the old colonial model, which is having the veneer of consent. It is to manufacture it. To manufacture poverty and then manufacture consent." –Russ Diabo

The colonial model is well known, time-tested extensively.

The Steven Harper government—the present government of the settler/colonizer of Canada—did what all prior Canadian governments have done, and has done it more aggressively. The Harper government deprives people of the basics of a dignified life: running water, critical infrastructure, stable health and food security.

Canada—like its American counterpart—does this by systemically appropriating the resources of Indigenous communities, militarizing those communities, bringing in new para-militaries to the borders of those communities, insuring long-term health instability in those communities, draining intellectual capital from those communities (through educational and financial institutions) and never investing in infrastructure. Then, they offer the community only one choice.

That choice is embedded in a series of laws and way-too-friendly courts and gun-barrel diplomacy that supports the intensification of resource extraction. And, it turns out that what Canada does in Canada to Native people is what Canadian corporations do around the world, perhaps having learned well from their neighbor to the south.

It's an important point in history because 75% of the world's mining companies today are Canadian-based, and –in the present era—we've seen the inefficient and extravagant consumption of North American First World countries (especially the US and Canada) drive a level of resource extraction which will not only require additional planets to continue, but ultimately destroys the land and water upon which we live.

One more time: Canada is the home to 75% of the worlds mining corporations, and they have tended to have relative impunity in the Canadian courts. Canadian corporations and their international subsidiaries are being protected by military forces elsewhere, and this concerns many.

According to a U.K. Guardian story, a Quebec Court of Appeal rejected a suit by citizens of the Democratic Republic of the Congo against Montreal-based Anvil Mining Limited for allegedly providing logistical support to the DRC army as it carried out a massacre, killing as many as 100 people in the town of Kilwa near the company's silver and copper mine.

The Supreme Court of Canada later held that Canadian courts had no jurisdiction over the company's actions in the Congo when it rejected the plaintiffs' request to appeal. Kairos, a Canadian faith-based organization, concluded that the Supreme Court's ruling would have "... broader implications for other victims of human rights abuses committed by Canadian companies and their chances of bringing similar cases to our courts."

The North American economy consumes a third of the world's resources, with perhaps a tenth of the worlds' population. That level of consumption requires constant interventions into other countries, and constant violations of human rights.

To continue on their present course, Canadian companies will need legal impunity, as there is no way to extract the remaining fossil fuels without drastically accelerating the damage that's already been caused, and there is no compensation for what has been done already.

Take the case of the Ecuadorian government versus Chevron Corporation. It is a bit confusing, but let's say that Chevron buys the Texaco company's assets in the country, and Texaco has left a large mess, rivers full of oil, toxins in holding ponds, piles of oil garbage, and a lot of people who are not able to eat fish from their rivers, and a lot of people who are sick.

Anyway, Texaco is bought up by Chevron, and the villagers now have to go after Chevron. After a long legal battle, (which Chevron wanted in Ecuadorian courts), the Courts ruled that Chevron was liable for $9.5 billion in damages. Chevron continued to appeal, and the Court then doubled the fine, suggesting that the lack of remorse by the company, essentially, is causing additional hardship to the plaintiffs, who have been awarded this settlement.

Then, as the New York Times notes: "Chevron said ...that it had no intention of apologizing for the environmental damage to the Amazon rain forest for which an Ecuadorian court ruled it responsible. Attorneys for both sides have said that if Chevron apologized, its legal liability of $18 billion would have been cut to $9.5 billion." Chevron's position: "Chevron does not believe that the Ecuador ruling is enforceable in any court that observes the rule of law."

That's corporate ethics in this day and age, and that's just the beginning of the damages.

Consider that we've consumed one half of the world's known fossil fuels, everything that is relatively easy to extract, and so what remains is largely difficult to extract, requiring extreme measures, and with very little net gain in terms of energy.

Copper mining is close to the most inefficient product to produce from a big dig. In other words, you need to remove 1,000,000,000 tons of material to recover 1.6 tons of copper. The only substance with a lower recovery rate is gold.

Copper mining projects in northern Anishinaabe territory will now take copper, creating vast rivers of sulphuric acid. The Ramu Nickel Mine proposal in Papua New Guinea will dump its mining waste into the depths of the ocean, destroying life indiscriminately.

Both projects, the mines in Anishinaabe Akiing and Papua are built for Chinese markets, illustrating how global market forces and inefficiencies impact us all. Whether the companies are Canadian or Australian, the markets today are often in China. In turn, much of what will be produced may end up coming back to North American markets in the form of the multitude of trade goods North America continues to purchase from China.

The rate of extraction these companies are pursuing is not only unsustainable; it is ecologically and economically disastrous.

"When Indigenous peoples oppose the destruction of our ecosystems. We get challenged as people who are saying, 'Let's go back to the stone age,'" Caleen Sisk, Winnemem Wintu Chief tells me. "The fact is that these guys with their extraction and pollution will put us (back) before the Stone Age. We won't even be able to eat..."

Which is to say, there is a monetary economy and then there is an economy based on clean air, clean water, and food, or quality of life.

Fossil fuel extraction practices illustrate the worst of addiction and overconsumption:

- The North American economy has moved to blowing the tops off of five hundred mountains in Appalachia (known as mountain-top removal) to benefit markets as far away as India.

- Deep-water extraction is being pushed into the most pristine and untouched regions of the ocean, and with global warming accelerating, the retreat of ice has left more ocean accessible to high-risk extraction technologies.

- The foremost example of the Extreme Extraction Experiment gone awry is British Petroleum's Deep Water Horizon fiasco in the Gulf of Mexico. The extraction of oil and gas through fracking methods threatens groundwater the world over and the aquifers we rely on.

- And, finally, the aggressive push into the tar sands of the Athabasca River basin destroys an ecosystem, sickening all who live there for the benefit of international oil interests.

It is in this context that the resistance of Indigenous women is essential, and it is found wherever our people are.

Pamela Paimeta, a spokesperson for *Idle No More* in Canada, talks about the origin of the movement, which sprang from Canada's violations of basic human rights, in which the Harper government gutted laws which would protect indigenous communities. His administration launched an economic war against these same communities if they would not sign mining agreements by holding out basic transfer benefits for food, education, housing and health, and then dismantling the environmental laws of that country, in an infamous bill called C 45.

C 45 passed at the end of 2012. That bill and a series of related bills removed roadblocks in the legislative and regulatory arena within this First World country for the direct benefit of mining corporations.

Paimeta—a legal scholar—points out that treaty rights and the rights of Indigenous nations are essential for all Canadians to support, (despite all that they have been taught in the schools, and despite the teaching and implementation of the construct of white privilege) and urges the larger community to see what is occurring across the country as a reality check.

"The first Nations are the last best hope that Canadians have for protecting land for food and clean water for the future–not just for our people, but for Canadians as well. So this country falls or survives on whether they acknowledge, or recognize and implement, those aboriginal and treaty rights. So they need to stand with us and protect what is essential."—Pamela Paimeta

In some ways, the *Idle No More* movement's emergence—and the increasing visibility of Indigenous women—are essential steps in educating a larger non-Indigenous population.

Native women have historically been marginalized—definitely marginalized in the media—as the dramatic pictures of Native people on horse back or Native men in various occupations has captured media attention more than the pictures of Native women.

That is changing on the front lines as they become more militarized, and that is changing because there is a more enlightened North American feminist community.

Native feminism does not exist in the same paradigm as non-Native feminism.

At the basics, we would say that we are not fighting for a bigger piece of the pie, we want a different pie altogether. We want the world we were instructed to carry on by our ancestors, and by our traditions. In that world, we have a good and respectful life, and with the adaption of those values into a set of appropriate technologies, we are clear on our path and what we will accept and want.

The Chief Occupies

Now back to Chief Theresa Spence, and the implication of her hunger strike in the capital of Ottawa, Ontario. She hoped to meet with Prime Minister Stephen Harper, urging him to "open his heart" and meet with native leaders angered by his policies.

"He's a person with a heart but he needs to open his heart. I'm sure he has faith in the Creator himself and for him to delay this, it's very disrespectful, I feel, to not even meet with us," she said. Her actions encouraged the development of a movement, *Idle No More*, which emerged in Canada and quickly spread to the US and elsewhere.

The social movement known as *Idle No More* consisted of protests, marches, direct actions and often traditional round dances which would be "flash mobs" and appear in the spur of a moment at places like the Mall of America, the state capital of Colorado, and other public spaces and city centers.

The movement has captured the attention and imagination of many of the youth in Indigenous communities, and it has been propelled by using social media well, documenting stories, images and videos which otherwise never would appear in the mainstream media.

Frankly, Natives have been historically marginalized in the media so effectively, that the only stories about the Native community are stories of either arrests (a survey of northern US native papers will find that is the majority of coverage), or national coverage of Native poverty.

That, however, is a trend that may be changing with an increasing number of Native writers, radio stations in more reservations and reserves, and the increased usage of social media, reaching into and connecting remote communities.

Different than *Occupy*

Some have likened the *Idle No More* movement to the *Occupy* movement.

There is some shared terrain, particularly in terms of the significance and power of social media, and the access the information age poses for historically marginalized communities. They now control their own media. There is—in that vein—and in the youthfulness of the Indigenous movement (most of the Native community is under 25 years of age by and large), that is similar to the youthfulness of the Occupy movement.

The *Idle No More* Movement itself, however, is old, mature and evolving with technology, as is the larger movement of Indigenous peoples. Indigenous movements have been engaged for hundreds of years, but emerged politically with the rise of American Indian Movement in the 1960s, joined side by side with other anti-colonial movements internationally (SWAPO, PLO, ANC, Poliserio) and others.

The movement has gained sophistication in international realms while strengthening the community-based resistance to extraction.

Movements on the ground, like Northern Cheyenne's *Native Action*, *DINÉ Care* (Navajo), *Anishinaabe Akiing* (Anishinaabeg) and national alliances and organizations like the Indigenous Environmental Network and Honor the Earth, have reiterated the political agenda and deepened and coordinated resistance, often achieving good results. Mining projects and nuclear waste dumps have been stopped, and some sacred sites have been protected.

Much of the leadership at the grass roots, or community-based level, is being provided by Indigenous women.

This is to say that I do believe that the *Idle No More* Movement more resembles the *Zapatista* movement and the ongoing indigenization of western hemispheric politics, but with the added dimension of instant media and cell phone technology, of which there has been little or no access in Chiapas.

We have seen our youth break open spaces in which their voices and stories have been heard, and where they have opportunities to influence public policy and opinion, and to support one another and connect through shared experiences between remote communities.

"*Idle No More* is one of what masked Subcommandante Marcos called 'Pockets of Resistance, which are as numerous as the forms of resistance themselves'." –Kristen Moe, *Yes Magazine*

The Zapatistas are a part of the 500-year-old movement of Indigenous anti-colonial resistance which crested in the early 1990s. It has continued to grow, change and adapt in many South American countries, notably resulting with the election of an Indigenous president in Bolivia and the enshrining of the Rights of Mother Earth in the Bolivian constitution.

We share common histories of colonialism, and today with a continued globalized presence, where colonial powers Spain, England, Portugal and France have been replaced by colonizing corporate entities such as SunCor, BHP Billiton, DeBeers, Conoco, Enbridge and Trans Canada… we understand that our resistance is still essential to survival.

Indigenous resistance is in many cases the strongest front, and has the capacity to protect the land, a semblance of a land-based economy for all. Native women do not by any means have a monopoly on creative resistance to colonialism, but Native women have played a significant role in that resistance. There may be some historic reasons.

Indigenous Women Resist from the Intersection of Sexism and Colonialism

There is something about never having been enfranchised or privileged by the industrial society, which means that Indigenous women are perhaps less colonized than some of their male counterparts. It's an armchair sociologist's observation. American, British and it's descendent, Canadian colonialism, favored making treaties with men, dealing with men and naming men. After all, that is what the European monarchy and feudalistic system was accustomed to.

Euro-American men did not notice the clan mothers of the Iroquois Confederacy. Nor did they recognize the place of women in Anishinaabe or other Indigenous societies. Hence, when decision-making was put in that realm, and favoring and privileging resulted, it focused not on the status of women, but on the status of men.

This is how a clientele class is created in the process of colonization, where the colonizer has at some point so infiltrated the world of the object of his desire, that we the colonized become the colonizer ourselves.

We are "digested" (as the root of colonization is the same as "colon," yep), and in that digestion we come to emulate the colonizer. That is, we come to emulate the mindset of the colonizer.

There is a good argument to be made, however, that the status of Native men also diminishes with colonization, particularly as we are denied access to our lands, our waters, our food, and our ceremonies. It is a process of colonization, and the Indigenous movement is, therefore, a process of decolonization.

What I know is that the hierarchy of colonization finds it easiest to deal with a few appointed leaders, or those who meet the approval of the federal government or the Canadian government, perhaps. And a lot of decisions are made by those individuals—often after a good deal of indoctrination, disinformation, coerced "acceptance" of policies, and intrusions of gun-barrel diplomacy imposed on Native communities.

Some of this has been reflected in the militarization of Indian Country, which, it turns out, is heavily militarized, as old cavalry bases are turned into new weapons training centers, and more and more of our people have been pulled into the US military until we "enjoy" the highest rate of enlistment of any population in North America. They still test the most lethal weapons on our lands, and continue to take our lands for more military actions.

Gun-barrel diplomacy is embedded, intrinsic to Canadian Premier Steve Harper's full-scale assault on Native resources. Starving your community is very effective in demonstrating who is the boss of you. Gun barrel diplomacy is happening when your land is occupied by multinational corporations who want to frack your territory for oil and the Canadian government sends the paramilitary riot police into your small community, or watches impassively as super-militarized security forces back the frackers.

Gun-Barrel Diplomacy Leaves Little Room for Talking.

And so we find that many times the front lines of the Indigenous struggles to protect our land are led by women. That is because we have never had access to the privileging of big expense accounts of the federal government and corporations, and that is because, by and large, someone is still needed to look after our families and children–in the face of heartbreak, and in the face of colonization, the face of an all-out war which destabilizes our Native men.

Now, this is a story about some of that process, but also is a story of why our resistance as Native women is so strong.

The Economics of Colonialism

"Canada has demonized us. We 'lost' our land, we 'lost' our language, we 'lost' our heritage. We are these rambunctious, crazy people who just 'lose' stuff...that is not what happened, and that is not what is happening...." —Frank Molley, MicMaq

"In the colonial to neocolonial alchemy, gold changes to scrap metal, and food to poison. We have become painfully aware of the mortality of wealth which nature bestows and imperialism appropriates...." —Eduardo Galeano, Open Veins of Latin America. 1973

This is how it works. The verb is "underdeveloping." That is what is happening to Indigenous territories on an ongoing basis in North America. Tribal lands, resources and people are being mined and de-stabilized, as water is contaminated, territories are impacted by mega projects, and wealth is appropriated.

The military takes Indigenous lands and has taken them historically. In the US, the largest military power in the world, from Alaska, to Hawaii—where a full third of the state is held by the US military, and more expansions for the so-called "Pacific Theater" are under way.

Alaska alone has some 700 used military defense toxic sites, which tell a story of the Cold War and every war since. The levels of radioactive and persistent organic pollutants remaining in the environment impact people who are dependant upon the land for their subsistence way of life. Then, there are the impacts of economic colonialism and underdevelopment to consider.

Elsewhere, an estimated $100 million per year in revenues is extracted from the Barriere Lake Algonquins' territory in the form of logging, hydroelectric dams and recreational hunting and fishing. The First Nation itself, however, lives in Third World conditions. A diesel generator provides power, very few jobs are available, and families live in dilapidated bungalows. These are not the lifestyles of a community with a $100-million economy in its back yard.

The 600 Canadian First Nations have provided the lion's share of those resources, from oil and gas in Alberta to uranium in Saskatchewan, mega-dam projects in Quebec, Labrador and Manitoba, and old and new mines in Ontario.

Not to mention the trees. There used to be a lot more in Canada, but there are more stumps now, and fewer trees, and the money has not gone to Native communities.

The US is a ditto

One third of all uranium, two thirds of all western coal, four of the ten largest coal strip mines in the country, vast dam projects and land seizures are all gouged out of Indian lands.

All of this means a transfer of wealth and a destabilizing of traditional economics and communities. In turn, we occupy the poorest postal codes in both countries, and lack basic First World infrastructure. About 14% of reservation households are without electricity, 10 times the national rate.

Energy distribution systems on rural reservations are extremely vulnerable to extended power outages during winter storms, threatening the lives of countless reservation residents.

Reservation communities are at a statistically greater risk from extreme weather-related mortality nationwide, especially from cold, heat and drought associated with a rapidly changing climate.

Debbie Dogskin, for example, a Lakota woman living on the Standing Rock reservation, froze to death in February because she couldn't pay her skyrocketing propane bills and her propane ran out. Ironically, she lived only about 100 miles from the Bakken oil fields where they flare off so much gas that they light the night sky, they can afford to waste so much.

Fracking operations in the Bakken are so energy-inefficient that they deliberately burn off about 350 million cubic feet of natural gas every day, as reported by NBC News in August, 2014. That comes to more than $100 million worth of gas burned off into the sky each month.

Reservations need more than 200,000 new houses, and there is no money for them.

And then there is the case of Pine Ridge, South Dakota, the largest Lakota reservation, and the poster child of those who want to talk about how horrible the conditions of Native people are.

At Pine Ridge, 97% of the people live below federal poverty line. The unemployment rate vacillates from 85% to 95% on the reservation. At least 60% of the homes are severely substandard, without water, electricity, adequate insulation and sewage systems. It is hard to manage in these conditions in a First World country. And it causes stress to people.

Add to this the specter of Man Camps and the degradation and victimization of Native women that comes hand in glove with the energy booms. That is why we resist them. They have no consent, either for our bodies, or our ecosystems.

It is no stretch to say that this predator economics targets our lands and our very bodies.

There is the physical destruction of peoples. In the US, an epidemic of diabetes wreaks havoc on most tribal communities, with up to 1/3 of the population afflicted with the disease, burdening them with immense health costs and overall destabilization as people in the prime of their knowledge increasingly become impacted by a crippling disease. The physical destruction of the peoples as either a systematic or a secondary impact of an economics which views Native lives as external to their cost/benefit equations doesn't stop there.

The Lost Boys of *Aamjiwnaang*

"On an Indian reserve in Canada, girls rule the day-care centers, the playgrounds, the sports teams. The reason: For the past 15 years, fewer and fewer boys are being born. It may be the leading edge of a chemically induced crisis that could make men an endangered species." —Melody Petersen, The Lost Boys of Aamjiwnaang, *Men's Health*, 2009

There are some communities, in fact, where the environment has become so polluted that women will likely be the future leaders of those communities simply because there will no longer be enough men being born, and males die at a higher rate than females at every age.

One place like that is *Aamjiwnaang*, an Anishinaabe community on the north shore of the Great Lakes This community is bordered on three sides by Canada's largest concentration of petrochemical refining, polymer and chemical plants, a place called "Chemical Valley."

Worldwide and historically, males and females are generally born in close to a 50-50 ratio, with slightly more males than females, but in Aamjiwnaang, the ratio of males has dropped to the 30 percentile. Between 1993 and 2003, there had been two girls born for every boy to the tribal community, one of the steepest declines ever recorded in birth-gender ratio.

As reported in Environmental Health Perspectives in 2005, "The trend in the proportion of male live births of the Aamjiwnaang First Nation has been declining continuously from the early 1990s to 2003, from an apparently stable sex ratio prior to this time. The proportion of male births showed a statistically significant decline over the most recent 10-year period (1994–2003) with the most pronounced decrease observed during the most recent 5 years (1999–2003)."

This trend is international, particularly in more industrialized countries, and the odd statistics at Aamjiwnaang are indicative of larger trends. The rail line, known as the St. Clair spur, carries CN and CSX trains to several large industries in Sarnia's Chemical Valley. Usually four or five trains move through a day, all of which are full of chemicals.

In the spring of 2013, the Ojibwe blockaded the tracks of that plant at Aamjiwnaang.

Those tracks are full of chemical trains from some of the 62 industrial plants in what the Canadian government calls Industrial Valley. The Aamjiwnaang people would like to call it home, but they've a few challenges with toxic levels of pollution in their house.

"If the prime minister will not listen to our words, perhaps he'll pay attention to our actions," Chief Chris Plain explained to the media at the takeover.

The Ojibwe have faced a chronic dosage of poisonous, cancer-causing chemicals for twenty-five years, and are concerned about the health impacts. They are also concerned about proposals to move tar sands oil through their community in a pre-existing pipeline, known as Enbridge Line Nine.

There are some places which are still beautiful, and these places deserve to live. There are many of them, as Indigenous territories have been largely remote. An overlay, for instance, of biodiversity and cultural diversity means that there is a map which illustrates that Indigenous territories are ecologically diverse and teeming with life with our human lives, and with the lives of our relatives (whether they have wings, fins, roots or paws).

This is where the balance has been preserved by careful and mindful living.

There is no balance in the predator economics of industrial society.

Of the Defenders of the Athabasca River Basin and Tar Sands Destruction

"When you destroy the earth, you destroy yourself. This is the common thread in indigenous thinking all over the world." –Melina Laboucan-Massimo

Melina Laboucan-Massimo is from a village which has been inundated with oil spill, and is one of many young women who have voiced opposition to the destruction of the land and water for the benefit of profiting corporations.

The Cree call the vast, pine-covered region *niyanan askiy*, which means "Our land."

The Lubicon Cree, and the lands they represent, were left out of the treaty agreements made over 200 years ago when white settlers first carved and divided the land. Their rights to their traditional lands are still unrecognized, which means that they don't have the legal right to protect their lands from the tar sands extraction that has devastated their territory over the past four decades.

In 2012 testimony before the U.S Congress, Laboucan-Massimo described the devastation to her family's land, which now is dotted with over 2,600 oil and gas wells:

"What I saw was a landscape forever changed by oil that had consumed a vast stretch of the traditional territory where my family had hunted, trapped, and picked berries and medicines for countless generations."

The Cree and Dene people, who have lived in their traditional territories for millennia, have seen more than 80% of their traditional territory, their lands, rivers and lakes made inaccessible due to tar sands expansion. Although billions of dollars of investments and resources have passed through their lands, what trickles down to the people has been overall ruin and devastation. Corporations like SunCor, Trans-Canada and Enbridge have been emboldened in their unaccountability to the First Nations citizens of Canada by the Harper government, which has sanctioned a full-scale assault on vast reaches of the Athabascan River system.

High levels of toxic pollutants in Alberta's Athabasca River are linked to tar sands mining and a drastically increased cancer incidence in Fort Chipewyan, researchers have found.

And consider also what happens at the other end of the pipeline.

The Keystone XL and the Alberta Tar Sands

"All of our tribes have taken action to oppose the Keystone XL pipeline. Members from the seven tribes of the Lakota Nation, along with tribal members and tribes in Idaho, Oklahoma, Montana, Nebraska and Oregon, are prepared to stop construction of the pipeline."
—Debra White Plume

The most notorious of pipeline proposals from the tar sands is the Keystone XL.

"It poses a threat to our sacred water, and the product is coming from the tar sands and our tribes oppose the tar sands mining," Debra White Plume, an Oglala leader told the press. White Plume's family and many others have opposed the Keystone XL pipeline, along with a myriad of uranium mining projects proposed for the Paha Sapa, the Black Hills.

This past October, the Lakota rode portions of the proposed pipeline route in a series of three spiritual rides to honor the water and counter the oil organized by several grassroots and national organizations, including Honor the Earth, Owe Aku and 350.org.

The routes covered territory between Wanbli on the Pine Ridge reservation to Takini on the Cheyenne River reservation.

This ride was one of three rides (the other two were Minnesota-based pipeline rides on the Alberta Clipper and proposed Sandpiper route for fracked oil).

See Honor the Earth's video: The Triple Crown of Pipeline Rides: https://www.youtube.com/watch?v=1v6_1DLth9U

The Lakota will ride again, and the Anishinaabe will stand with them, and with our Dene and Cree relatives.

Lakota Oyate, and the Treaties to Protect All

The 1868 Fort Laramie Treaty is the treaty that governs relations between the US and the Lakota Nation. *Oceti Sakowin* treaty territory overlaps areas of Montana, North Dakota, South Dakota, and Nebraska. These lands and that treaty are sacred to the Lakota, and—across Indian Country—both tribal leaders and non-Indians are demanding that those treaties be recognized as the law of the land, since they are affirmed in the US constitution.

At one of several summits of the Lakota and their allies, they reaffirmed their opposition to the Black Snake, the Fat Takers Pipeline–also known as the Keystone XL, a project intended to benefit oil companies at the expense of the people and the planet.

Gary Dorr, from the Nez Perce Tribe in Idaho, spoke about opposition to the pipeline and his tribe's legal position on the tar sands. The Nez Perce tribe has already used its treaty rights to block the transport of so-called megaloads of mining equipment headed to Alberta's tar sands through its territory. The tribe launched blockades and won a court battle to stop the shipments from traversing its lands. At the nearby Umatilla reservation, people have also been arrested for blocking these loads.

That battle, about whether the megaloads can go north to feed the tar sands industrial complex, or the oil can come south, is raging in the Northern Plains.

Debra White Plume added, "This whole area of the Great Plains was retained by the Lakota in the Ft. Laramie Treaty with the United States. As far as our people are concerned, that treaty is still the law. We look at this area as ancestral, as sacred, and as ours to defend. The KXL skirts actual, federally-recognized reservation boundaries, but it is in our treaty territory and it is crossing our surface water and the Oglala Aquifer."

What has been revealed recently is that TransCanada needs to build part of its infrastructure, which includes a transmission line and power station, through the lands of the *Kul Wicasa,* Lower *Brule,* South Dakota and the *Sicangu* at Rosebud, South Dakota. Those power lines are part of its infrastructure, and these two bands of the Lakota Nation oppose tar sands, oppose the KXL, and they're refusing to comply with the development of the KXL infrastructure. So that's about the latest thing that's happening right now with our people.

Someone needs to explain to me why wanting clean drinking water makes you an activist, and why proposing to destroy water with chemical warfare doesn't make a corporation a terrorist.

Opposition to the Keystone XL pipeline has many faces, from ranchers in Nebraska and Texas, who reject eminent domain takings of their land for a pipeline right of way, to the Lakota nation, which walked out of State Department meetings in a show of firm opposition to the pipeline. All of them are facing a pipeline owned by TransCanada, a Canadian Corporation.

Fat Takers

In this part of the land it's just been recently been spoken about in different reports from the federal government, and this report talks about parts of Mother Earth that America and other capitalist thinkers refer to as resources.

They look at Mother Earth as a warehouse of resources for them to extract, and this is gas, oil, and uranium. This federal government report was published recently and says 1 trillion dollars' worth of extractable resources are in Red Nations lands. So, in looking at the long run, there will come a time when Fat Taker will be knocking at your door, wanting your gas, oil, or uranium. Without the skills and resources you need to defend yourself, that's going to be hard times. We've seen hard times come like that to many Red Nations.

Our land base is very large here, and from here to our nearest Lakota relative is an hour and a half, and that's the Sicangu on the Rosebud Reservation. It's about 4 hours to the four bands on the Cheyenne River Reservation. So the distances between our homelands are great, requiring hours and hours of travel. To protect ourselves, every community needs this training just because of the distance involved between us.

"As a Lakota woman, I do not see a division between myself and the environment. That's a concept I can't even comprehend, and that's how I feel toward the land and the water. In this area the whooping crane, the fox, and many relatives where they live, their communities of free range, is going to be affected by this pipeline. We speak for them and for the Standing Silent Nation – the plants. We know that for 500 feet on each side of the pipeline no trees are going to be allowed to grow. They're going to cut every tree in their path for all of those thousands of miles. They won't be allowed to grow back to protect the pipeline. That's part of their security, and that's criminal."
-Debra White Plume, Lakota

The Alberta Tar Sands and the Keystone XL pipeline amount to a criminal assault on our Mother Earth. We are witnessing the poisoning of an entire ecosystem and of the life that will depend upon it for generations to come. The wastage of clean water to steam out the bitumen and move it to market has damaged maybe beyond repair the ecosystem of the northern Athabascan River water basin as well as the boreal forest.

So as you look at the destruction already caused by the tar sands bitumen mines and now by this KXL pipeline, we have to see it in terms of how it impacts all of life. So to us it's an attack against Life itself. That's how I see it.

Summing up

We are here. And we are not going anywhere. That's what I will say about Indigenous women. We are also connected to the Earth in a way that the Fat Taker, the *Wasichu*, and the corporate predator economy is not and will never be.

That is because we understand our relationship and honor our Mother. We understand that what corporations would do to the Earth is what corporations and armies have done to our women, and we give no consent.

At the same time, we are visioning and creating the world we wish to live in, and that we will live in. We are in the midst of doing the work to restore local food systems, restore and strengthen health, housing and energy systems in our Indigenous communities.

And, we are working at the level of policy for the creation of laws which protect water, seeds and indeed, the rights of Mother Earth. That is what we will need, not only our strong and entrenched resistance, but the creative power of humans, of unfettered and unencumbered women, children and men. That is how we will survive.

GIIJIMIJ HARPER:
CANADA ESCALATES WAR ON FIRST NATIONS
(with Frank Jr. Molley)

"It's blackmail and it's the most illegal thing ever done...We told the Minister it's like you're putting a gun to our head and telling us to sign."
—CURTIS BARTIBOGUE,
COUNCILOR, MI'KMAQ FIRST NATION

A small Mi'kMaq reserve in Nova Scotia may be the first battle in a new round between the Harper government and First Nations. The Harper government, feeling piqued by international support for the *Idle No More* Movement, has thrown down the gauntlet one more time, this time in terms of a "Starve or Sign" set of consent agreements with First Nations. Burnt Church is one of the first reserves to stand up and face down the Harper agenda.

At stake is title to lands, minerals, and a host of choices on the future direction of Canada, at the center of which First Nations are exercising their rights. While the Canadian government moves ahead with a legislative and policy agenda intent upon de facto termination and confiscation of many rights and assets, United Nations observers are closing in on Canada, and asking for some accountability to international law, and—for instance—the UN Declaration on the Rights of Indigenous Peoples, which Canada in fact signed.

Although the United Nations has asked Canada to admit Special Rapporteur on Indigenous Issues James Anaya into Canada, the Harper

Government had not yet allowed entry. The UN Rapporteur has asked to come to Canada to take formal testimony beginning in 2012, and has yet to receive a formal invitation. It turns out that doesn't mean there aren't problems.

As the story unfolds, the Harper government is facing much more opposition than they had expected. In short, things aren't exactly rolling Harper's way. And frankly, First Nations Band Councils may have their own awakening now as a movement that was sparked in the deep of Winter grows and takes root in Spring.

Burnt Church *(Esgenoopetitj)*

Burnt Church is a Mi'kMaq First Nation, which has some bragging rights. They are the poorest postal code in all of Canada: Poverty ranking number one.

In mid-March they received an annual contribution agreement form from the Canadian Ministry of Aboriginal Affairs, a usual set of transfer agreements which come as a part of peace treaties signed and legal issues negotiated between the Crown, Canada and First Nations. This time the agreement was different: it looked different and was clear in intent, which is to have First Nations sign away their rights in return for money.

What happened next surprised many, perhaps the Harper government most of all. Despite the dire conditions of the community of Burnt Church (i.e., some 80% unemployment, and essentially full dependency on the promised funding allocation), Burnt Church said "No", that it would not sign the agreement with the Harper government.

The Band Council spoke with the community and found deep concerns with signing what is an essential agreement, but which had been presented with some significant changes.

"It's blackmail and it's the most illegal thing ever done," says Councilor Curtis Bartibogue. "We told the Minister it's like you're putting a gun to our head and telling us to sign. He just said if we sign there will be no funding problems." Bartiboque's words were echoed by Chief Alvery Paul and eight of twelve Council members from Burnt Church First Nation.

Burnt Church is not alone. Manitoba Chief Ray Robinson is on a hunger strike and all across Canada there is opposition. In Saskatchewan, Cree similarly decided to say "No." "One of the council members took the whole appendix home and read it all. There were a lot of conditions never seen before. Some signed and some didn't," Christine Dieter, a First Nations woman in southern Saskatchewan, told a reporter. The appendix allegedly requires the bands to support federal omnibus legislation and proposed resource developments as a condition of accessing their funding.

Some bands have already signed the funding agreements out of necessity, noting that they did so under duress, and at least two others allegedly did not. "As of April 1, 2013," one source said, "they will have no funds because they did not sign the agreement." Thus far, two bands, the Peepeekisis Cree Nation and the Onion Lake Cree Nation, had not signed in Saskatchewan. These funding agreements make up the general operating budget for the reserves.

"The government—through its contribution agreements—is trying to get First Nations to sign onto [their policies] or else be cut from their funding," Chief Allan Adam of the Athabasca Chipewyan First Nation in Alberta, told a Hill Times reporter. Adam said his Nation refused to sign its contribution agreement, worth more than $1 million, because it doesn't agree with the federal government's omnibus budget implementation legislation and bills such as C-27, the First Nations Financial Transparency Act. .

The Harper Agenda

Since the eruption of the *Idle No More* Movement in early December, the concern has always been a myriad of new amendments to existing laws affecting aboriginal peoples' rights and their traditional lands, rhetorically entitled "Canada's Economic Action Plan."

Although dubbed a long-term plan to strengthen the Canadian economy, the majority of this will come at the expense of Aboriginal peoples' rights over lands and resources. In order to meet these economic goals, Aboriginal Affairs and Northern Development Canada (AANDC) has employed a tough approach.

The government seems to be trying to undermine the traditional "derogation" provision, a clause that Chelsea Vowel, writer for *Apihtawikosisân* and Metis scholar explains, "...is central to every agreement between First Nations and the Canadian government."

A non-derogation clause in Aboriginal law generally reads like this: *"Nothing in this Agreement shall be construed so as to abrogate or derogate from the protection provided for existing aboriginal or treaty rights of the aboriginal peoples of Canada by the recognition and affirmation of those rights in section 35 of the Constitution Act, 1982."*

The agreements are the staple of financial support for First Nations, providing essential health care, education, housing and social assistance funding. "Some new agreements with the Bands are designed to force a land surrender," says Wilson. "In other cases, basic rights, like the right to potable water—which is not available in a number of First Nations—are being linked to a diminishment of rights." These agreements are being applied without prior notice or consultation. A once-fiduciary obligation under the law is now being utilized in an unfair advantage in getting what Canada wants: compliance and consent.

In one article, *Are you alarmed? You should be,* Vowel explains, these new "my way or the highway" agreements include language that is, "typical legal double-speak. Your rights are protected... unless we need to violate them to carry out this legislation that we did not create with adequate consultation with you and further, we will not consult with you as we carry out these legislative duties."

All this comes at a time when many First Nations are in dire financial straits. "We have been receiving very minimal support for services in our communities," INM co-founder Nina Wilson explains. "[Federal appropriations are] based on prices that date back to the last millennium. For instance, one community gets $4,000 a year for snow removal, and in fact is spending $36,000 a year. That money has to come from somewhere. It has snowballed into a debt, and bands have no way of taking care of it. Bands now are being faced with new financial negotiations, and many bands are in the red, because of the low-ball appropriations".

The Omnibus Budget Implementation Bill is overarching, and has been criticized by opposition MPs as subverting the democratic process. The bill was rushed through Parliament. Among the supplementary bills, nine directly affect aboriginal peoples and their lands. Of concern to First Nations are changes to legislation on water rights, matrimonial law, the Indian Act, education, health, privatization of Indian lands, taxation on reserves and on the matter of financial transparency and accountability.

Cree attorney Sharon Venne is an international human rights lawyer. Her experience in dealing with the feds is extensive, most notably as Chief Negotiator for ten years in Canada's Northwest Territories. She held a presentation in early October in Kahnawake, Mohawk territory. Venne explained the federal plan intends to absolve federal fiduciary obligations, based on a notorious set of policy recommendations dating back to the 1960s called the White Paper.

"What they are doing [now] is 'frustrating' the application of S.91(24) in the British North American Act, 'Indians and Lands Reserved for Indians,' by transferring this stuff to the Provinces and they are doing it through all kinds of mechanisms. It's not only through legislation, but, it's through the [annual] contribution agreements," Venne explained.

This positioning would diminish the nation to nation relationship, in particular legal jurisdiction and responsibilities towards all First Nations. "...because they're going to shove us into the Provinces. And they're going to accomplish what they said in the White Paper. And that's what they're pushing us towards," she said.

What Underdevelopment Looks Like

The reality is that 200 years of Canadian development has left underfunded First Nation economies. Canadian mining and forestry have essentially stripped Aboriginal resources for a paltry sum. Today, many of Canada's 617 first nations live in Third World conditions. Negotiations are too often uneven. As prominent Native scholar Russell Diabo wrote, "...it seems the negotiating First Nations are so compromised by their federal loans, and dependent on the negotiations funding stream that they are unable or unwilling to withdraw from the tables en masse and make real on the demand that the Harper government reform its Comprehensive Claims and Self-Government policies to be consistent with the articles of the UNDRIP."

This is where the UN Special Rapporteur on Indigenous Issues James Anaya comes in, the agreements are non-compliant and non-consistent with the UN Declaration on the Rights of Indigenous Peoples. While the agreement itself is non binding, *what would be the point in even signing it, Indigenous attorneys wonder, if the government has no intent of even attempting to carry out the intent?*

Canada Needs to Manufacture "Consent"

"We've existed in this territory for millennia. We don't have a land claim - it's beyond that, actually. Our rights exist throughout all of our territories," Arlen Dumas, Chief of the Mathias Colomb Cree Nation

Basically, Canada needs to manufacture consent. What's at stake is hundreds of billions of dollars worth of minerals, oil, gas, access for pipeline companies and water. Canada's domination of a world minerals market is at risk, because First Nations are saying "no" and are making demands. And both Canada's human rights record, and frankly a well-managed public relations campaign which suggests that First Nations are essentially impoverished beggars, is being challenged by a grassroots movement.

Canada is the world's top potash producer and the second largest producer of uranium, not to mention a host of other precious metals and the world leader in tar sands of the Athabascan River delta, all Aboriginal territory. That's already a $120 billion-a-year national industry. Status depends on stability, and for the first time in six years, Canada failed to top the mining industry's list of the best mining jurisdictions in the world.

Surveyed companies said they were concerned about land claims. "I would say one of the big things that is weighing on mining investment in Canada right now is First Nations issues," said Ewan Downie, chief executive of Premier Gold Mines, which owns numerous projects in northern Ontario.

Prior and Informed Consent

There is a legal term called "Prior and Informed Consent" which makes agreements possible under the law (as opposed to under the gun), and now—with an increasingly educated and empowered Indigenous community, evidenced by the *Idle No More* Movement—that consent is not looking so easy to secure.

This is particularly true as communities themselves challenge what has become, essentially, entrenched power, often at a level of Indian Act leadership and chiefs. As Professor Pamela Palmater of Toronto's Ryerson University explains," This movement was about educating First Nations to say 'no', that's not what happens when you're an owner of the resources. An owner of the resources gets resource sharing," The owner of the resource can also say no.

In fact, the ability to say no has already slowed or derailed at least a half dozen energy and mining projects in British Columbia. "It's the project killer, the investment killer," Clayton Thomas-Muller, with the Indigenous Tar Sands campaign, explains.

Mathias Colomb Cree Nation cut off access for HudBay Minerals, Inc. to its Lalor project in early March. Protesters cut off access to the gold-copper-zinc mine, demanding talks with the company on an ownership stake in the $773.84 million project, which had started limited production.

To the north, mining companies have flooded into the James Bay lowlands and remote Northern Ontario communities, an area being dubbed the Ring of Fire. There is gold and the diamonds of Attawapiskat and Kashachewan, the home of Chief Theresa Spence, and the DeBeers Diamond Mine.

The mining holds the promise of thousands of jobs over the next decade, if not longer, as long as the proposals can pass environmental muster and garner the support of the region's first nations.

Chief Eli Moonias of Marten Falls First Nation is in the center of the Ring of Fire. Moonias knows well the problems with water- his community has had a water crisis for five years, with no potable water. Boiling is required, or bottled water is imported into the community. The community is concerned about new mining projects, and also wants a water treatment plant and a road into the community, none of which have been forthcoming from the Harper government, nor the mining companies.

Moonias looks at development in the oil sands and hears about the inedible fish and the poisoned Athabasca River. He vows never to let anything like that happen to the Albany and Ogoki rivers that flow through the muskeg and meet at Marten Falls.

"It's not only fish, it's the animal kingdom. It's not only us, it's everybody. It's the planet. You can't jump [with] a careless plunge into development. You have to know what you're doing to your future."—Chief Eli Moonias, Marten Falls First Nation

More to come, and the 617 First Nation communities have provided a lions share of those resources from oil and gas in Alberta to uranium in Saskatchewan, mega dam projects in Quebec , Labrador, and Manitoba, and old and new mines in Ontario. Not to mention the trees. There used to be a lot more in Canada, but there are more stumps now and fewer trees, and the money has not gone to Native communities.

That's the challenge. Multinational mining corporations are eying vast reserves and deposits throughout northern Ontario as world gold and minerals markets grow, and new hydro-fracking proposals are inundating everywhere there is natural gas.

It is an era of Extreme Extraction of Indian lands and Native scholars are pointing out an even more extreme detraction from treaty obligations with Canada and First Nation peoples. Native peoples are also pointing out that treaty rights echo sacred agreements between Indigenous peoples and Creation.

"The protection of water is a sacred obligation to indigenous people. Without clean water, life will cease to exist. Our obligation to protect water is an overall respect for life itself."—Chief Isadore Day, Serpent River First Nation.

Back east there is a clear movement for accountability and caution. Burnt Church is right in the thick of it. Canadian interests in hydrofracking are knocking on the door of the community and more extreme suggestions are on the way.

As if it couldn't get any more heated, New Brunswick's Premiere David Alward took a trip this January out to Alberta, where he enjoyed Premiere Alison Redford's company, dined with executives of oil, gas and pipeline companies and returned with an idea—a big one— a new pipeline to the east.

Alward announced his plan without discussing it with the Chiefs and political leadership of the Maliseet and Mi'kMaq peoples, despite the fact that the pipeline would go directly through their unceded territory. The Honorable Premier is also the Minister responsible for Aboriginal affairs in the Province, an area that has been host to seven of the ten poorest postal codes in the country, all of which are Mi'kMaq and Maliseet communities.

UN Special Rapporteur for Indigenous Peoples, James Anaya has been requesting to formally enter Canada since early 2012. Anaya is completing a report for the United Nations on extractive industries and Indigenous peoples, and Canada is one of the largest flashpoints in the world. Among the many concerns, Grassroots First Nations are gearing up for a series of challenges regarding the proposed west-to-east oil pipeline that would bring Alberta oil to Quebec and New Brunswick via an underused natural gas pipeline.

In the meantime, the INM movement that began in the deepest of winter last year has emerged this spring with new force, an Indigenous Spring, so to speak, and is challenging the power of Harper and some entrenched leadership.

It is the power of informed Indigenous peoples with access, for the first time, to a way to break their isolation: electronic media and smart phones. The Movement seems to be taking strong root from eastern Canada's Burnt Church to northern Saskatchewan. What seems clear is that Native people have learned that consent cannot be manufactured by federal threats, and the Harper government may have met its match in a grassroots movement sweeping the country.

WHEN THE NATIVES ARE RESTLESS

Late October 2015's crushing defeat of Canadian Prime Minister Steven Harper had many causes, but in the midst was a resounding Indigenous turn out. The October 29 election was historic: 10 Indigenous MPs were elected, and 54 ran for office. Overall, the Canadian vote was the highest in history, reminiscent of the Obama election in 2008. In both instances, people who had traditionally been disenfranchised voted in large numbers. In the 2008 US election, people stood in line for hours to vote. In Canada, ballots had to be flown in and delivered to communities.

The Canadian election changed the demographics of power, and it may dampen some of the oil and mining industry's seemingly all-access pass to power, at least, that is what it looks like.

Not unlike the emergence of the *Idle No More* Movement, the Native Canadian *Rock the Vote* Movement, emerged from the 671 reserves and urban communities and has made a monumental shift in Canadian power. The election strategy had some brilliance: *get people to vote, and give them candidates they are interested in.* In a carefully orchestrated plan, a record-breaking 54 indigenous candidates ran for office. Each candidate ran in one of 51 swing ridings identified by the national Assembly of First Nations or AFN. The AFN identified locales where the aboriginal vote could make a difference between a majority and minority government. "We have to say our people got engaged, got involved, and they were tired of what they were seeing in the last six years especially", Sheila North Wilson, Chief of the Assembly of First Nations told reporters. At least five First Nations reportedly needed extra ballots brought in to accommodate the numbers.

"In other southern communities, we are told, in fact, that ballots ran out," Wilson told reporters. Voting was up by as much as 20 per cent in some reports. Among the major Conservative upsets was Aboriginal Affairs Minister Bernard Valcourt, who was ousted by Liberal candidate Rene Arsenault and joined newly elected Liberal Prime Minister Justin Trudeau, son of the long time Prime Minister Pierre Trudeau.

Manitoba's Grand Chiefs believe the huge response was attributed solely to a desire to oust Stephen Harper from office. The fact is, Harper government actions spurred the *Idle No More* Movement, and now the vote. Three years ago, *Idle No More* representative Clayton Thomas Muller referred to "the extremist right wing government of Steven Harper", noting the government was intent on selling the natural wealth of the Canadian (Aboriginal) north to the highest bidders in a multinational market. The passing of the omnibus budget Bill C-45 gutted thirty years of environmental legislation and violated tribal rights. The bill was combined with significant fiscal cuts to First Nations. Put it this way: Before the passage of Bill C-45, 2.6 million rivers, lakes, and a good portion of Canada's three ocean shorelines were protected under the Navigable Waters Act. After, eighty-seven are protected. First Nations suffered significantly.

Harper had also ignored repeated requests to investigate the 1200 Indigenous women murdered or missing, and why Native women comprise two percent of the population, yet account for one in four murder victims.

Other significant Native issues included the National Truth and Reconciliation Commission which, after six years, had taken testimony from over 7000 survivors of a brutal era of residential schools. While Harper had issued an apology to residential school survivors, saying "We are sorry," in five separate languages, for the 150,000 Native children who suffered in the schools, Harpers government declined to release records of investigations into residential school abuses and seemed to have no intention to adopt any of the 94 recommendations made by the Commission. The administration also cut funding to Aboriginal Health Research, and neglected food programs to the far north, which served exclusively Native communities.

Clayton Thomas Muller is pleased with the change but cautious, as Premier Justin Trudeau has not made public any major moves on issues like climate change. Trudeau, however has promised significant upswings in Aboriginal appropriations and infrastructure needs, as well as proposing to legalize marijuana. "Massive voter turnout, by Canadians and First Nations people changed the face of Canadian politics this year. People are tired of seeing politicians in bed with industry, and the disregard for human rights. We know the people must continue to press for actions, but the message is clear to politicians and industry." Noting the significant concessions made in federal policies to the mining and oil industry, Muller continues, "Cleaning up after these damaging legacies will take time and effort. But the fact that politicians like Harper are now being shown the door is cause for hope that people-powered efforts …are beginning to work."

Fallout in Corporate Land

The large oil pipeline companies are Canadian: TransCanada, Kinder-Morgan and Enbridge. Some 75% of the world's mining companies are also Canadian-based, including highly controversial Polymet, whose corporate headquarters are in Toronto. All have benefited significantly from the Harper administration. It is not clear if there will be implications, but there are perhaps some rumbles.

Enbridge's proposed Northern Gateway Pipeline, intended to move tar sands oil from Alberta to the West Coast has new problems, besides opposition from First Nations and many local citizens. This past May, with the election of Rachel Notley as Premiere of Alberta, Calgary-based Enbridge found it did not have the strongest support. "Gateway is not the right decision. I think that there's just too much environmental sensitivity there and I think there's a genuine concern by the Indigenous communities," Notley said in an April interview with the Calgary Herald. "It's not going to go ahead. I think most people know that."

It is not clear how this may impact Enbridge's financial standing, especially when combined with what is now at least a two-year delay in projected Sandpiper and other lines in Minnesota. Just after the Canadian election, TransCanada, the company seeking to build the Keystone XL oil pipeline, asked the Obama administration to suspend review of the project, possibly giving Obama a pass, but also signifying what may be some cooling of benefits to Canadian corporations. In a statement, TransCanada said it would be "appropriate" for Secretary of State Kerry to suspend the current review of the Keystone proposal as Nebraska's Public Service Commission deliberates over the pipeline's route. Anti-Keystone groups saw this as a favorable sign, but no one seems to trust TransCanada. Less than a week later, President Obama denied the essential presidential permit for the Keystone pipeline.

Back in the North Country

2016 may be the year to Rock the Native Vote. A number of northern politicians have come out squarely and often against tribal interests. Representative Steve Greene, for instance, represents White Earth reservation. Greene formally opposed the tribe's attempts to purchase land around the tribal cultural treasure Rice Lake. Green blocked approval of the tribal land purchase with Minnesota Legacy Funds. More recently, Attorney General Lori Swanson opposed tribes and environmentalists in appealing the (unanimous) Minnesota Appeals Court ruling which ordered a full Environmental Impact Statement on the proposed Enbridge Sandpiper line. Ironically, just after the Canadian election results came in, Enbridge itself called for an environmental impact statement on the pipeline proposals. There are more.

The 2016 election will be a huge battleground nationally, with the ultra conservative David and Charles Koch planning , according to press reports, to put $900 million into the elections. In Minnesota, Wisconsin, Montana, South Dakota, North Dakota (where Senator Heidi Heidkamp narrowly won, largely on a Native vote), and elsewhere, it may be time to bring out the Natives. After all, as both the Canadian and Obama election should have taught us, massive amounts of corporate money can only be overcome by massive numbers of people.

Add to that, a carefully orchestrated strategy of running Natives for office, and some things may really change. A Canadian reporter commented on the lessons from Canada, "this is ...an enormous blunder and moral failure for Harper, who ... massively underestimated the cultural and political resurgence of Indigenous Canadians. He's been treating them like victims, all the while forgetting they are, in fact, survivors."

South of the 49th, with populations and voting numbers growing, Native people are also survivors. We will see how the vote is rocked.

TOP: *Winona LaDuke on Luna, Pipeline Ride. (Photo ©Keri Pickett)*
ABOVE LEFT: *Frank Wahn, Lakota musician. (Photo ©Keri Pickett)*
RIGHT: *Winona with Tommy James' (Tlingit) warclub. (Photo ©Keri Pickett)*

Killing the Black Snake, ledger art by Michael Horse

Killing the Pipelines,
illustration by Gord Hall

Black Snake and the Pipeline Chronicles:

**NORTHERN GATEWAY, KEYSTONE
AND THE ENBRIDGE GREAT LAKES LINES**

THE SPIRIT BEAR AND THE PIPELINE

"You know what it's like sitting down to negotiate with the Canadian government? It's like sitting down to talk with a cannibal. You can make as much small talk as you want, but in the end, you both know what he is thinking."
— First Nations chief

I am writing this story because of a bear—a white bear. The Spirit Bears are white bears in a clan of black bears; one out of every ten of these bears is born pure white. Called *Moksgm'ol* by the *Tsimshian* people, there are only 400 Spirit Bears in the Great Bear Rainforest in northern British Columbia. Their territory surrounds the town of Kitimat, the proposed end of yet another tar sands pipeline, which means large equipment, pipes, possible spills, and a lot of infrastructure may soon be invading the home of these bears.

There are few routes for tar sands oil to travel from the point of extraction in central Canada to the ports that are gateways to global markets. One is the controversial Keystone pipeline, heading south to the Gulf of Mexico. Another is the proposed Northern Gateway pipeline, which would travel west from Alberta through British Columbia to Pacific Ocean ports—straight through sensitive watersheds, temperate rainforests, and millennia-old communities of First Nations peoples.

In January 2012, just two weeks after President Barack Obama announced that the United States would not move ahead with the proposed Keystone XL pipeline from the Canadian tar sands down to the Gulf Coast, Enbridge Inc. was scrambling to show that its proposed Northern Gateway pipeline was a sure thing—and maybe, just maybe, Enbridge was also hoping to scare U.S. policy makers back to the table for another round of negotiations on the Keystone project.

With some very quick maneuvering after Obama's announcement, the Canadian government set up a National Energy Board (NEB) panel that started hearings on the highly contentious terrain of the proposed Northern Gateway pipeline. It would run from Alberta to British Columbia, crossing 785 rivers and streams, tunneling through the Coast Range twice, and spanning the headwaters of three of the continent's most important rivers—the Mackenzie, Fraser, and Skeena.

The pipe would also punch through the heart of the Spirit Bears' home. Upon reaching the coastal town of Kitimat, the oil would be pumped into holding tanks and then into colossal oil tankers called Very Large Crude Carriers (VLCCs, if you are an insider), which would then chug over the wreckage of a large government-owned passenger ferry—Queen of the North—that is still leaking oil into the ocean, as it has been for six years. After snaking through 120 miles of fjords, making a few tight turns offshore of the largest remaining temperate rainforest on the planet, the VLCCs would arrive at an open ocean that has record-setting tidal fluctuations. Beyond that, it's a clear shot to China. None of that was mentioned at the National Energy Board's Enbridge hearings held thus far.

Negotiating with Cannibals

In a hotel conference room in Edmonton, Alberta, filled with families from Cree communities in northern Alberta, Enbridge officials listened to testimony from members of the communities that would be touched by the Northern Gateway pipeline. Cree villagers talked about their land being overrun with roads and power lines, poisoned by oil and its by-products—and about their rivers and fish already exhibiting signs of stress, and long stretches of days when the fish are inedible and full of tumors.

Panel officials politely nodded while Enbridge attorneys and public relations flacks scribbled notes. I sat next to the Enbridge representatives, and as I watched them I recalled what a First Nations chief from British Columbia once told me: "You know what it's like sitting down to negotiate with the Canadian government? It's like sitting down to talk with a cannibal. You can make as much small talk as you want, but in the end, you both know what he is thinking."

The hearings were interesting in a number of ways. Enbridge is pushing for quick regulatory approval of the Northern Gateway pipeline without providing cost and market analysis, adequate assessment of alter- natives, or environmental impact studies. Enbridge is pushing for hearings with the support of the NEB, without any discussion of either the broader ramifications of the pipeline, such as the anticipated massive increase in production at the tar sands, or the transport of that oil through innumerable delicate ecosystems. Another intriguing fact is that this would be a pipeline to nowhere, since there are no ready markets for the oil. Despite that, Canadian Prime Minister Steven Harper has said the pipeline is "of national interest."

Peter Okimaw walked up to the microphone. He is a middle-aged man from the village of Driftpile, a Cree reserve around 250 miles north of Edmonton. "When I was a kid, I used to drink from those creeks and rivers," he said. "Now I have to go to Walmart and buy water when I go into the bush by those creeks. When I turned 18, I started to work for the oil industry at Fort McMurray [Alberta]. I cleaned up oil spills. If I tell my son something, it is: Do not work on those oil spills. The last one I worked on was at Slave Lake. We got hired on power-saw operations for ten to twelve hours a day. My brother and I, we were working in power-saw pants. We did not have proper equipment. We were walking in the oil in the creek for ten to twelve hours a day without proper equipment."

During this portion of the testimony, the Enbridge representatives made few notes and wrote very slowly.

Okimaw continued: "I had seen the beaver there going crazy. I said to my brother that we wouldn't go crazy. We would go to our hotel room, and our eyes and our skin would be burning. Now I am wondering if that is going to do something to me in the future. It is all changed now. Like our river, no one swims there now because it is contaminated. Sure we'd like to take our children to swim, but where? We have to go to Edmonton to swim in a pool. It's our traditional land and we should keep it that way. We should save the rest. Once you've taken the heart of Mother Nature, then where do we stand? The world will be looking at us in Alberta. They will say, 'Boy, it was good while it lasted.'"

The Invisible Hand of the Invisible Market

Here are a few major problems with the Northern Gateway pipeline project. To begin with it has no customers. It is a pipeline for the sake of building a pipeline. There is a glut in export pipeline capacity in western Canada. Current oil production in western Canada leaves 41 percent of existing export pipelines empty, according to a report by the Natural Resources Defense Council, which says, "Based on industry production estimates, no additional export pipelines are needed out of the tar sands for at least another ten years."

The panicked response in the American press and from some U.S. politicians is that this Canadian oil will be sold to China, but the 525,000 barrels out of the Northern Gateway pipeline would amount to just 6 percent of what China used in 2010, and there is the real possibility that China may be content to buy cheaper oil from Iran. The U.S. Energy Information Administration says, "Iran's best customer is China, which took about 22 percent of Tehran's oil exports during the first half of [2011]" and is "one of the few nations on friendly terms with the Islamic republic. China's demand will continue to grow, but there are a number of sources for this oil."

Is it truly in Canada's "national interest" to spend around $6 billion on a pipeline without committed buyers for that oil? Or is it a *Field of Dreams* strategy: If you build it, they will come?

Safety Last

Those VLCCs, which can hold 2.2 million barrels of oil and are as large as the Empire State Building, would be deployed to move oil from the pipeline through the port of Kitimat. There could be up to 200 shipments each year, and on every journey the VLCC's captain would have to navigate challenging straits which have never been traversed by anything that large.

Then there is the pipeline problem. Enbridge's track record for spills is not stellar. According to Enbridge's own data, between 1999 and 2010 there were some 804 reported spills, which released 161,475 barrels of hydrocarbons into wetlands, farms, and waterways— approximately half the oil spilled in the Exxon Valdez disaster.

In July 2010, an Enbridge pipeline ruptured near Kalamazoo, Michigan, spilling more than 840,000 gallons of tar sands oil. Enbridge's operators were unaware of the spill at first and did not shut the pipeline down for a full 17 hours.

A year after the spill approximately 200 acres of river sediment were still contaminated and a nearly 40-mile stretch of the Kalamazoo River remained closed to the public. Kalamazoo has infrastructure and a relatively large population, so the response there was good by industry standards. It is unlikely that the spill response would be nearly so prompt in the mountain passes or rainforest traversed by the Northern Gateway pipeline.

Nigeria of the North

Prime Minister Harper is from Alberta, where he worked for an oil company. A majority of Alberta's politicians come from oil families, oil money, or families who worked in the oil business. According to Eriel Deranger, a Dene mother and activist from Fort McMurray in the heart of the tar sands, Alberta is so serious about being a petrol state that the Canadian government has actively sought to limit renewable-energy businesses in the region by changing legislation, making special permits, and limiting access to subsidies.

Here's another way of looking at the Northern Gateway pipeline proposal: Think of Alberta as the *Nigeria of the North*. (Well, there are a lot more white people in Alberta, and Canada's military hasn't killed anybody to protect the oil business.) Both economies have been increasingly dominated by oil. In 2009 Nigeria exported around 2.1 million barrels of oil per day; Canada exported 1.9 million barrels per day.

Environmental regulation of the oil industry in both Nigeria and Alberta is lax, and the industry has been actively opposed by Native people—the *Ogoni*, in particular, in Nigeria and the Cree in Alberta. In the early 1990s, battles between the Ogoni and the oil companies escalated, with the Indigenous people demanding some $10 billion in damages, compensation, and denied royalties. They also called for an "immediate stoppage of environmental degradation." Those demands were answered with military action that led to the deaths of an estimated 2,000 people, including noted Ogoni poet and political leader Kenule "Ken" Saro Wira.

In Alberta, death and oil have a more subtle relationship. Alberta has the highest suicide rate of any province in Canada—127 percent higher than the rest of Canada, with a 400 percent increase in the past fifteen years. All of this is worsened, arguably, by the Tar Sands. Consider that an estimated 40 percent of the drivers of equipment are on some sort of illegal drug, which of course means these drugs are now increasingly available in the northern Native communities. According to investigative journalists, approximately $7 million worth of cocaine now travels up Highway 63 every week on transport trucks to the north, which is where the aboriginal people live.

Not surprisingly, since it is a petrol state, Alberta has the largest disparity of wealth of any province in Canada, and the gap there between the average income of a non- Native resident and that of a Native resident is equally appalling—the average Alberta family makes six times the income of an on-reserve Native family. This is somewhat similar to the income disparities in Nigeria. Nigeria is Africa's top oil producer, but the number of Nigerians in dire poverty rose to 61.2 percent in 2010 from 51.6 percent in 2004, the Nigerian National Bureau of Statistics said in a recent report. "It remains a paradox ... that despite the fact that the Nigerian economy is growing, the proportion of Nigerians living in poverty is increasing every year," said Yemi Kale, the head of the Nigerian statistics bureau.

"Hard of Hearing" Hearing

Back at that hearing held at the hotel in Edmonton: Chief Brenda Sam from Driftpile Cree First Nation steps up to the microphone. She reminds the panel of the history of the province, the treaties, and the duality of responsibility. She also reminds her audience of the long history of problematic relations with settlers, including pervasive sexual abuse in residential schools. "The treaty said we should not molest the newcomers. We kept our end of the bargain, but who molested whom? Think about the residential schools? Who molested whom? Our concerns are about impact. We may have not had the right to live as equals in this unjust society, but we have the right to an opinion."

Next, Gene Chalifoux comes to the podium. She is married to a community member, but, from what I can tell, she came from New Brunswick a very long time ago. She says she has moved in with the Natives, and found it a quite delightful place to live. Her Cree name is *Kakiwaksquo*, "Dry Meat Woman." She explains that she is proud of learning how to live in the North. She boasts about her trap line of squirrels. "It was just a real exhilaration to be a mean old woman and see all these little squirrels hanging by their neck because I did it myself." And then she laughs. We all laugh.

But she also made the crucial point that needs to be pondered throughout Canada: "The people here in front of you signed Treaty with the government of Canada about 113 years ago.... Those people that signed Treaty had a belief that they would be treated fairly and that this land would be theirs.... They got the short end of the stick, the same as my ancestors, the Montauks did... If you give these people another eight generations, at the rate things are going, they won't exist either.... If you don't deal with them fairly, they won't exist seven generations from now."

And there it is, a fundamental question for Canada, for all of us: If a people disappear in seven generations does that mean responsibility disappears too?

There is a proposal for a massive pipeline for no apparent reason, and a people may disappear because of it. Make that peoples—the Driftpile Cree First Nation is just one of more than 130 First Nations in western Canada who have publicly stated their opposition to the pipeline and the tankers. At least 70 of them have declared bans on the transport of tar sands crude through their traditional territories. It will be interesting to see if corporations and governments respect these bans.

The Keystone XL pipeline was pitched as a way to provide Americans with oil and much-needed jobs. The Northern Gateway pipeline is being pitched on the promise of sales to foreign markets. Here in Edmonton and in the far North, Alberta's Petrol State is hoping that no one will notice the threat to the aboriginal people, the water, and the Spirit Bear.

Tar Sands, Pipelines, and the Threat to First Nations by Winona LaDuke with Martin Curry was published originally in Indian Country Today; ©2012 by Winona LaDuke, used by permission of the author.

A PIPELINE RUNS THROUGH IT

"This is land that has been in my family for decades. It is prime Red River Valley agriculture land. It was handed down to me by my mother and father when they passed away, and I'm intending to hand it down to my children when I pass away... My wife and I have...told our children that we will pass this on. Of course, if 225,000 barrels of oil bursts through this thing, that certainly is the end of this family legacy."
—JAMES BOTSFORD, FAMILY FARMER, NORTH DAKOTA
LANDOWNER IN ENBRIDGE SANDPIPER RIGHT OF WAY

While the national press has kept a focus on the controversy over the Keystone XL pipeline, something is going on in northern Minnesota. This has to do with the Enbridge Corporation, a Canadian company that is determined to move oil from places where there is no infrastructure, and that is showing its determination in some ways which Northerners may not like. That oil is destined for Lake Superior. Lots of it.

Enbridge's Sandpiper will carry far more than a single Keystone XL pipeline, like four times as much oil and something called "dilbit," diluted bitumen that is far more corrosive than crude oil.

Here's a bit on the math and the pipelines: Between Gretna, Manitoba and Clearbrook, Minnesota, there are eight Enbridge pipelines already in a 160-mile swath. Then we get down to a few less lines, but those are all being upscaled and expanded. Enbridge (also known as the North Dakota Pipeline Company and several other dba aliases) is now proposing three pipeline expansions: Line 3, Line 67, Line 13 aka the Southern Lights (that goes the other way, carrying dilutents to the tar sands, but still can leak) , and a new line called the Sandpiper.

This expansion would amount to an increase of over one million barrels or 42 million gallons of oil per day.

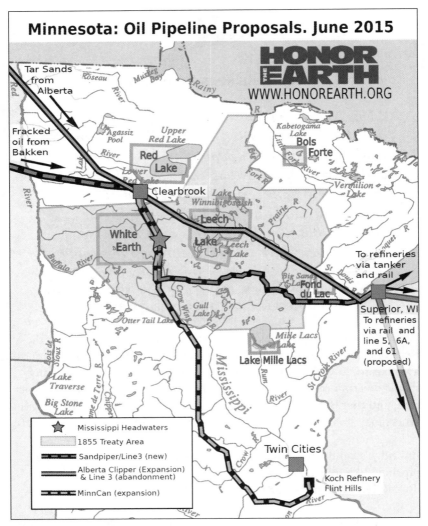

Minnesota: Oil Pipeline Proposals. June 2015

HONOR THE EARTH
WWW.HONOREARTH.ORG

Tar Sands from Alberta

Fracked oil from Bakken

Clearbrook

White Earth

Leech Lake

Bois Forte

To refineries via tanker and rail

Fond du Lac

Superior, WI
To refineries via rail and line 5, 6A, and 61 (proposed)

Lake Mille Lacs

Twin Cities

Koch Refinery Flint Hills

⭐ Mississippi Headwaters
◻ 1855 Treaty Area
▦ Sandpiper/Line3 (new)
═ Alberta Clipper (Expansion) & Line 3 (abandonment)
▦ MinnCan (expansion)

"Northern Minnesota is becoming the super highway for oil," Attorney Paul Blackburn tells me. Paul has provided policy analysis and strategic advice on a variety of pipeline matters and authored reports on pipeline safety and oil spill response.

If all the lines go through, the sum total of oil traveling over northern Minnesota's lakes and waters could be about four million barrels per day. This is about 200 times more than the amount of oil spilled in the Kalamazoo Enbridge spill in 2010. Not surprisingly, there are a number of increasingly concerned Northerners.

Do some math, and help me out: All of this oil—say four million barrels a day—will end up in Superior, Wisconsin, where we find the Calumet refinery with a capacity for 46,000 barrels per day is located.

That means more oil moving from Superior into an expanded-yet-aging infrastructure in the Great Lakes (a whole bunch of 50-year-old pipelines that need updating and that apparently will need to be doubled in size), and then there are the tankers.

Gichi Gummi, or—as we call it, Lake Superior—is unique in depth and purity and also doesn't change the water much, so one spill and well, that's not a good thing, risking one fifth of the world's fresh water, where the bones of more than a thousand ships already lie on the bottom.

Let's not dwell on that, but do note that there are 17 refinery expansions proposed for the Great Lakes region, and that is a lot of oil. That is a lot of oil proposed to be moved by a company which has had so very many safety violations, and that holds the record for the worst land (plus 30 miles of river) oil spill in US history.

The Road to (and from) Kalamazoo

That would be the Kalamazoo Spill, where in 2010 one of Enbridge's 30-inch pipelines ruptured, pouring almost a million gallons of oil into the river before their controllers could respond, creating a catastrophe requiring a billion-dollar cleanup.

Enbridge pumped more than 20,000 barrels of oil into the Kalamazoo that day despite the company's claims that their so-called "advanced" safety systems were top-notch and infallible. The spill went on for 17 hours, because the company thought there was a misreading of the indicators. The pipeline began leaking on July 25, but it was not until July 26 that a local gas company employee discovered the leak and reported it to Enbridge.

The federal Pipeline and Hazardous Safety Materials Administration's (PHMSA) investigation found Enbridge had committed "multiple violations of its hazardous liquid pipeline safety regulations related to integrity management, failure to follow operations and maintenance procedures, and reporting and operator qualification requirements."

Now, that "integrity management" problem Enbridge has, that's a big problem all by itself.

Two years later, on July 2, 2012, PHMSA proposed to smack Enbridge with the largest civil penalty in agency history, $ 3.7 million, and a list of 24 actions to be taken; and, on July 10, 2012, the National Transportation Safety Board (NTSB) reported its own findings, stating: "The NTSB's recommendations support the findings of PHMSA's own investigation, which found multiple violations of federal pipeline safety regulations *and lack of a safety culture at the company,* which culminated with a breakdown in communications."

The NTSB further concluded that Enbridge's response to past management-integrity-related accidents "focused only on the proximate cause, without a systematic examination of company actions, policies and procedures."

Among the many pages of problems the PHMSA investigation found under the category of "Control Room Management", were systemic failures in understanding roles and responsibilities among Enbridge's own employees, *who may not be qualified to operate the systems they are operating,* the report stated.

PHMSA rules require that "Each operator must define the roles and responsibilities of a controller during normal, abnormal, and emergency operating conditions", in order to "provide for a controller's prompt and appropriate response to operating conditions...."

The investigation found, however, that Enbridge controllers could at any time be monitoring or controlling pipeline systems for which they are not qualified or not been fully trained, and that "The difference in abnormal operating condition detection and emergency actions required between pipeline systems is not clearly identified in the (Enbridge's) plan."

As reported in the Federal Register on May 6, 2014, PHMSA found that "Due to the rapid growth of Enbridge's pipeline system, Enbridge hired additional control center staff without objectively assessing whether that growth in personnel would affect safe operations.... The leak detection process was prone to misinterpretation, and control center analysts and operators were not adequately trained in how to recognize or address leaks, especially during startup and shutdown... the control center ignored warnings from field and operations personnel that there was a possible leak.... Control room personnel did not follow the established procedure to shut the pipeline down if column separation couldn't be resolved within 10 minutes.... Enbridge failed to train the control center staff in team performance, which resulted in poor communication and lack of leadership."

So, that is what was happening *inside* the Enron bubble, but how did Enbridge protect the interests of the public? PHSMA reported that "Enbridge's PAP (Public Awareness Plan) failed to effectively inform the affected public, including citizens and emergency response agencies about the location of the pipeline, how to identify a pipeline release and how to report suspected product releases."

PHMSA found that "The Enbridge plan did not adequately provide for response to an emergency regarding 911 notifications when a leak is detected or notification of a leak received." That "lack of a safety culture at the company" was demonstrated again less than two weeks later, on July 27, 2012, when Enbridge's 24-inch Pipeline 14 ruptured in Adams County, Washington.

PHMSA described the incident as "hazardous to life, property and the environment."

Now, just to give the US system of regulation some credit, in a rare move, PHMSA the Pipeline and Hazardous Safety Materials Administration (PHMSA) issued a system-wide corrective-action order against Enbridge a year ago, because of the number of safety violations the company had accrued.

Part of the lack of regulatory oversight problem may be that PHMSA has only about 120 inspectors, and 2.5 million miles of pipelines to inspect.

What we know for sure is that there is a lot of oil and dilbit that Big Oil wants to move, as it is land-locked, and on the cusp of becoming what is called "stranded assets" as the US and other nations move away from dependence on fossil fuels.

The pipeline-building frenzy has been promoted as necessary "for America's energy security", but that may be a bit questionable. The US is now one of the largest producers of oil, and we're already exporting six times as much finished petroleum products (2.1 million barrels per day) as the alleged "need" for the Sandpiper, for example, is supposed to fill (350,000 bpd).

When the Polar Bear and the Seals Escaped

I remember when the polar bear and seals escaped from the Duluth Zoo. Or, at least this is the picture in my mind. It was a good one, and a strange one, and it had a lot to do with climate change and infrastructure, two basics concerns in our society. As it turns out, I am not opposed to pipelines. In fact, I like infrastructure. It would be nice to be able to rely on it.

According to the American Society of Civil Engineers' latest Infrastructure Report Card, the US has earned a "D" in infrastructure generally, a "D" on drinking and wastewater infrastructure, and a "D+" on energy infrastructure.

Duluth itself had a few infrastructure problems, we found out, when the Big Deluge hit the city, and the polar bear and seals escaped from the zoo. Climate change shows our weaknesses, and there is more to come.

The reality is that infrastructure failure is causing natural gas explosions and water main ruptures around the country. Infrastructure failure is happening when the I-35 Bridge collapses in Minneapolis and an I-5 bridge falls into the Skagit River in Washington, and infrastructure failure is when ten thousand gallons of oil spills in downtown Los Angeles, 7,000 barrels spill in Mayflower Arkansas, or a train track crumbles under the weight of its load.

We have an infrastructure problem generally in the country. Some folks would say we should fix old pipelines before we make new ones. One example of that might be Enbridge Line 3, which is—according to the *Bemidji Pioneer*—46 years old, and has been "undergoing almost constant maintenance", or that 50 year old Enbridge line running under the Great Lakes. I'd take a look-see at that one.

There is something called the PIG, or the Pipeline Inspection Gauge, by the way, which Enbridge does use to check the lines... but then they have to repair them. It turns out that the company knew about weaknesses in the Kalamazoo area, but failed to take corrective action, according to the National Transportation Safety Board.

There was a study done on the Keystone XL route which asked some of these questions and found some interesting answers. The study found that spending money on unmet water and gas infrastructure needs in the five relevant states along the KXL pipeline route will create more than 300,000 total jobs across all sectors, or five times more jobs than the KXL, with ninety five times more long term jobs.

Similar statistics might apply in Minnesota, which has a reported $6 billion in unmet infrastructure needs, about the equivalent of projected Enbridge investments into oil pipelines. "It's sort of a question of which infrastructure and jobs we want," Michael Dahl, an Anishinaabe who works on the pipeline issues explains, "If we want infrastructure for Enbridge, or infrastructure for our towns, cities and homes."

THE ENBRIDGE WAY:
LACK OF A SAFETY CULTURE AND EMINENT DOMAIN

"I got a call from the attorneys at Enbridge recently, advising me that they are about to file a condemnation suit against us. This was followed by a Fed Ex package with a final offer.... The Enbridge attorneys said they could file their suit within a week or two. I reiterated that I was not going to give them anything, they would have to take it."
— JAMES BOTSFORD, FAMILY FARMER, NORTH DAKOTA

James and Krista Botsford are standing up to Enbridge on the Sand-piper line—literally standing on the line—as Enbridge is claiming that they have a right to drive their pipeline through the Botsford's family farm.

They are looking at a huge legal battle, and Enbridge has told them directly that "our rights trump your rights" after the company filed a restraining order against Botsford to prevent him from enjoying his own land. The Sandpiper, as a new line, is very contentious, as the other Enbridge lines all cross Red Lake, Leech Lake and Fond du Lac reservations, along the Highway 2 Corridor. This one is new terrain, through the south, and across North Dakota.

At last count, Enbridge needs 2000 easements and rights of way and a lot of permits for the Sandpiper. All of those can be difficult to get, denied or challenged. Besides that, the Sandpiper would cross 137 public lands, including Mississippi Headwaters State Forest, and 76 public waterways. That is a lot of public water and treaty-protected water. And – very disturbingly – Enbridge is proceeding confidently, even without an approved route, clearing land, setting up outposts, etc.

It is possible that Enbridge is a bit concerned about process, or might be, since the Keystone routing fiasco of this past February. That's when Nebraska court judge Stephanie Stacy declared unconstitutional a law that had given Nebraska Govenor Dave Heineman the power to push the project through private land.

"The interests in oil profits should not supersede the rights of property owners....It is not in America's national interests to allow a foreign oil company to condemn American farms and ranches to take foreign oil to the Gulf Coast for sale on the global market," wrote Senator Rob Hogg in a letter to Congressman Bruce Braley of Iowa's First Congressional District.

Meanwhile, in Minnesota there are a growing number of landowners who are concerned about the Sandpiper proposal. That's because the pipeline proposal runs through the lakes with the highest water quality in Minnesota, outside of the boundary waters.

Among them are the Carleton County Landowners Association, Friends of the Headwaters and a number of lakes associations.

As well, Honor the Earth, a national Native environmental organization, has intervened in the Public Utilities Commission process, and six Anishinaabeg governments have come out opposing the project.

"It is not possible to identify—let alone to avoid—sites of historic, archaeological and cultural significance, without consulting with the Tribal Historic Preservation Office. Not doing so raises serious concerns about Enbridge 's ability…" Susan Klapel, Commissioner of Natural Resources for the Mille Lacs band of Ojibwe, would write in a letter to the Public Utilities Commission.

The pipeline route runs through the center of wild rice territory. All of the Ojibwe bands are concerned, and most have also questions if the Public Utilities Commission would have the sole authority to grant permits over tribal lands within reservation borders, and also within the 1855 treaty area. "I ask you to not grant Enbridge (Sandpiper) permits through the proposed southern route," Klapel wrote.

A Flawed Process

Native people are not the only ones concerned about the Enbridge way or the Public Utilities Commission. In mid April, twenty state legislators wrote a letter to the PUC asking "that all federal, tribal and state laws be followed," and expressing concern about the process.

"That process has been designed largely to fast-track permitting, and seems to be set up for the company," Willis Mattison, a technical advisor to the Friends of the Headwaters says. Mattison is a feisty retired guy. He retired as a regional director of the Minnesota Pollution Control Agency and the pipeline goes through his region. He is not pleased, either with the company or with the state agencies.

Let's put it this way: The Sandpiper project was announced with a very short timeline and with only a few public meetings in the plan. There was no public meeting held on the White Earth reservation, which specifically requested one, despite the tribe's specific request, which was totally reasonable since the pipeline crosses the reservation. Then there was a lack of access to information, and only a short period of comment on the 610-mile route. The route was announced, however, there was no detailed map associated with it.

Here's how it worked: Bob Merritt, a former Minnesota Department of Natural Resources hydrologist, requested the GIS Shape File for the proposed Sandpiper line and was refused on the basis that the information was declared a "trade secret" and protected by the Code of Federal Regulations covering sensitive public infrastructure vulnerable to terrorist attack.

The response from the PUC reads: "Thank you for your e-mail to the Minnesota Public Utilities Commission. Enbridge will not provide GIS shape files, as it deems this information as Trade Secret (Minn. R. 7829.0500). This information falls under Critical Energy Information (18 C.F.R. § 388.113) and is exempt from mandatory disclosure under the Freedom of Information Act. You may certainly contact Enbridge to request this information."

That's what Brian Swanson of the PUC explained to Mr. Merritt. It's hard enough to comment on the hydrology of a 610-mile pipeline in a couple of months, it's harder without a map.

Willis Mattison explained the problems to the PUC: "The overall experience of Friends of the Headwaters members throughout their involvement in the matter of the proposed Sandpiper pipeline has ranged from frustration to befuddlement, to confusion, rejection, and exclusion. Having our state government department staffs perform in ways that have been outwardly defiant, defensive, obfuscating and off-putting has created a deep sense of distrust, suspicion and at times utter outrage. Our members' and organization representatives' attempts to fully participate in the decision-making process have been rebuffed on numerous occasions....This defiance of citizen's right to be heard on the part of government agencies not only violates First Amendment rights but works to destroy the general public's trust in fair and equal treatment under the laws that govern us as a people".

It appears that there are a lot a lot of lakeshore owners who are realizing that after a 30-inch fracked-oil pipeline runs near your land, property values are going down, and that is even without a spill. This is a measure of the distrust that Enbridge has earned itself. And some of those affected property owners feel like they should be able to make comments. The Enbridge Company, however, has opposed any extension of the public comment period.

WHEN TREATIES MATTER: *MANOOMIN*

Manoominikewag "They are making wild rice." There are few places in the world with the wealth of the North. One fifth of the world's fresh water lies in the Great Lakes. Oil and water do not mix. There is wildlife, a fishery worth hundreds of millions of dollars, tourism, and wild rice. That is the food that grows on the water and is central to Anishinaabeg people and culture as well as to the ecosystem. Wild rice is a gift, an amazing gift. There is no cultivation required. Our rice grows naturally, but we must care for the lakes.

Nimanoominike omaa "I harvest wild rice here." In fact, I harvest wild rice on the Crow Wing chain, because it is abundant, and because it ripens earlier than the manoomin on my own reservation. That is how our people have been, have always been. We go to where the rice is, and that is not always on the reservation, but on our ceded lands.

Those are places where our reserved treaty or usufructuary rights apply, protected in perpetuity by the "supreme Law of the Land", by the U.S. Constitution itself.

It turns out that these are places where Enbridge wants to put its pipeline, and the Sandpiper line goes not only there, but also would pass within a mile of the largest wild rice bed in Anishinaabeg territory: Rice Lake on the White Earth reservation.

Enbridge's pipeline would cross lakes, creeks and watersheds, including those where tribes have worked long and hard to restore native sturgeon populations and to protect wild rice.

Imagine that one day you wake up and find out that a pipeline company wants to run a thirty-inch pipe pumping 375,000 barrels of oil per day under high pressure through your burial grounds, sacred sites, medicinal plant harvesting areas, and no more than a mile from your biggest wild rice harvesting areas. And, they didn't even bother to mention it.

Are We (You) Protestors, or Protectors?

That's pretty much what Mille Lacs found out. Then the Mille Lacs band was also probably a bit surprised to find that Enbridge had hired Randy Jorgensen, an attorney who specializes in Indian fighting in this millennium, and who was a lead counsel for landowners opposing the Mille Lacs band in the landmark Supreme Court case.

Jorgenson argued on behalf of his new client Enbridge at the PUC, that tribal rights and interests should not be considered by the PUC.

It's a rather small world in Indian fighting apparently, and an expensive one.

The proposed Enbridge Sandpiper line is within the 1855 treaty area of the Anishinaabeg, and the rights to harvest wild rice in that region remain with the Anishinaabeg. Those rights were never relinquished.

Anishinaabe tribal member Michael Dahl was asked if he was protesting the pipeline proposal, while he was riding his horse along one of three pipeline rides taken this past fall by Honor the Earth (see Honor the Earth Triple Crown of Pipeline Rides https://www.youtube.com/watch?v=1v6_1DLth9U).

"We are not protesters, we are protectors," Dahl replied.

Wild rice needs clean water, and perhaps the treaty (and federal trust responsibility) will help protect it, along with Michael Dahl.

"Treaties are the law, equal in statutes to federal laws under the US constitution, and … the US has the responsibility to honor the rights and resources protected by the treaties." –Bob Perciasepe, Deputy Administrator of the EPA

Bob Peciasepe was writing to all EPA regional administrators in 2013. He continued: "While treaties do not expand the authorities granted by the EPA's underlying statutes, our programs should be implemented to protect treaty covered resources where we have the discretion to do so."

It would appear that the EPA has a broader obligation scope than it has been taking, and for that matter the EPA might want to consider thinking about the cumulative impact of pipelines and mines on the Lake Superior Basin.

Got a Plan?

Consider that there's about 2.65 billion barrels of oil in the Bakken. There are possibly 3.73 billion barrels of oil in the Three Forks, which underlays the Bakken. The US uses around 6.8 billion barrels annually, twice as much as the whole asset. So, that $2.5 billion 30-inch pipeline called the Sandpiper, for a twenty year oil boom is a bit of a wonder in the math. Enbridge will likely use the line for Tar Sands oil, if they can, and when the Bakken runs out. The company just hopes to have customers, to keep a level 10 % profit, pretty much guaranteed under federal regulations.

Then there is the spill question. Actually, there is no question about the spills. There will be spills because Enbridge has been responsible for more than 800 spills in the past fifteen years, and they have that lack of a safety culture problem, and they have that integrity management problem, and all these problems with the infrastructure they are already operating, so leaks and ruptures are a given.

The way it works with pipelines is that the profit is at the beginning and at the end; the middle is a lot of risk. Someone told me that pipelines are better than tankers. Then someone else said, "It's like the choice of driving the car with bad brakes, or driving the car with bad steering."

That's the choice between moving oil from the Bakken by train or by pipeline. These choices are not good, and maybe we need to all have a bit of a discussion on what's going on here.

For instance, Minnesota oil consumption has dropped ten percent in the past decade, and that is making some folks wonder why the North should have to take on all of this risk without a clear benefit. All in all, it might be time to have a good discussion about oil, infrastructure, and water in Duluth, before another 4 million barrels of oil heads this way.

THE FAT TAKERS PIPELINE:
NATIVE PEOPLE, THE KXL, THE COWBOY AND INDIAN
ALLIANCE AND THE CONSTITUTION

"No Keystone XL Black Snake Pipeline will cross Lakota Lands. We will protect our lands and waters and we have our horses ready."
—Brian Brewer, President of the Oglala Sioux Tribe

"It will be obvious, it will be concrete, and I think once it starts and they start building you will start to see the momentum and the force of the tribal people.... It is an epic project, it will have an epic response from the tribal people."
–Gary Dorr, Nez Perce Tribe

In mid-February, the Keystone XL Pipeline—*the Black Snake*—found some stronger adversaries:

"It poses a threat to our sacred water and the product is coming from the Tar Sands and our tribes oppose the Tar Sands mining," Debra White Plume, an Oglala leader told the press.

White Plume's family and many others have opposed the pipeline, along with a myriad of uranium mining projects proposed for the Paha Sapa, the Black Hills.

"All of our tribes have taken action to oppose the Keystone XL pipeline. Members from the seven tribes of the Lakota Nation, along with tribal members and tribes in Idaho, Oklahoma, Montana, Nebraska and Oregon, are prepared to stop construction of the pipeline," she said.

This past October, the Lakota rode some of the proposed pipeline route in a series of three rides organized by grassroots and national organizations, including Honor the Earth, Owe Aku and 350.org. The routes covered territory between Wanbli on the Pine Ridge reservation to *Takini* on the Cheyenne River reservation, spiritual rides to honor the water and counter the oil.

This ride was one of three organized on the Alberta Clipper and proposed Sandpiper routes (See https://www.youtube.com/watch?v=1v6_1DLth9U). The other two rides took place along Minnesota pipeline routes.

The Lakota will ride again. That is, if the pipeline project gets President Obama's approval and if the Nebraska and Iowa lawmakers don't stop it first, because of the little constitutional problems of eminent domain. And, that is also if the Environmental Protection Agency doesn't close it down.

The Keystone XL Project took a big step forward for oil companies when the State Department announced that the pipeline had passed the most recent environmental review. The State Department Inspector General, however, is investigating potential conflicts of interest on the part of ERM, the contractor hired to conduct the study, because of its close relations with TransCanada, the company building the pipeline, in the past.

All in all, there is a lot of confusion about this. At a national level—in theory—the project will now go into a final phase which focuses on whether Keystone XL "serves the national interest."

The KXL pipeline's environmental, cultural and economic impacts will be weighed in this phase and at least eight agencies will have input on the outcome, including the Departments of Defense, Justice, Interior, Commerce, Transportation, Energy, Homeland Security and the Environmental Protection Agency.

And then there are the tribes, and there is the matter of the treaties.

Lakota Oyate

The 1868 Fort Laramie Treaty is the treaty between the US and the Lakota Nation. *Oceti Sakowin* treaty territory overlaps Montana, North Dakota, South Dakota, and Nebraska.

These lands and that treaty are sacred to the Lakota, and—across Indian country—tribal leaders and non-Indians as well are demanding that those treaties be recognized as the law of the land, since they are defined in Article Six, paragraph 2, of the US Constitution as *"the supreme Law of the Land."*

When judges and others elected to public office swear to support the Constitution, this is the agreement they are making:

ARTICLE VI of the United States Constitution

1. All Debts contracted and Engagements entered into, before the Adoption of this Constitution, shall be as valid against the United States under this Constitution, as under the Confederation.

2. This Constitution, and the Laws of the United States which shall be made in Pursuance thereof; and all Treaties made, or which shall be made, under the Authority of the United States, shall be the supreme Law of the Land; and the Judges in every State shall be bound thereby, any Thing in the Constitution or Laws of any State to the Contrary notwithstanding.

3. The Senators and Representatives before mentioned, and the Members of the several State Legislatures, and all executive and judicial Officers, both of the United States and of the several States, shall be bound by Oath or Affirmation, to support this Constitution; but no religious Test shall ever be required as a Qualification to any Office or public Trust under the United States.

At the mid-February summit, the Lakota and their allies reaffirmed opposition to the Black Snake. Gary Dorr, from the Nez Perce Tribe in Idaho, talked about opposition to the pipeline, and his tribe's legal position on the Tar Sands.

"The Tar Sands is already affecting the people (of Fort Chipewyan in Alberta); climate change is already obvious. To facilitate that is not something the Native people of the U.S. are going to do. We are not going to sit idly by and let it happen." –Gary Dorr, Nez Perce

The Nez Perce tribe has already used its treaty rights to block the transport of so-called megaloads of mining equipment headed to the Alberta's Tar Sands through its territory. The tribe launched blockades and won a court battle to stop the shipments from traversing its lands.

Among the voices at the conference were treaty council representatives Faith Spotted Eagle (Yankton), Russell Eagle Bear of Rosebud, Jay Taken Alive of Standing Rock, and Leonard Little Finger of Oglala Treaty Council as well as other traditional chiefs and leaders. They reminded participants of the Mother Earth Accord that Indigenous leaders and allies signed at Rosebud in 2011 and the International Treaty to Protect the Sacred from the Tar Sands Project they signed at Yankton in 2013.

They also stressed their willingness to resort to direct action if President Obama approves the pipeline.

Is there a National Interest in Moving "Dilbit"?

The Administration's decision on whether to approve a Presidential Permit for the Keystone XL Pipeline will be based on whether the proposal is "in the national interest."

Robert Gough, secretary of the Intertribal Council on Utility Policy, asked and answered the question: "Whose national interest is at stake? No place more than here", he said, referring to the Lakota Nation and the region.

"The pipeline would carry bitumen diluted in toxic slurry (dilbit) across the route of the rural water pipeline that provides drinking water supplies on the reservations in South Dakota, as well as across the Cheyenne River, and across the Ogallala Aquifer," Gough said.

"TransCanada's first dilbit line spilled 14 times in its first year of operations after receiving a Presidential Permit to pass from Alberta across North Dakota, South Dakota, Nebraska, Iowa and Illinois.

"Even if it (dilbit) wasn't spilled, it's a death knell for the planet we as humans have lived on for thousands and thousands and thousands of years," Gough said, referring to the global carbon impact of the Tar Sands themselves.

TransCanada countered: "The incorporation of 59 special conditions and dozens of other extra spill prevention and mitigation measures will ensure that Keystone XL will have a degree of safety over any other typically constructed domestic oil pipeline system under current code."

That sort of thinking might hold up in TransCanada's mind, however, leaks are continually bursting open on the oil pipelines they've already buried in the ground, already poisoning the water as Big Oil pushes to increase their capacity to scorch the Earth.

And, it appears that only some 20% of pipeline spills are discovered by the companies that own or operate them; the remainder usually found by people who are not equipped to stop spills: farmers, people living in their homes.

Accepting the Word

Besides that, the Lakota point out that the Oglalla aquifer is the sole drinking water source for not only humans but everything else. There is no way that a people who have lived in this area for a thousand years are going to accept the word of a fifty-year-old pipeline company when their water supply is on the line.

Percy White Plume, leader of both the Big Foot Memorial Ride and this past Fall's ride on the Keystone XL pipeline asks:

"If our children and grandchildren have no water and have to drink bottled water because of the contamination of the pipeline, or a leak, what will our horses be able to drink? What will the wildlife drink?"

Then there's the matter of the Environmental Protection Agency. It appears that the EPA just woke up to a legal responsibility, and seems to be taking it seriously.

In 2013 Bob Perciasepe, Deputy Administrator of the EPA, wrote to all regional administrators: "... treaties are the law, equal in statutes to federal laws under the US constitution, and ... the US has the responsibility to honor the rights and resources protected by the treaties. While treaties do not expand the authorities granted by the EPAs underlying statutes, our programs should be implemented to protect treaty covered resources where we have the discretion to do so."

It would appear that the EPA has a Constitutionally-mandated broader scope of obligation regarding the treaties than it has been taking with the Environmental Impact Statement process for the Keystone XL. And, that Constitutionally-mandated treaty protection scope might cover the pipeline.

This is true, since the EPA might have found its mojo again. This is how we know the mojo might have been found: During the last week of February, the EPA took action to consider the impact of the proposed Pebble Mine project on the Bristol Bay fishery in Alaska. It's a very controversial project. That fishery provides about a third of the sockeye salmon to the US consumer, and would be destroyed by the proposed mine. After 150,000 comments were submitted, the EPA decided to intervene.

Back in the Northern Plains, there's a similar discussion that is about what people will drink, wondering about not just what they will eat but where their water will come from if Bakken crude poisons the aquifer. The Bakken oil field extraction is already contaminating water supplies in a state with little water. And, it turns out that people may not want to drink the Kool-Aid.

Drinking the Kool-Aid

"Drinking the Kool-Aid." That's a term that came from the Reverend Jim Jones, I believe, and it is something you don't want to do. His Kool-Aid killed around 900 people, his ardent followers, some voluntarily, some not so.

There is a new Kool-Aid, some would say. The TransCanada/Koch Brothers/Enbridge/SynCrude/KXL Kool-Aid is the story they are peddling that proclaims there are a lot of jobs in the pipelines, that the US economy will be saved, and we'll all be more secure with the pipeline.

This is not actually true. It turns out that mega projects are not necessarily employment opportunities. I'd say that the last mega projects which really were employment opportunities were the building of the Egyptian pyramids by Jewish slave labor. This might be a little different, but a lot of people don't like being a slave either to the Egyptians or to the oil companies.

Let's think about what $7 billion could buy if we thought about investing in the economy and energy infrastructure of this country. A just-released study analyzing employment from the Keystone XL proposal versus needs and employment for other options found some rather large holes in industry claims.

The study found that spending money on unmet water and gas infrastructure needs in the five relevant states along the KXL pipeline route will create more than 300,000 total jobs across all sectors, or five times more jobs than the KXL, with 95 times more long-term jobs.

Think of it this way: In its latest Infrastructure report card, the American Society of Civil Engineers gave the nation a D on drinking water and waste water infrastructure and a D+ on energy infrastructure. Infrastructure failure is causing gas explosions and water main ruptures around the country.

Infrastructure failure is when your I 35 Bridge collapses in Minneapolis, and infrastructure failure is when an Exxon Mobil pipeline ruptures in Mayflower Arkansas, spilling 7,000 barrels of oil into a suburb. We have an infrastructure problem generally in the country. Some folks would say we should fix old pipelines before we make new ones, particularly pipelines which don't serve our towns, cities, or homes.

And then there is tribal infrastructure. About 14% of reservation households are without electricity, 10 times the national rate. Energy distribution systems on rural reservations are extremely vulnerable to extended power outages during winter storms, threatening the lives of reservation residents. Reservation communities are at a statistically greater risk from extreme weather related mortality nationwide, especially from cold, heat and drought associated with a rapidly changing climate.

For instance, Debbie Dogskin, a Lakota woman on the Standing Rock reservation froze to death in February, when she couldn't pay her skyrocketing propane bills. Her propane ran out. Ironically, she lived about a hundred miles from the Bakken oil fields where they flare off gas, they've got so much.

Reservations need more than 200,000 new houses, and there is no money for them. And then there is the special case of Pine Ridge, the largest Lakota reservation, and the poster child of those who want to talk about how horrible the conditions of Native people are. 97% of the people at Pine Ridge live below the federal poverty line.

The Fat Takers Pipeline

At Pine Ridge, the reservation Brian Brewer, Debra White Plume, Percy White Plume live on, no one believes in the White Man's pipeline. They call it the Fat Takers' pipeline, the pipeline of the *wasichu*.

The unemployment rate vacillates from 85% to 95% on the reservation. At least 60% of the homes are severely substandard, without water, electricity, adequate insulation and sewage systems.

Basically, the Lakota—like many other Native people—see a big infrastructure project like the KXL pipeline, which moves profits from one corporation to another across their land, as more than a Black Snake of the Fat Taker. It is a threat, and there is no new water.

The Constitution

Finally, there is that pesky problem of the Constitution. It's a problem with Indian treaties, and it is a problem with the Keystone XL Pipeline, largely because, it seems that in Nebraska the governor was just too excited about approving the pipeline, and violated the constitutional rights of Nebraska citizens.

The eminent domain questions have been ongoing and challenging, but in February, Nebraska district judge Stephanie Stacy declared unconstitutional a law that had given Nebraska Gov. Dave Heineman the power to push the project through private land.

This past week, two Iowa state legislators, Senator Rob Hogg and Representative Bobby Kaufmann, called on Congress to oppose the proposed Keystone XL pipeline because of the use of eminent domain in the development of the project.

"I urge you to stand with those landowners who do not want this pipeline running through their property," wrote Rep. Kaufmann in a letter to Congressman Dave Loebsack of Iowa's Second Congressional District. "The interests in oil profits should not supersede the rights of property owners."

"It is not in America's national interests to allow a foreign oil company to condemn American farms and ranches to take foreign oil to the Gulf Coast for sale on the global market," Senator Hogg wrote in a letter to Congressman Bruce Braley of Iowa's First Congressional District. "The Keystone pipeline threatens America's land, water, and wildlife. Congress should say no, the State Department should say no, and President Obama should say no."

This past spring a gathering of ranchers and Natives came together, forming what is called the Cowboy and Indian Alliance, representing Nebraska and South Dakota ranchers, and Lakota, Ponca and other Native people. They too are intent upon stopping the pipeline. So there you go: the Fat Takers' pipeline, the Wasichu Black Snake, is facing new adversaries, and they are daunting, they are tough, and they are your neighbors.

Postscript: November 2015, President Obama denies the Presidential Permit required for the KXL pipeline.

ENBRIDGE PLAYS UNFUNNY GAME WITH OIL PIPELINE

A long time ago, the Royal Canadian Mounted Police called my house. That was up in a remote Cree community in northern Canada, where I lived with my husband and children. The RCMP inspector asked for me and said they would like to talk to me about a missing person case. I said, "Who's missing?" They said they couldn't divulge that, as that was part of the investigation. I said I couldn't help them.

We've got a similar challenge. The comment period for Enbridge's proposed Sandpiper fracked oil pipeline route through North Dakota and Minnesota is coming to a close; that is, to comment on the route or alternatives. The problem is that no one knows the route; we can't get a copy of mapping for the proposed route to comment. Enbridge won't release it.

Bob Merrit, former Minnesota Department of Natural Resources hydrologist, requested the GIS Shape File for the proposed line and was refused on the basis that the information was declared a "trade secret" and protected by Code of Federal Regulations covering sensitive public infrastructure vulnerable to terrorist attack. This is the correspondence from the Public Utilities Commission:

"Thank you for your e-mail to the Minnesota Public Utilities Commission. Enbridge will not provide GIS shape files, as it deems this information as Trade Secret (Minn. R. 7829.0500). This information falls under Critical Energy Information (18 C.F.R. § 388.113) and is exempt from mandatory disclosure under the Freedom of Information Act. You may certainly contact Enbridge to request this information."

That's what Brian Swanson of the PUC explained to Merrit. This is a problem. As Willis Mattson, another former state regulatory official, quips, "The PUC and Enbridge cannot reasonably withhold this data set while simultaneously shifting the burden onto the public to find, evaluate and advocate alternative routes for the pipeline. The public is hampered in its time, expertise and technical resources and certainly is no match for the capabilities that large corporations like Enbridge possess. Yet, this is what the process requires of the public."

What to Do?

So what's a girl to do? Or what is the public to do? The process grinds on, and the Enbridge proposal is to put a 24- or so inch pipeline next to spring-fed lakes and shallow aquifers, crossing close to pristine wild rice harvesting areas, places full of native prairie and medicines, and to fill that pipeline with some of the most volatile stuff known to humans.

And, adding to that, the gigantic Canadian company that proposes it, Enbridge Corporation, has 800 spills under its belt already; and less than 20 percent of pipeline spills are actually found by the company. They are found by folks like you and I, who become First Responders.

In the meantime, we aren't even allowed to know where the pipeline is proposed to go, and we can't figure out what we are commenting on. The national security bit is a bit of a hoax because we don't actually have a pipeline in.

I'd sure like to know what aquifers, what endangered prairie (like that pristine 960 acres near Grand Forks) the proposed pipeline would cross, and what alternatives would be. Can't do that without a map.

I don't know if the RCMP ever found that missing person. I hope they did. It was funny at the time. But I'll tell you what, Enbridge's lost pipeline, or the one under that cloak of invisibility, is not so funny.

The public has a right to know. The comment period should not continue without a full disclosure of the route.

FACING PIPELINES AND MINES, TRIBAL GOVERNMENTS PUSH AHEAD

"The oil companies say they've got all this great technology, all this computer equipment and remote sensors that will detect a spill instantly and shut it off. Well the truth is there's been studies done about this. I believe it's less than 20 percent of the spills are detected by the technology, by the super-system. So the rest of them are detected by guess who? The people who live there, local emergency response folks, by people who smell the spill."

—PAUL BLACKBURN,
ENERGY AND ENVIRONMENTAL LAW ATTORNEY

In Anishinaabe Akiing some new mining proposals and pipelines threaten the water and land of this region. This past month, tribal governments stepped up to issue some big challenges to those plans.

In late February, the White Earth Tribal Council issued a resolution, stating it "…is opposed to the application filed by the North Dakota Pipeline Company with the Minnesota PUC with respect to a routing permit for the Sandpiper Petroleum pipeline between Tioga, North Dakota and Superior, Wisconsin."

The White Earth tribe is concerned not only because the pipeline would be in Nora Township (one of the most northeastern townships within the 1867 treaty reservation) just upstream from Rice Lake, the mother lode of ricing on White Earth. The tribe is also concerned because this pipeline, like the proposed expansion of the Alberta Clipper line, impacts the 1855 treaty area lands, which White Earth tribal citizens need to feed our families and earn a modest living.

Ecological Ignorance

In early February, the Minnesota Chippewa Tribe admonished the Minnesota Pollution Control Agency, for "ecological ignorance," wherein the PCA seems to be trying to re-designate some of the waters where wild rice is found, so that those waters can have diminished water quality. In short, Norman Deschampe said in a letter to John Linc Stine, Minnesota PCA commissioner, "Waters used for the production of wild rice…must remain on the wild rice waters lists for regulatory purposes. They cannot be pulled off and dropped instead onto the proposed watch list, in effect delisting them as class 4 status of the state with the stroke of a pen."

So it seems like the state of Minnesota might have been trying to pull a fast one on the tribes, and it doesn't look like it worked. In another building in St. Paul, the Minnesota PUC is considering issuing some permits for two big pipelines, the Sandpiper and the Clipper, and the state and federal government are considering Minnesota's first copper mining proposal, one which will require water treatment for 250 to 1,000 years or so. The copper mining industry is anxiously awaiting the outcome of the environmental review as there are six or more similar and even larger and more polluting copper mine projects waiting in the wings. One might ask the question if these agencies have sole jurisdiction, based on the 1837, 1854 and 1855 treaties and court decisions which reaffirm the Anishinaabe rights in this area.

It's more than a bit confusing, as both state and federal agencies like boxes. If you ever try filling out a federal grant application, you know this to be true. It turns out that ecosystems and Indigenous peoples do not live in boxes.

EPA, or the Environmental Pollution Permitting Agency?

Enter the Environmental Protection Agency. In late January, I paid a visit to Region 5 EPA, sort of like an individual tribal citizen would. I came to ask a few questions of the EPA, which, in my mind was the one branch of the federal government which would protect the environment. After all, that's its name. The conversation I had was disturbing.

First, I asked why the proposed PolyMet copper mine had been given an "F" rating, rare as that may be, in their 2009 Environmental Impact Statement and if there was any way to not fail with that project.

The F-listed hazardous wastes are known as "wastes from non-specific sources" like degreasers and cleaning solvents, as opposed to K-listed hazardous wastes, which "includes certain wastes from specific industries, such as petroleum refining or pesticide manufacturing. Certain sludges and wastewaters from treatment and production processes in these industries are examples of source-specific wastes."

So, they are saying with the F listing that they wouldn't be able to identify where the hazardous wastes produced by the project were coming from.

A 100% Record of Violations

A study of modern sulfide mines in the U.S. found that 100 percent of open pit mines in climates similar to northeastern Minnesota violated water quality standards. In the U.S. as a whole, 84 percent violated water quality standards; of these only 16 percent had predicted a high potential for contaminant leaching. Among sulfide mines predicting low acid mine drainage potential, 89 percent in fact resulted in onsite acid mine drainage. The hard rock mining industry is the largest source of Superfund liability to taxpayers, costing more than $2.6 billion so far. The EPA estimated the cost of remediating existing pollution at hard rock mining facilities is between $20 and $54 billion. It would seem like these facts would not change.

In PolyMet Northmet proposal, the EPA gave the PolyMet project a failing grade. The EPA gave this low a rating to less than one percent of similar projects. Undaunted, mining proponents spent over $20 million to reissue a supplemental draft of their environmental impact study.

So I asked the EPA, "What could PolyMet ever do to not fail the regulatory process?" I asked this, because water quality impacts, like the sulfuric acid which would come from the proposed mine would peak, say 500 years from now. And, I wasn't really sure, which junior Canadian mining company was going to be around to take care of that.

I was told by one of the EPA reviewers that I should be thinking about mitigation, basically, not preventing. This has bothered me ever since. Then, perhaps more bothersome was the lead officer there telling me that the EPA was really the "Environmental Pollution Permitting Agency." That was their job nowadays. I basically said, "Say it ain't true ... after all, this is my agency." So, what is this to say? In my opinion, it is to say that the EPA may have lost its way and needs a bit of encouragement to enforce some of those federal laws like the Clean Water Act.

It turns out that this is actually a big thought coming down from somewhere in Washington, and this will also have possible implications for treaty rights, maybe even for Region 5 EPA, if they want to abide by the U.S. Constitution.

In 2013 Bob Perciasepe, Deputy Administrator of the EPA, wrote to all regional administrators, "Treaties are the law, equal in statutes to federal laws under the US Constitution, and the US has the responsibility to honor the rights and resources protected by the treaties. While treaties do not expand the authorities granted by the EPA's underlying statutes, our programs should be implemented to protect treaty covered resources where we have the discretion to do so."

It would appear that the EPA has a broader scope than it has been taking, with the EIS process for the PolyMet mine. And, that scope should likely be considered as the pipelines, mines, tankers and increased need for coal impacts the whole region. I am hopeful.

Pipelines Take Two

Back on the pipelines. Enbridge wants to expand the Tar Sands pipeline because it suggests there is a need for this for their customers – far away, and the second is the Sandpiper line, which is a new pipeline of fracked oil coming from North Dakota (the Fort Berthold Reservation) and will be full of that highly volatile stuff and that will run up almost against Rice Lake, the mother lode of ricing on White Earth. This is what White Earth is very concerned about.

Tribes might have made some decisions to take money the last time for the Enbridge, but they don't need to do it again. Leech Lake in fact had a $ 10 million settlement, which ended up in a pretty controversial trial – about $ 2.4 million of that was used by then Secretary/Treasurer Mike Bongo and former tribal Legal Director Eric Lochen and Executive Director Robert Aitken as an uncollateralized loan to Moondance Ranch, for their summer concerts. It was a fiasco and the Leech Lake Band of Ojibwe Tribal Council voted to prosecute their own tribal citizens for the unapproved loan. I hope the tribe got some good box seats in the least.

The Fond du Lac Band made a different agreement, although it did accept the proposal. Its agreement had to do with previous Enbridge lines which were put in 50 years ago and it is rumored that Enbridge threatened to leave those aging pipelines and instead create a line just south of the reservation, but nevertheless impacting the tribe. It was a tough negotiation, but Fond du Lac ended up with a line. Today, Chairwoman Karen Diver is very prominent in her opposition to the mining proposals. But it is not clear what position the band will take on an expansion of the Clipper pipeline, based on agreements with Enbridge. It is unlikely however that Enbridge wants to negotiate again with the band on anything.

These difficult agreements were made, perhaps binding the tribe into whatever Enbridge would propose. Times and information have changed and we know more, particularly about risk, as the volume of dilbit oil (from the Tar Sands) doubles in the lines which cross these reservations. As attorney Paul Blackburn explained in an interview, "The Alberta Clipper pipeline is the newest one … As pipelines get old they do tend to corrode and when they corrode, there's a bigger risk of them rupturing." Dilbit is highly corrosive.

A Few Other Recent Findings:

Minnesota, or Anishinaabe Akiing, is the primary superhighway for Canadian (tar sands oil) to come into the U.S. There are seven pipelines running through the 1855 and 1854 treaty areas, as well as the Fond du Lac, Red Lake and Leech Lake reservation territories.

As Blackburn explained, "They're shipping sort of the equivalent of the Exxon-Valdez amount of oil across Minnesota each day and some of those pipelines are quite old. So if you think about two million barrels of crude oil potentially coming into the United States, they can bring in a huge amount of oil into the United States through Minnesota and most people don't know that. It is the primary interstate highway in from Canada to the United States to bring in crude oil."

And the spills problem: There are the spills that have not been reported. There's the 865,000-gallon spill in the Tioga farm field, and that one seeped up from six feet down in a six-inch pipe that they said maybe got hit by lightning with a thumb-size leak in it. It leaked for weeks. That's a lot of not monitoring. Pipelines are generally monitored by the companies. They have this thing called the PIG: The Pipeline Inspection Gauge. Reassuring.

And then they have a super-remote monitoring system, which doesn't seem to work. As Blackburn explained about the largest spill in U.S. history, the Enbridge Kalamazoo Spill, "…went for 17 hours. The oil companies say they've got all this great technology, all this computer equipment and remote sensors that will detect a spill instantly and shut it off. Well the truth is there's been studies done about this. I believe it's less than 20 percent of the spills are detected by the technology, by the super-system. So the rest of them are detected by guess who? The people who live there, local emergency response folks, by people who smell the spill." That is, possibly a bit of a local concern for fire departments. Better have a lot of disposable diapers and paper towels; that's the standard for spill clean up as of last year.

At stake is the future of one-fifth of the world's fresh water and the people, land and animals that live there. It is the Anishinaabe universe. It is worth protecting. This spring, tribal governments appear ready to take on that challenge. On the tribal citizen front, Honor the Earth intervened to become an official party to the PUC proceedings for the pipelines with attorneys Peter Erlinder of the International Humanitarian Law Institute, law professor William Mitchell and Frank Bibeau, free range civil rights attorney and White Earth Tribal citizen. Working together might help all of us.

ENBRIDGE EPIPHANY

Ziigwan bidaagoshin … It is spring, the time of some of the most promising winds in our region, and I cannot help but ask: If the Enbridge Corp. were to invest $16 billion in renewable energy in Minnesota, as opposed to in fossil fuels pipelines, would we like them more? I answer "yes."

According to Enbridge's 2014 annual report, the company with the longest and most complex oil pipeline system in the world hopes to have a carbon neutral footprint. This seems challenging, in light of the proposals to move well over 2 million barrels of new high-carbon oil across the North in the upcoming years.

The company moves more than half of Canadian Tar Sands oil toward the U.S. So let us help re-imagine the company. In the company's annual report, they discuss their $4 billion in renewable energy investments since 2002, including the 2014 purchase of a $650 billion wind portfolio in Indiana, and 150 megawatts of solar in Nevada. In Canada, Enbridge is helping Ontario generate power from the methane in landfills, all good stuff, in a world that has been getting warmer and choking more on greenhouse gases every year.

Looking at the annual report, pipeline costs are at around $16 billion for Minnesota alone, not including a contentious pipeline called the Gateway in British Columbia. If Enbridge spent $16 billion on renewable energy in Minnesota instead of pipelines, this is what we might see: 265,142 homes with 5 kw of solar panels, or 1,325 two-megawatt wind turbines, generating about 8 billion kilowatt hours per year, just to begin with. If we just put that into "nega-watts" of efficiency, we could retrofit 662,857 homes with about an $8,000 retrofit job each, saving each home about $300 a year. That is a good deal, as climate change approaches and fossil fuel access becomes more challenged.

As far as jobs? Enbridge, like other pipeline-peddling companies, likes to refer to pipeline projects as job creators. Their promotional materials for the Line 67, Sandpiper and Line 3 replacement projects—

according to the company—will generate 3,100 anticipated construction jobs, in the large type, but in smaller type Line 67 expansion (Clipper) will have up to 100 construction jobs. (There were 45 jobs in building phase one of this pipeline). The Sandpiper and Line 3 replacement projects should employ 1,500 construction workers. This sounds good; however, jobs in fossil fuel pipelines are short term and capital intensive. In other words, it takes a lot of money in steel and lawyers for big projects and less goes for labor.

Infrastucture vs. Standard Assets

When an engineering research group looked at the ill-fated Keystone XL pipeline, they found that spending money on unmet water and gas infrastructure needs in the five relevant states along the KXL pipeline route will create more than 300,000 total jobs across all sectors, or five times more jobs than the KXL, with 95 times more long-term jobs. That was a $7 billion project.

Just think about if we used those union pipe fitters for infrastructure in Minnesota.

Think of it this way: The American Society of Civil Engineers, in its latest infrastructure report card, gave the country a "D" on drinking water and waste water infrastructure and a "D+" on energy infrastructure. Infrastructure failure is causing gas explosions and water main ruptures around the country. Infrastructure failure is when your I-35 Bridge collapses in Minneapolis, and infrastructure failure is when the apartment buildings in the East Village are leveled because of gas leaks.

And then there is tribal infrastructure. About 14 percent of reservation households are without electricity, 10 times the national rate. Energy distribution systems on rural reservations are vulnerable to extended power outages during winter storms, threatening the lives of reservation residents. I mention this because tribal communities are most impacted by the risk of pipeline leak liability.

So, give me a hand, Enbridge; give us all a hand. Don't waste our time, your money and our collective ecosystem of water and wild rice on pipelines. Those pipelines will be stranded assets in a decade – a waste of steel and a liability for all of us. Evolve and resurrect. It's spring and the best and clearest winds are blowing.

Dale Greene and Tania Aubid. Photo by Sarah Little Red Feather.

On Foods

DEAR GOVERNOR DAYTON

We would like to eat. Our people have been jailed for snaring rabbits and hunting, and have lost our boats and nets. It is time to evolve our relationship with the state. This last week, your Department of Natural Resources decided to issue some citations to Ojibwe people for ricing on Hole in the Day Lake. That is, after the cameras were gone. The officers went out to track down Morningstar and Harvey Goodsky, citing them for harvesting wild rice off the reservation without state permission. Sort of like "poaching wild rice." This is out of line. Let me do my best to explain why.

When my ancestors signed the treaty of 1855, Anishinaabe Akiing—our land—was in good shape. We could all drink the water from these lakes; wild rice grew throughout our territory; fish, moose and wolves were abundant, and the maple trees were in their glory. That treaty was with the US government, and somehow you are now managing the assets of the 1855 treaty, or most of them. You are failing to care for what we love.

This is what I see. Some 90% of the wetlands have been drained. The western third of Minnesota, including the 1855 treaty territory was once covered with wetlands. Today, even though Minnesota is spending millions annually, the state is still losing more than it restores.

About the Fish

Fish. Well, these days a pregnant woman or a child can eat one meal a month of walleye (under two feet), bass, catfish or northern, none of the larger ones. Coal-fired generation causes that. The rest of us can eat once a week, before we have to worry about methyl mercury poisoning. Wow.

Now your Fisheries Department has managed to crash the Mille Lacs Fishery. Let me remind you that the Mille Lacs band did not do that, and has volunteered to forgo tribal harvest for next year. This crash resulted from the folly of your politics and the 2006 decision to increase the limit, despite scientific and tribal expertise which set the limit at 350,000 pounds. Minnesota Fishery's staff secured legislative approval for 550,000 pounds. Nice work. The walleye population in 2014 was its lowest in 30 years. And, many of your lakes are dying from agricultural runoff and invasive species.

Anishinaabeg people have always lived with the moose and the wolf. You have allowed their destruction by corporate and special interests-driven myopic management policies. Let me be clear: In July of 2015, the Center for Biological Diversity and Honor the Earth filed a request to list the Moose as endangered. In just 10 years' time, moose numbers in Minnesota have dropped from nearly 9,000 to as few as 3,500. Why? Habitat destruction caused by mining and logging industries and over-harvesting. Now, scientists agree that the greatest threat which could virtually eliminate moose from Minnesota within five years stems from climate change. Yet the state continues to forward a fossil fuels-based energy policy, from dirty oil pipelines to a "clean energy plan" which uses coal gasification as a centerpiece of stupidity.

Frankly, your forest management policies alone could have almost wiped out the moose. A 2006 study found that six of the 12 known wildlife corridors in the Mesabi Iron Range will likely become isolated, fragmented or lost completely, and almost 9,000 acres of habitat will likely be destroyed. That's what new logging and mining projects will do to the Moose.

Minnesota has made a mockery of stewardship and respect by failing to understand the nature of the wolf in the North and the centrality of the wolf to Anishinaabeg people. In 2014, DNR announced an increase in wolf hunting permits: 3,800 hunting and trapping licenses available for the coming season, up from 3,500 last year, allowing up to 250 wolves to be killed before the season closed. This forced federal court action, but also compelled the Ojibwe tribes to declare wolf sanctuaries on our reservations and push for the same in our treaty territories.

You have cost us many of our trees. Our chief Wabunoquod spoke of how the great pines had been stolen from our people and cried at the loss, as they were our ancestors. The maple basswood forest system is in serious decline, and many of our most productive maple sugarbush areas in the 1855 treaty territory have been cut, without regard for us. This leaves families without food and sugar.

Now you come for the wild rice. You have cost us 50% of the manoomin in the North. Let us be clear, this is the only grain indigenous
to North America and is far more nutritious than GMO crops. Yet
dam projects destroy our precious food, and now the state intends to
weaken sulfate standards which protect our waters and wild rice so
that you can open up mining in the north for Canadian, Chinese and
other foreign interests.

Then there are the baffling pipelines: four of them through our best
wild rice territories, all pushing through the entirely dysfunctional system of the Department of Commerce and Public Utilities Commission
which will not even speak formally with tribal governments.

Please explain to me again why our people should be arrested for
harvesting wild rice? The state has shown no regard for the North. We
would like to eat and continue the life we were given by the Creator.

GROWING THE HERB: MARIJUANA, HEMP AND INDIAN COUNTRY

*"You have an unmotivated person and you
become more unmotivated on cannabis. I am
afraid that the self esteem of our people is not
going to handle legalizing it well."*
—KEVIN SHORE, WHITE EARTH TRIBAL MEMBER
AND GULF WAR VETERAN, USING VA-PRESCRIBED
THC FOR HIS CHRONIC CONDITION

*"I think that decriminalizing recreational use
would benefit our people greatly since so many
of us use it and many have been incarcerated for
possessing it. The tribes certainly could gain by
better controlling how it exists within our communities as well as financially with sales and*

possible taxation...We have retained aboriginal rights to utilize medicines within our communities the way we see fit. "

—Martin Reinhardt , Professor,
Northern Michigan University

"We've already seen a decrease in violent crime within the jails. Snack food contraband is up 300 percent but that's to be expected. We will continue to monitor the marijuana program, but so far so good."

—Tom Norton, Warden,
Colorado Department of Corrections

It's time to reconsider the regulation of marijuana and hemp. With the Pinoleville Pomo tribe of California initiating the first tribal commercial marijuana grow operation, and the Department of Justice's announcement that it would not prosecute for marijuana or hemp, the door has been opened to look at the regulatory scheme.

This December, Justice Department Director Monty Wilkinson announced, "The eight priorities in the Cole memorandum will guide United States Attorneys' marijuana enforcement efforts in Indian Country, including in the event that sovereign Indian Nations seek to legalize the cultivation or use of marijuana in Indian Country."

In turn, the Pinoleville Pomo tribe, which is located in Mendocino County, one of the largest marijuana-growing counties in the country, announced a commercial venture with two partners, Colorado-based United Cannabis and Kansas-based Foxberry Farms. The 250-member tribe announced that it will grow thousands of plants for the medical marijuana business on its 99-acre reservation.

What's the catch? There are a lot of them, especially in any states which have not yet legalized marijuana. Attorney General Cole, for instance, states that the Department of Justice will retain the right to prosecute individuals who engage in the distribution of marijuana to minors, where revenue is going to criminal enterprises, drugged driving, or diversion to a state where it is not legal.

While some tribes are looking to this as a highly lucrative business, others are considering just the local economics and pros and cons of the industry. In the least on the cautious side, tribal police are already pretty busy and under funded, so the keeping of marijuana to within reservation borders may be a bit of a challenge for any regulatory authority. And, that "Driving While Indian" thing that occurs when you leave the reservation boundaries, is going to be supremely tested if tribes go ahead. There is not an easy path in any case.

The Economics

I am told that 40% of my community smokes the herb. The fact is we're spending millions of dollars a year importing marijuana from largely unsavory characters onto the reservation, creating a great loss to our tribal economy. This is undeniable in every reservation. I haven't done complete studies, but in order to buy marijuana from dealers elsewhere, conservative estimates indicate that $60,000 a week is draining from my own reservation, White Earth. With a little math, it looks like around $3 million annually is drained from the reservation for purchases.

That is coming out of tribal pockets, pockets in some of the poorest counties in the state. That is part of our challenge. Could tribes curb that economic drain with a local marijuana economy? There are some larger economic benefits, for both hemp or marijuana, as well as risks.

Hemp Economics — Supply and Demand

Over 30 nations grow industrial hemp today, including Canada, France, England, Russia, China, Germany and Australia. China is the largest producer of industrial hemp. On the other side, the U.S. is the largest consumer of hemp products, with total annual retail sales in 2013 of $580 million. Between 60% and 90% of the raw hemp materials imported into the US come from Canada, which legalized hemp production in 1998.

This is some old stuff. The Declaration of Independence was drafted on hemp paper. I don't know if our treaties were written on hemp paper, but maybe. Both the Navajo Nation and the Oglala Sioux Council passed ordinances and resolutions on hemp, but at that time, the Drug Enforcement Agency came down with a heavy hand—particularly on the White Plume Tiospaye—which grew 0 percent THC hemp in 2000-2002 on their family allotments.

That crop had been legalized by the Oglala Sioux Tribe, however, in all three years the crops were raided by DEA SWAT teams, destroying thousands of dollars worth of seed. Federal prosecutions were extensive, but the family escaped imprisonment, although they were barred from any more hemp farming. Ironically, the raids had dispersed seed throughout their land, and the crops remain today, although the family is barred from harvest. That was then. It's not clear what that means in light of the change in Justice Department policy.

Marijuana Math

Tribal communities would be unable—under the present regulatory scheme—to sell marijuana off reservation, unless the state they find themselves in has legalized it. This is the case of the Pomo, or a tribe in any state with medical or recreational use. It is not clear as of yet the licensing, but when the state of Minnesota held its informational meeting on the new medical marijuana policy, regulatory officials stated that tribal sovereignty would dictate growing in that state, but no word on distribution or sales off reservation. This is likely to be determined in the upcoming year. The question of a local tribal economy in marijuana, however, is worth some considering.

The marijuana economy is a robust deal in Colorado, where the state is likely to haul in around $43 million this year from marijuana taxes. That is a 27% tax on marijuana. And that's taxes, not business. It's got a huge ripple through the economy for sure, from growers to hydroponic suppliers to bakers. Colorado is sort of unique in its situation and demographics, but it is a booming industry and we are all looking at it

Costs of Marijuana Prosecution

Marijuana has accounted for nearly half of all total drug arrests in the US for the past 20 years, according to FBI crime statistics. Washington state data indicated that the arrest rates grew substantially until in 2010, arrests were three times that of two decades before. The majority of those arrested were white and young, but Natives were arrested at a rate of 1.6 times higher than that of whites, although African Americans were arrested at twice that rate. The possession arrests, according to a Washington state study were at about $200 million in a decade ending in 2010. That's an expensive proposition. It also is a social problem.

A marijuana possession arrest creates a permanent criminal record easily found on the internet by employers, landlords, schools, credit agencies, licensing boards, and banks. A criminal record for the "drug crime" of marijuana possession creates barriers to employment and education for anyone, including whites and the middle class.

There is also the question of tribal enforcement priorities. I talked to tribal officers on White Earth reservation who told me, in effect, that they had a lot more important things to do than arrest tribal members for possession of marijuana. This makes some sense, considering the rest of the domestic violence, DUI and other issues in tribal communities.

As well, there is the concern about drug testing for work at any federally-funded tribal facility (that is, all of them). This means that there are employment issues for tribes who will need to regulate. "We sign an agreement to be a drug free workplace," Tara Mason, Secretary Treasurer of White Earth tells me when I ask her about the regulations, "that is not going to work well." It appears that those who would work for tribal agencies should not smoke marijuana and that would not change. "A lot of us don't work for the tribe", another tribal employer tells me, which I assume is true on most reservations.

Konvict Kush and Good Math

If you're going to federal prison, you might want to look at Colorado. For many years, it had one of the largest prison complexes in the nation, until the state began to look at sentencing and parole. Now, the Colorado Department of Corrections is allowing inmates to grow and consume recreational marijuana, in accordance with state law. In an interview with Rocky Mountain News, prison Warden Tom Norton explained, "We've already seen a decrease in violent crime within the jails. Snack food contraband is up 300 percent but that's to be expected. We will continue to monitor the marijuana program but so far so good." Each inmate is allocated one gram of marijuana per day but additional weed can be earned through good behavior and prison work programs.

Dubbed "Konvict Kush", all the marijuana is grown on prison grounds. "The inmates enjoy the agricultural part of growing the cannabis plants," Norton said. "We have a waiting list of prisoners wanting to trim the buds." With rising prison costs, the economics of marijuana production makes good math. "We keep half of the crop and the rest goes to local Colorado pot dispensaries. Our current projection indicates prison weed sales will cover thirty percent of the incarceration cost by 2020." Colorado prisoners have been so successful with their cultivation that Konvict Cush has qualified for the prestigious Cannabis Cup Award for the year's best marijuana.

Drug Wars

Bad date idea: Taking your mother to see Oliver Stone's *Savages*. It was horribly violent, and drove home the deadly price of the drug wars, and how much I love Benicio Del Toro…. Put it this way, since 2007, around 80,000 people have lost their lives as a result of the fighting between drug cartels and Mexico's armed forces, according to Reuters. And according to the Department of Justice (DOJ), a large portion of the US illegal drug market is controlled directly by Mexican cartels.

In 2012, a study by the Mexican Competitiveness Institute found that US state legalization would cut into cartel business and take over about 30 percent of their market. Vice News did an interview with retired DEA officer Terry Nelson and found that legalization was effecting the drug trafficking and cartels.

"The cartels are criminal organizations that were making as much as 35-40 percent of their income from marijuana," Nelson said, "They aren't able to move as much cannabis inside the US now." Minnesota's Native Mob has historically been involved in marijuana, as well as a host of other drugs and weapons. While prosecutions landed many leaders of the Mob behind bars in 2010-13, it is not clear in a state like Minnesota what the effect on Native gang activity would be, and that is worth considering.

Addictions and More Addictions

"It is a powerful medicine. Like sugar, and alcohol abuse creates family problems. Feel we should always have the choice of what we put into our bodies...." Rachel Montour Ballard, *Akwesasne*

"When my mother met her second husband (my stepfather), he used to smoke it occasionally. Then he would watch something silly on TV and fall asleep. She didn't want him to get caught with it, so she insisted he only drink. This was a really bad idea, since it didn't relieve his stress and made him angrier and more violent. He would start looking for something to focus his anger on as he got drunk, which would almost always be one of his stepchildren. While drunk, he lost all sense of how hard or long he would beat us. When he was high, I don't think he ever hit us at all. The law as it stands has probably put many children and spouses in this position...." –Anonymous interview

That's probably a snapshot of a lot of houses. I surveyed a lot of people on the question of addictions and the impact of legalization and got many opinions. What we know is that our tribal communities suffer from epidemics of addictions. We alter our consciousness because of many things: the pain of historic trauma, boredom, lack of cultural and community strength, and because we like it. The root causes of our drive need to be changed; that is long term work and healing. We need solutions to our problems, and we all know that drinking a six pack or smoking a bowl is not going to make your life better. It might help you forget for a few hours, but we have to change our communities and ourselves.

Frankly, it's easier to get IHS prescription drugs on the reservation and snort them up your nose than probably anywhere else in the country, and that's been a pretty bad idea. Sam Moose, Mille Lac Band Commissioner of Health and Human Services talks about the epidemic which is claiming new victims in the Mille Lacs area: babies born addicted to opiates, both prescription painkillers and illegal drugs like heroin.

According to Moose, the reservation is one of the hardest hit communities in Minnesota. Twenty-eight percent of babies with Neonatal Abstinence Syndrome (NAS) in Minnesota are born to Native Americans, even though Native Americans make up only about two percent of the state's population. In other words, American Indian newborns are 8.7

times more likely than white babies to be born with NAS. Add to that Fetal Alcohol Syndrome (FAS), and we've got a pretty dire situation for the next generation.

What would marijuana do to this? Dr. Melissa Gorake, told me: "As a researcher of FAS and now a doctor of clinical psychology...I truly believe, on a personal, community and societal level, that legalizing marijuana will decrease rates of FAS expression within our communities. Hands down. Access to marijuana will decrease women's use of alcohol during pregnancy which is the most violent teratogen (any agent that can disturb the development of an embryo or fetus) to brain development which lasts a lifetime. It's a start and it's simplistic, but it's something."

That's an interesting thought, but many people remain opposed to "transferring addictions." At the same time, from my limited study, marijuana use is pretty prevalent on the reservations.

The Highest Risk for Marijuana: Teenage Boys

"It is extremely rare to see kids who are chronically using pot doing well in school." Dr. Brett Neinebar, a family and emergency ward physician near Brainerd Minnesota, told me. It might have to do with this neurotransmitter called dopamine.

"Dopamine is the neuro transmitter which is associated with the rewards center of your brain. If you do something well, like get an A , or win a race, you get a good feeling and that stimulates the reward system...marijuana stunts that. Because those who get that reward tend to be high achievers, the loss of it is a problem. Marijuana use really stamps out the dopamine." In lay person terms, it's sort of like when your kid says "whatever" and rolls their eyes, and that becomes permanent. How horrible.

A new medical study quantifies this. "This study suggests that even light to moderate recreational marijuana use can cause changes in brain anatomy," said Carl Lupica, PhD, at the National Institute on Drug Abuse. "These observations are particularly interesting because previous studies have focused primarily on the brains of heavy marijuana smokers, and have largely ignored the brains of casual users."

The team of scientists compared the size, shape, and density of the nucleus accumbens and the amygdala — a brain region that plays a central role in emotion — in 20 marijuana users and 20 non-users. Each marijuana user was asked to estimate their drug consumption over a three-month period, including the number of days they smoked and the amount of the drug consumed each day. The scientists found that the more the marijuana users reported consuming, the greater the abnormalities in the nucleus accumbens and amygdala. The shape and density of both of these regions also differed between marijuana users and non-users."

Marijuana can also cause an early onset of schizophrenia in young men, who are genetically pre-disposed to "and normally you would have gotten it at 25, Dr. Neinebar explains, "you will more likely get your first psychotic break at 13 … which is a problem because the longer you have it the more debilitating it is …The problem is that schizophrenics and people who are pre-disposed to it … are really drawn to drug abuse."

A Plant is not a Criminal

"I have seizures and don't have epilepsy. Marijuana helps ease these seizures. When the restrictive medical marijuana law is put into effect, I won't be able to afford what they will be trying to sell to me. It's all disappointing. I am sick of Big Pharma meds…" –Anonymous interview

Marijuana is a medicine. Marijuana or *peje* (a nice Lakota word for grass) does not solve all problems. It does not cure everything, make you prettier or smarter. It is a plant and it is a medicine. As much as our community deals with tobacco abuse, tobacco as a medicine, or peyote, as a medicine, everyone agrees that need to restore our relationship to our plant relatives in a respectful manner. Indigenous peoples know plants have spirit and power, and need to be addressed with reverence. Abuse is always not going to work out well.

There's clear evidence of the benefits of marijuana in the treatment and pain relief of glaucoma, fibro myalgia, epilepsy, rheumatoid arthritis, seizures, PTSD (and remember we have the highest number of living veterans of any community) and a host of other medical conditions.

My friend Kevin Shore suffers from Gulf War Syndrome, and he is struggling with a host of major medical conditions. "Actually they call it rheumatoid variant disease at the VA, because—like in Vietnam—they don't want to call it an Agent Orange syndrome. They tried putting me on morphine, oxycodone, all of that didn't work well. I found that cannabis was the least harmful to my body as the side effects go."

Because Kevin is being treated by the Veterans Administration, he cannot smoke marijuana, or take it in any form. So the VA provides him with a synthetic form of marijuana. "I'm hoping to have a good case, because a federally recognized doctor has prescribed synthetic THC." While medical studies indicate that marijuana is helpful in many cases, it is clearly not a panacea for all illnesses.

Exploiting the Plant

Some of the heaviest cultural criticism if the plant is legally grown would be the exploitation of the plant. For instance, today, probably about 90% of the marijuana available in commercial or black markets is grown with chemicals, much of it indoors, pushing the plants to their capacity. It's sort of like a feedlot of industrial marijuana farming. I traveled to Denver this past year, and did some window shopping at facilities.

At one organic marijuana retailer I asked what they used. The salesman didn't know, and there was, in my limited review, little interest in that discussion. The environmental impact of larger cultivation is comparable to other industrial agriculture, adding energy use of grow houses. Washington and Oregon, for instance, are projecting a surge in power use, simply from grow houses. Slow-grow, outdoors and organic is pretty much the preference of the connoisseurs, and illustrates the conflicting relationship with the plant: commercial, medicinal, cultivated, home use, etc.

A Regulatory Scheme in Oregon

What is clear is that regulation is essential. Either we as tribes keep the same historic criminal standards for marijuana and hemp, or we change them. In either case, we still regulate.

Oregon's recently passed law explains that state's reasons for legalization and offers an example:

(a) To eliminate the problems caused by the prohibition and uncontrolled manufacture, delivery, and possession of marijuana within this state;

(b) To protect the safety, welfare, health, and peace of the people of this state by prioritizing the state's limited law enforcement resources in the most effective, consistent, and rational way;

(c) To permit persons licensed, controlled, regulated, and taxed by this state to legally manufacture and sell marijuana to persons 21 years of age and older, subject to the provisions of this Act;

(d) To ensure that the State Department of Agriculture issues industrial hemp licenses and agricultural hemp seed production permits in accordance with existing state law; and

(e) To establish a comprehensive regulatory framework concerning marijuana under existing state law.

So, to make it happen, Oregon's Control, Regulation, and Taxation of Marijuana and Industrial Hemp Act removes penalties for adults 21 and older who possess, use, and grow a limited amount of marijuana

Once the law takes effect, adults 21 and older can possess up to eight ounces of marijuana and grow no more than four marijuana plants in their households. Those amounts are total limits for the household. Each adult can possess up to an ounce in public. Individuals 21 and older may also gift — but not sell – up to an ounce of marijuana, 16 ounces of marijuana products in solid form, or 72 ounces of marijuana products in liquid form to other adults. The purchase limit will be one ounce, or the amount set by the liquor commission, whichever is lower.

Four types of marijuana businesses will be allowed and regulated by the Oregon Liquor Control Commission: "Marijuana producers" will cultivate marijuana for wholesale; "Marijuana processors" will produce marijuana extracts and products; "Marijuana wholesalers" may purchase marijuana and marijuana products to sell to marijuana retailers and other non-consumers; Lastly, "marijuana retailers" are allowed to sell marijuana and related items to individuals 21 and older.

Talking about it is key. Careful regulation, honesty, and courage may be an answer.

A HARD RAIN IS GONNA FALL: GMOS, ORGANICS AND OUR HARVESTS

"When it rains in Chicago it rains Atrazine, when it rains in Washington DC it rains Atrazine...."

People visit me. Anthony Suau, a journalist who spent twenty years working for *Time* magazine and is working on a new film called *Organic Rising,* profiling the why and how of American organic farmers and the growth of the industry. He came to interview me about the ancient corn varieties that we grow, like our Bear Island Flint, a hominy corn with twice the protein and half the calories of sweet corn and rocking B vitamin levels, among other cool things.

So, it turns out that he was more interesting than me. Not surprising. Three revelations:

One: The Chinese military no longer serves genetically modified foods to military personnel.

Two: Organic farmers in Illinois produced yields equal to industrial farmers in this years' corn harvest, around 220 bushels per acre, with 45% less energy use.

Three: Organic farmers receive four times as much for their crops than conventional farmers.

1) On feeding China's military personnel: China's military is the world's largest, with nearly 2.3 million in uniform. In 2014, China announced there will be no more genetically engineered foods served to their troops. In 2013, China began rejecting GMO corn shipments; now the concern has moved to soybeans, a big North Dakota crop.

According to Mi Zhen-yu, a former vice president of the China Academy of Military Science, China imported more than 63 million tons of GMO soybeans from the U.S. and other countries in 2012.

"The glyphosate residue contained in GMO soybean food oil [and GM soybean protein powder processed from GMO soybean cake, a by-product of GM soybean food oil] eaten three meals a day, continuously penetrates the bodies of most Chinese, including children at kindergarten, primary school and middle school, university students and teachers, staff members and soldiers of the Chinese army, government staff members and other consumers," Zhen-yu wrote in an April paper titled, *We Must Face the Harm Caused by Imported GM Soybeans to 1.3 Billion Chinese People*. Glyphosate is the active chemical in Round Up. China's not having it.

2) On GMO vs organic crop yields: Anthony Suau explains "Harvesting is now underway and reporting record GMO corn yields. Illinois GMO farmer Tom O'Connor is bringing in a record 200 to 220 bushels an acre. That said, the Schock organic farm in Yorktown, Illinois is also bringing in 200 to 220 bushels an acre. Identical yields are decimating the notion that the world needs GMOs and their related pesticides to feed the world."

This is a really interesting thought, because a lot of the media and public relations around GMO crops is based on a higher yield. It is now possible to produce the same yield organically, and—it turns out—with 45% less energy and a much smaller carbon footprint, which makes a lot of sense in a time of climate change.

3) On GMO vs organic crop prices: Suau tells me that he has just interviewed farmers in Illinois who reported that "GMO corn is selling for $2.94 a bushel...In comparison organic corn feed is now selling from $10.50 to $14 a bushel (in some areas $18 a bushel). The increase in prices appears to be coming from the U.S.' demand for organic dairy products: organic milk and eggs," Suau explains. Seed distributors have also seen a massive switch this year from GMO to conventional seeds.

So it's a time of putting harvests to bed, and I am hoping a time for thinking about what we are doing in the future. Monsanto (which sells 90% of the world's GMO seeds) has been busy selling us glyphosate-laden Round Up. Some 800 million pounds of it were put in our soil, water and crops this year, with diminishing results for weed reduction and increasing persistent organic pollutants in our water supply and probably in our rain.

In turn, Atrazine, commonly used on potatoes and other crops in the North Country is brought to us by Syngenta. I find it interesting that it is still being used in the US, although in October of 2003, it was banned in the European Union because of ubiquitous and unpreventable water contamination.

And, that water contamination is not just in the ground water. It turns out it is in the rain. Atrizine also evaporates into the air, and in a process called "volatilization drift", it settles back into waterways.

USDA scientists found Atrazine residues in 87.9% of the drinking water tested in 2012.

So here I am wondering what we're doing. China and Europe are not liking the GMOs, atrazine and glyphosate, and farmers are getting less for their crops sold using those chemicals and GMO seeds.

I think I'm going to stick to my heritage corn and bean crops. They worked pretty well for my ancestors, and I think they will pan out for my descendants. And, I like visitors.

EAT, PRAY, FARM

I watch a man. He is plowing a field with an ox. Barefoot, tilling soil. Fertile soil. An egret walks behind him, then more. It is a peaceful place: quiet, rich soil, no noise just the breathing of the man, the ox, the creak of some equipment, and the birds. I watch in wonder. I have come to learn, and what I learn is eat, pray, farm. I am not Julia Roberts, but I have come to India to understand a movement to keep the seeds, to keep the egret, and to protect the farmer.

There are a lot of them. There are 800 million farmers. Almost 70% of the people farm in the country. And, they eat well. It is something to consider and to learn from.

The place I find myself is Navdanya, founded in 1984 by farmers of India, including Physicist Vandana Shiva who saw the need to protect the seeds- not only to eat, but also because Indian agriculture was entering a crisis as farmers were forced into industrial agriculture. The crisis has been a result of federal and international agriculture policies pushing small farmers to grow crops with chemicals. The farmers entered a cycle of debt, loss of soil fertility, increased poisoning of their lands, and ultimately, many have committed suicide. According to a recent *Al Jazeera* article, the last 20 years nearly 300,000 farmers have ended their lives by ingesting pesticides or by hanging themselves. That is enough. It is time for peace with the land and peace with the farmers.

Navdanya means "nine crops" that represent India's collective source of food security. Navdanya in thirty years has established 54 community seed banks across the country, and trained approximately 500,000 farmers in sustainable agriculture and "food sovereignty" over the past two decades, and helped establish a large fair trade organic network in India. Perhaps I have come here to find out how to return to Indigenous agriculture, or how the return occurs in a large scale. We need to do that at home. Navdanya is an inspirational model. Their operation is simple and elegant, no million dollar seed bank- metal and glass containers. The seeds, representing ideas and actual seeds are nurtured and held in a number of communities. That is security. The top soil, the foundation of life, is healthy, that is the future.

This is a moment in Indigenous agriculture in North America. There is a resurgence, a recovery of Indigenous farming, native harvesting, food security, sovereignty, producers and chefs. Seed savers like Rowen White, Carolyn Chartrand and the Minneapolis based Dream of Wild Health are part of a strong movement to restore seeds, bring them out of hiding, and bring them back to the land and people. There is a resurgence in tribal food work- the Grand Ronde Food Sovereignty Project, Hopi Permaculture Project, Oneida Nation Farms, White Earth Land Recovery Project, and a growing number of Native farmers, from Clayton Brascoupe with the Traditional Native American Farmers Association, to Aubrey Skye on the Standing Rock Reservation, gardening for his family and community. Harvesters are working together- the fishers of the north, the wild ricers of Minnesota, and the Ojibwe Maple Syrup Producers Cooperative. There is a growing movement on tribal food policy- led by organizations like the Native Food Sovereignty Alliance, and on the ground producers, and production facilities like those at the Taos Community Economic Development Commission. Stories are being told and shared, and international work is underway- like many of us who have come to the Slow Food Movement, a movement in over 132 countries for food which is fair, clean and just. The seeds, the foods are coming home, or maybe we are just re-establishing our relationship with them again.

Why is this moment important? Because we have lost a great deal, and we will not be able to feed ourselves if we do not find it, find the seeds, take care of the land and water the food comes from, and in the process, find ourselves.

This moment is also important because US policy issues like that of the Keepseagle v. Vilsack lawsuit come to light. Decades of depriving Native farmers of access to the resources to capitalize their production forced many off the land, resulting in many non Indians having cheap access to tribal lands. People have died waiting for settlements, and still we see that the lawsuit must crawl through a federal process in the US, with potentially $380 million left over from individual allocations to put to Indigenous agriculture. The Keepseagle Lawsuit is known as the Native Farmers v. USDA, followed a similar lawsuit by the Black Farmers, against the USDA, which had systematically denied loans to Black, Native, Mexican, and Hispanic farmers. That is a long story, only part of which will be told here. I suggest it is possible that in not being entirely sucked into the industrial agriculture system, we may have a chance to restore our own food security and dignity, with good intent. Now would be the time.

The State of Native Agriculture

The US Agricultural census reports 60,000 Native farmers today. These are farmers supporting their families in livestock, grains, and food production — in structures ranging from the massive Navajo Agricultural Product Industry, Gila River Enterprises, Tanka Bars, to

Tohono O'odham Community Action, the White Earth Land Recovery Project, to a farmer. This is food production at a scale which feeds people, and nations, in many ways, some sustainable- in the practice of nurturing soil, water and people, and some in a corporate model. There would be more, but the checker-boarding of tribal lands, and the fact that most tribal agricultural lands are in fact leased to non Native interests, causes us a problem in long term food security.

Add to that ecological destruction, catastrophes like the EPA-caused massive mine tailings spill (three million gallons of mine slurry waste, impacting water supplies for Navajo farming families). Navajo Nation President Russel Begaye stated that "Navajo harvest was diminished by as much as two-thirds compared to 2014." And, Navajo officials told reporters that roughly 1,000 farmers on the reservation suffered losses. This would be on top of the massive Navajo Livestock reduction programs, which diminished Diné herds by two thirds between 1936 and 1952, and continuing programs today. At this point with our populations increasing, we should be increasing our food security, not diminishing it. After all, my friend Sugar Bear Smith explained to me once, "You cannot talk about being sovereign if you can't feed yourself." In short, it is clear that our food systems have been colonized, deconstructed, and our wealth taken by others. Now is the time to decolonize our food systems.

Keepseagle

When I began to write this story, two years ago I thought about the seriousness of the discrimination against Native farmers in the US- the lack of access to financial resources to grow crops, equipment, loans. The Keepseagle basic settlement is relatively simple: The government will provide $680 million in compensation to settle a class-action lawsuit by Native American farmers against the U.S. Department of Agriculture. George and Marilyn Keepseagle, lead plaintiffs, were unfairly denied operating loans and had to sell portions of their sprawling farm on the Standing Rock Reservation in North Dakota. Largely, according to the settlement, because they were Native. In the meantime, the same USDA would give loans to non Native farmers who would lease and often come to own Indian land. "This is a great day for us, not only for us but our people," Marilyn Keepseagle told reporters at *Indian Country Today*. "It's been a long time brewing and finally today it came to a positive end. And I'm happy about that."

"Today's settlement can never undo wrongs that Native Americans may have experienced in past decades, but combined with the actions we at USDA are taking to address such wrongs, the settlement will provide some measure of relief to those alleging discrimination," Secretary of Agriculture Vilsack said in his statement. Of the settlement, almost half remains still un-allocated, and as that process moves ahead.

This essay is, in fact about how our agriculture might move forward with capitalization like that available through the USDA settlement. We will need money to undo the loss. And we will need the courage an vision to restore ourselves.

I grieve the justice and equity denied And, then consider that, in retrospect, this may have been a favor. Why? Because we are, by and large not in the industrial agriculture world. We are not, by and large beneficiaries of Monsanto, Syngenta and Dupont, and because of that, we are less entrenched, have compromised ourselves less and have a chance, to restore that which is most valuable to us as cultures, as peoples, including our foods. And to protect our ecosystems and biodiversity- because it turns out that is where food security is found.

What Have We Missed?

There is a war on the land I drive from my home on a quiet lake, in the midst of my reservation, White Earth. It is such named for the white clay found here, and came also to be known for our soil, soil left by the glacial retreat, a rich black soil, which is part of the very corporate agriculturally productive Red River Valley.

Our people fed ourselves and the settlers well. As Mary Winyerd would write in her book, *North Country*, "Dakota and Ojibwe women were deep into commercial enterprise ... They peddled sugar, wild rice, pumpkins, corn, squash and other agricultural products to the traders and the military. With virtually no food produced for the market by whites in Minnesota country in the 1840s, and fresh produce in high demand, Native women entrepreneurs could set premium price on their small surplus harvests ..."

Like many Indigenous peoples, our wealth was the source of our poverty; our lands stolen through the allotment era, the prairies, cut, plowed into farm land. That was then, a hundred and twenty years ago- a people, my people made into refugees as our great lands were taken.

Today, as I drive to the south or to the west, I see equipment that I cannot identify. I am told the giant insect-looking machinery is chisel plows or huge chemical sprayers. The giant equipment is cultivators, combines. They are as big as a house, and they are upon the land. They move down the quiet rural roads. And then they take over the road, and take over the field. They have done much damage.

An old farmer, my neighbor shakes his head at me, when I ask him about the plan for the future of agriculture on the Ponsford Prairie, near my house. He acts as if I am not intelligent enough to know how to farm. *That is the lot of being a tribal person on your own reservation; a white farmer will act as if he knows better.* The fact is this is not true. They have in fact, led us to a place where our ability to feed the future generations is threatened.

The Threat

Let us begin with Minnesota. *Some 90% of the wetlands have been drained.* The western third of Minnesota, including the 1855 treaty territory was once covered with wetlands. Today, even though Minnesota is spending millions annually, the state is still losing more than it restores. The Minnesota Pollution Control Commission released a daunting report noting that a fourth of southern Minnesota's lakes and rivers are too tainted to use as drinking water. The Minnesota Pollution Control Agency (MPCA) reported overall, 41 percent of Minnesota's streams and lakes have excessive nitrogen, all of them in the state's southern and central regions. The nutrient, which is used as fertilizer in agriculture and comes from wastewater treatment plants, can be toxic to fish and other forms of aquatic life.

That nitrogen is a primary cause of the vast oxygen-depleted area in the Gulf of Mexico known as the Dead Zone. That Dead Zone is about a thousand square miles, of destroyed ocean. And, that, of course, is only the tip of the iceberg or a small part of the plume nationally and internationally. Minnesota's industrial agriculture caused some 70% of the destruction of water quality in Minnesota lakes, and the soybean and corn mono-cropping of the state is a microcosm of national and international problems with industrialized agriculture.

Soil not Oil

That's the name of my colleague Vandana Shiva's book which discusses the intersection between a fossil fuels economy, and the destruction of soil. It turns out that soil is what you need to live: good, healthy soil. The more things which end with "cide" we put on them-pesticides, fungicides, herbicides, insecticides (all fossil fuels based), combined with the more nitrogen-based fertilizers which are added to the soil, the worse things get. After all, if it says "cide" one can only equate it with homicide, suicide, or genocide. In short, a cautious person would not want to have the root word "cide" associated with something we eat. Without delving into the ecological, human health and natural world impacts of "cide" on our world, let us say that systemically, the entire system of industrial agriculture is flawed, and it is time to move on.

Industrialized agriculture is not only toxic, it is unsustainable. The fossil fuel use of agriculture from seed to table results in up to one quarter of all carbon dioxide emissions which are causing global warming. It is said that – in reverse – if we were to move our world to an organic agricultural system or systems we would sequester one quarter of the carbon. That is pretty much what we need to do in this climate-challenged era.

Changing the Pig

It is common sense that you cannot fix a problem with the same mindset which created it, and that's what industrial agriculture attempts to do. It will not work. Or perhaps better said by Trevor Russel, Watershed Program Director for the Friends of the Mississippi, "Current plans to attack the problem by persuading farmers to adopt expensive and not very effective methods... are just lipstick on a pig... At some point we have to change the pig."

I live in what is called Minnesota. It is here, that Norman Borlaug, known as the "Father of the Green Revolution" made his plans and his work. The University of Minnesota has a Borlaug Hall, and is well underwritten by industrial giants, whether Cargill or Monsanto. This way of thinking and this war on the land, is based on the practice of growing single crops intensively on a very large-scale monoculture.

That is what the USDA wanted us to do as Native people, and it has not worked out, either for the land, or for us. Corn, wheat, soybeans, cotton and rice are all commonly grown this way in the United States. It is the exact opposite of biodiversity and agrobiodiversity in Indigenous farming. It is also absolutely counter to everything that we know is true as Indigenous people. *You cannot treat a plant like a machine. It is a living being, and you cannot disrespect the animals, whether they have wings, fins, roots or paws.* You cannot create the conditions where there are more antibiotics served and injected into healthy animals than given to sick humans in a country. It will, frankly, not work out over the long term for any of us.

In terms of related problems, or a mindset which come up with false solutions: Genetically Engineered crops pose spiritual as well as health and ecological problems for our people. Dana Eldridge, Diné scholar, has been analyzing food systems for the Navajo Nation, explains. GMOs, she says, threaten both the ownership of Native seeds and the spiritual aspects of food. "Corn is very sacred to us—it's our most sacred plant. We pray with corn pollen--in our Creation story we're made of corn—so what does it mean that this plant has been turned into something that actively harms people?"

In response, to this and many other problems of GMOs, Mexico banned GMO corn entirely as of 2013, with a fall of 2015 court decision, despite 100 challenges by transnational agribusinesses like Monsanto, reaffirmed the ban. Opponents of growing genetically modified corn in Mexico, the country known for over 30 varieties of non-GM maize, have prevailed. Elsewhere, in 2014 the island of Kauai passed an ordinance mandating a full disclosure of all chemicals being used on the island by major agribusiness. That is just the tip of the iceberg

Indigenous Foods, Farmers, and the World

"Connected to the land is connected to the past." —Phrang Roy, Indigenous Terra Madre

"Biodiversity, regenerative agriculture, community ownership and in-digenous seeds- lose these and you lose your health." —Toby Hodges, IFAD, at Terra Madre, Shillong India Fall 2015.

"Don't clear crop a whole piece. We have to leave some for the plants and animals." —Sean Sherman, the Sioux Chef

I have once again, returned to India, it is 2015. The setting is Megha-laya, perhaps one of the most ecologically diverse and culturally diverse places in the planet. The gathering is the second Indigenous Terra Madre, an international gathering to talk of food, and our future. Tremendous speakers come to the gathering, up to 1600 people from farming, harvesting and Indigenous communities world wide. I am inspired, to say the least, but I am more than that. I am grateful for the work ahead.

Indigenous agriculture is really the only future of agriculture; that is, agro-biodiversity, a multitude of crops adapted for the land, not adapting the land for industrial crops. That agriculture, as explained by Toby Hodges, must be connected to community land and seed ownership and biodiversity. It is, in other words, not just the seeds, but the ecosystems and the people.

There are several reasons for this: First, Indigenous peoples continue to live in a restorative and sustainable food system, when we con-trol our lands, and our seeds. Second, Indigenous food producers and farmers are already adapting crops in the face of climate change through the intelligence of seed selection and cropping systems which have been passed down through the millennia. Third, Indigenous farmers are already producing up to 70% of the food eaten in commu-nities, while industrialized agriculture, with it's upwards of $13 trillion in investments (according to Pat Mooney of the ETC), cannot actually feed the world; and Fourth, our food is cool. Let me explain more:

Cool Foods

Pat Mooney, a scholar from Canadian based ETC group (Mooney won the international Right Livelihood Award from the Swedish Parliament in 1987) tells the Terra Madre gathering, that "Indigenous people work with 7000 crops and one million varieties, while the majority of industrial agriculture has whittled this down to 135 major crops and 103,000 varieties." Mooney explains: "My generation is the first generation in the world that has lost more knowledge than it has gained." Why is this important? Because plants are magical beings simply stated, with complex nutrients, medicinal values, cultural and spiritual connections, and they feed the soil and the world.

"Corn beans, squash and tobacco grew from the body of Sky woman, the daughter of the mother of the Creator of the world," Teena Delormier tells the gathering. She is Mohawk, and a professor at the University of Hawaii in Manoa. She adds, "Women could veto war by withholding food. When settlers came to North America we were people with food security."

The very foods we grow or harvest have very special powers to combine. As Harriet Kuhnlein an internationally recognized nutritionist, from McGill University explains." Like corn, beans and squash, some are nitrogen-hungry and some are nitrogen-producing: that is the relationship between corn and beans." Make a meal and all is balanced. "Singularly tortillas are at 62 on the glycemic index, and beans are at 22," Kuhnlein explains. Put together into a meal, they are at 32. The magic of foods is a real medicine. "There are over 300 natural medicines in plants to reduce blood sugar," Dr. Daphne Miller from San Francisco State explains to the Terra Madre conference.

Harriet Kuehnein's study in northeast India finds that in areas where there is significant reserves of biodiversity there are lesser levels of anemia. Similarly measurements for malnutrition, micro nutrient deficiencies, and dietary inadequacies, as well as hypertension are much lower where people live with their indigenous foods. In one area she found that tribal people used over 327 foods of which 138 were cultivated and 185 were wild, including 83 types of vegetables and fruits and 24 mushrooms, and an amazing soup of frogs which was served as a post partum comfort food, with an extremely high vitamin content. All of this is, it seems, better than vitamin drinks.

Looking at rainfall and climate change in the Sahel, Toby Hodges found that tribal people had adapted their crops to continue their harvests. As the major corporations like Monsanto, and Syngenta talk about climate change adapting varieties they are introducing; the fact is that tribal people have been adapting their varieties for the last twenty years. In another ecosystem, he notes, "One village had 165 rice varieties growing and ten taro varieties" In a time of confusion in climate, those varieties will provide some food security. In addition to that, each variety often has distinct nutritional attributes. "Agrobiodiversity has everything to do with health, food security and economic security for people. How land is being used affects biodiversity and challenges a communities ability to keep diversity," Hodges explains. In turn, industrialized agriculture is sucking up billions of dollars to create "climate smart varieties." Pat Mooney explains that corporations like Syngenta and Monsanto are working on this so-called climate smart agriculture. "136 million is the average cost for climate smart seeds per species."

A rhetorical question might be asked: What if we used that for supporting indigenous and sustainable agriculture?

Omaa Akiing: On our Land

"Don't talk about profits , talk about gifts." —Hassan Roba, Christensen Fund Program Officer, Ethiopia

There are people who connect us and their numbers are growing. Carolyn Chartrand is a Métis woman who, has been looking for the heritage seeds of her people. It is believed that in the 1800s, the Métis grew some 120 distinct seed varieties in the Red River area of Canada. Of those, Caroline says, "We ended up finding about 20 so far."

In Canada, three-quarters of all the crop varieties that existed before the 20th century are extinct. And, of the remaining quarter, only 10 percent are available commercially from Canadian seed companies (the remainder are held by gardeners and families). Over 64 percent of the commercially held seeds are offered by only one company; if those varieties are dropped, the seeds may be lost.

That's the reason Caroline is a leader in the Métis Heritage society and Indigenous seed restoration in Canada.

A recent article by a prominent Canadian writer suggested that agriculture in Canada began with the arrival of Europeans. Caroline had to ask her, "What about all that agriculture before then?" Caroline is a committed grower in the effort to recover northern Ojibwe corn varieties that once grew 100 miles north of Winnipeg—the northernmost known corn crop in the world. That's some adaptable corn.

Maybe my favorite story is the squash: *gete okosomin,* is what I call it, or the really cool old squash. First given to me by Luis Salas, and then by Frank Alegria from the Menominee reservation in Wisconsin, I was told that it had been found in an archaeological dig, near Green Bay, Wisconsin. Cached away in a clay ball, the squash seeds were carbon-dated 800 years old. I grew the squash, then in enthusiasm have passed the squash on to others. Now, each year, I am sent pictures of the squash. Two and a half feet long or so, the size of a large zucchini, it is orange in color with a set of stripes on it. We feast with the squash now at many of our gatherings, and it flourishes. The resilience of seeds is a miracle; reborn in this generation in the hands of loving farmers. I look at the pictures people send me, lovingly, like a gramma admiring her progeny.

"Those seeds are the old ways. They gave our ancestors life for all those years," said Frank Alegria, Sr. The son of migrant farm workers, Frank has been gardening since he could walk and farming on the Menominee reservation in Wisconsin since he was sixteen. Now an elder, he continues to grow native varieties, including *gete okosomin.*

Deb Echohawk tells the story of the sacred corn seeds of the Pawnee. By combining efforts with the descendants of settlers who live in the traditional Pawnee homelands in Nebraska, the Pawnee are recovering varieties thought to be lost forever. Deb and others have been formally recognized as Keepers of the Seeds.

Likewise, the White Earth Land Recovery Project has created a seed library, working with local growers to increase the varieties of all vegetables grown on the reservation, and particularly focused on corn varieties, including the Bear Island Flint (never a crop failure), Manitoba White flint, and others which have short growing seasons, are short of stalk and are frost, drought and wind resistant. They have had some success. Ronnie Chilton who farmed for the project for several years, tells me that even the deer prefer the Indigenous varieties to the field corn of the industrial famers. "I've been seeing deer strut past a field of GMO corn to feast on our corn."

Indigenous farming also restores social relations in our communities. At the Shillong Terra Madre conference, the role of women in seed keeping is discussed. "Women are the best at selecting the seeds. They not only know how they grow, but they also know how they cook." That is a far cry from an industrial lab at Monsanto or Syngenta. Eldridge also points out in an article in *Indian Country Today*, that growing food in a community helps to heal from the historic trauma." What I've learned during this food research is you can't produce food by yourself. You need people, you need family, you need community and relationships, so a lot of it is about rebuilding community and reconnecting with the land and I think that's a very important healing process for our people."

"One of the things that I think Native people recognize and have passed down culturally is that you need to have human beings within food production ecosystems for all of those reasons—safety, quality, a relationship with your food. The principles of safe food are indigenous and inherent in Native communities," Pati Martinson of the Taos County Community Development Corporation, a local food hub, tells the reporter from *Indian Country Today*.

In the big picture, P.V. Satheesh, founding member of the Deccan Development Society, describes a network of 5,000 small-scale women farmers in India. Those women are producing food for many, beyond their own households. "Self-sufficiency…starts at the farming house-hold. Once that household becomes self-sufficient, it starts spreading to the community, local area and then the larger, regional area." So, this is to say that restoration of food economics strengthens communities.

Patti Martinson and Terri Bad Hand have been leaders in establishing the Native American Food Sovereignty Alliance. That Alliance, working with a number of local organizations and a sixteen member founding board, hopes to promote Indigenous food policy at a national level. This, combined with work with Slow Food to form a Turtle Island Slow Food Nation, or a North American consortium of producers, will help support the growing and resilient movement of Indigenous agriculture.

This year, I held some rice in my hand from Onamia Lake in Minnesota. The seed had been dormant for 17 years, and like our *gete okosomin,* seeds dormant for centuries, can return and flourish. This year, I planted my corn field with a horse, tilled in fish fertilizer from the lakes, and had a bountiful harvest. Unlike my counterpart in India, I cannot use an ox. The seeds I plant, like other old seeds, flourish in a pre-industrial and a post-industrial world. Those seeds, our communities and our prayers, I believe, are not only the future of our food, but the future of food for all in this world. *Mi'iw.*

Tributes and Gratitude

TO THOSE WHO HAVE JOINED THE ANCESTORS

During the time that many of these stories were written, I lost many people whom I was close to. My father, my sister and my husband passed to the Spirit World. I send them greetings there. And, here are some of the stories of others who passed during this time. May they smile down upon us and give us guidance.

Randy Kapashesit with Waseyabin and Ajuawak Kapashesit.
Photo by John Ratzloff.

RANDY KAPASHESIT: A GREAT CHIEF PASSES ON

"While his passing is a shock and tremendous loss for the people of MoCreebec and the leadership circles he shared, Chief Kapashesit's strong vision and dedicated efforts will carry on through the younger generations he helped lead."

—National Chief Shawn A-in-chut Atleo
of the Assembly of First Nations

When Chief Randy Kapashesit returned this time to his remote community in northern Ontario, the earth shook. Tremors of 4.4 magnitude shook the region, where earthquakes are very rare, and Randy came home for the last time.

Chief Kapashesit died unexpectedly on April 25 in Minneapolis, leaving a loving companion, Donna Ashamock; two biological children, Waseyabin LaDuke Kapashesit and Ajuawak Kapashesit, both residents of the White Earth reservation of Minnesota; and a grandson, Giiwedin Buckanaga.

He also left a community of Cree in northern Ontario, which he had led for some 25 years.

MoCreebec Chairman Allan Jolly wrote: "It wasn't long after joining MoCreebec that his peers/colleagues noticed his intelligence, his ability to express and articulate ideas, his skill to understand aboriginal issues of the day and to formulate strategies in how best to approach in dealing with those issues especially as it concerned MoCreebec."

"(Chief) Kapashesit was instrumental in drafting the constitution that would form the basis of how MoCreebec Council of the Cree Nation would operate and function as a political organization, which was based on the cultural history, traditions, values and beliefs as central in the political, social and economic life of the MoCreebec people.

"(Chief) Kapashesit is remembered as a tireless supporter of Aboriginal rights and the environment, as well as a promoter of indigenous economic sustainability. He was also chosen as the representative for the United Nations North American Indigenous Caucus, serving on the planning committee for the United Nations 2014 World Conference on Indigenous Peoples."

Other First Nations leaders also felt the loss of Randy Kapashesit's passing, as posted on the MoCreeBec Nation website:

Mushkegowuk Grand Chief Stan Louttit: "The passing of Chief Randy Kapashesit is a huge loss to the MoCreebec Nation and also for the Aboriginal people in North America…This huge sudden loss in our lives is being felt throughout the Mushkegowuk Nation."

NAN Grand Chief Stan Beardy: "It is a great loss to the community and for the First Nations at large…He was a well-respected and dedicated leader who accomplished a lot for his community particularly in environmental and eco-tourism sectors. He has definitely left a legacy for many of us to follow."

The MoCreebec Council of the Cree Nation exemplifies in many ways the depth of challenges First Nations face. The Cree Nation had lived well for many generations on the shores of James Bay, adapting with the coming of the Hudson Bay Company; Anglican, Catholic and a multitude of later-arriving churches; the founding of Canada itself; freighter canoes and snowmobiles.

Nothing in their long history has so impacted the MoCreebec community, perhaps, however, as the construction of the vast Hydro-Quebec James Bay project dams of the1970s, and well into this millennium. Hydro-Quebec is a government-owned utility that builds and operates dams; James Bay is one of the largest hydroelectric projects in the world.

The dams put under water the lifestyle of the *Eeyou*, the Cree of eastern James Bay, drowning trap lines, places where medicines were gathered, where ancestors were buried, and a history of a People and a Place.

The dams also hailed the advent of a new politic in Canada, where new "treaties" were negotiated over resources and over the future. The infusion of hundreds of millions of dollars of compensation transformed Cree communities, but also caused divisions between the People, and between the People and the Land.

The MoCreebec people were excluded from consultation under the James Bay Northern Quebec Agreement (1974), despite their origins in the northern territory.

Their residence in Ontario—largely a result of unwilling displacements caused by fur trading posts and forced immersions in residential schools—was used against them in determining who would have a voice in the negotiations. This meant that the MoCreebec Cree would not receive benefits although their trap lines and way of life had also been largely destroyed.

It was not only that the financial benefits were denied to the MoCreebec people, but also their ability to oppose new mines and dams in the region (or—in effect—to be self-determining in their own ancestral Cree territory) was undermined.

Most of this generation of MoCreebec was born in what was called "Tent City," essentially a northern refugee camp in the island village of Moose Factory.

MoCreebec formed as an organization in the 1980s to address basic human rights of the community, and became a political government of the Cree, using traditional governance systems.

MoCreebec people who speak the "y" dialect of Cree have always been in this part of the world, generations even before the start of the organization.

Brenda Small, sister of Randy, spoke in the eulogy of how Crees in both the west and east coasts of James Bay have traveled and lived together long before border and assimilation policies became entrenched.

These were forefront issues that impacted the lives of MoCreebec people, and Kapashesit was the chief since 1988. MoCreebec took a route which was different than many other First Nations in Canada or the US: The MoCreebec affirmed their own self-determination through their governance and practice, not through recognition under Canada's Indian Act.

Randy understood that MoCreebec's work was part of the recovery work of the larger Cree Nation. MoCreebec's website discusses their Constitution and political structures of the community, shaped by a deep reverence for Cree culture:

"Recognizing the supremacy and will of the Creator, the people who have chosen the name MoCreebec renew the social contract of Sharing, Kindness, Strength and Honesty, which was the basis for the first meeting of Aboriginal and European peoples...We reaffirm the aboriginal rights guaranteed by the Canadian Constitution, asserting that these rights also embody a sense of community, equality, a need for independence and self reliance."

MoCreebec's constitution reaffirms traditional governance, and has been a very successful example of self determination in practice.

Over twenty five years, MoCreebec has created a political entity to represent the interests of the Cree people of the community, outside of the "box" offered by the Indian Act of Canada, somewhat akin to federally recognized tribal governments in the US.

For example: extended family governance systems, representational governance and self-determination are all key principles of the MoCreebec community. Through this work, the government of MoCreebec has succeeded in housing tribal members, creating economic development opportunities, and growing from a $30,000 budget in 1986 to a $6 million budget in 2012.

Chief Randy Kapashesit was honored by his community, and by national and international dignitaries in a packed school auditorium in the community of Moose Factory.

Kapashesit was remembered for "how he loved his people." Angus Toulouse, representing the political communities of 132 First Nations in Ontario, spoke about how Randy "reminded us of our relationship to the environment. We weren't going to get more land, nor any new water...."

Grand Chief Louttit of Mushkegowuk Council commented, "You couldn't take the puck away from him on the ice, and you could never take a puck away from him at the table. Randy never gave in." His international work at the United Nations was recognized by a number of national and international organizations.

Randy's memorial service included both traditional Native and Anglican as Kapashesit was the "Chief of All the People." The service also included readings from the Dalai Lama and Malcolm X.

When a great leader passes on, families mourn, communities mourn, and the Creator has brought home someone who made a difference in the lives of a People. On the morning of May 4, Chief Randy Kapashesit was laid to rest in the cemetery on his island.

A snow had fallen in the night, unusual for the region at this time of year, but, perhaps the favorite weather of the Cree chief.

Chief Randy Kapashesit is also survived by his sister Brenda Small and her husband Gerald Rayner (Thunder Bay, Ontario); his father, James Small; mother of his children, Winona LaDuke (White Earth); adopted children Ashley and John Martin, and Winona's son Gwekaanimad Gasco, and many cousins and relatives in the northern Cree communities of Canada.

FOR PETER MATTHIESSON

"For all those who honor and defend those people who still seek in the wisdom of the Indian way…"

—Peter Matthiesson,
from the dedication of *In the Spirit of Crazy Horse*

He was a writer among writers up to the last. Peter Matthiesson lived in an era of grand adventure writers, storytelling in words, and he lived it well.

I remember thinking these thoughts of our times together, walking, talking and watching him in his craft. I knew him as a friend, and loved him as a courageous and gifted man.

Peter died this past week, after living a gifted life. As a young writer, I admired his style and his agility. The word and the story is what he loved, a careful art, trampled often by today's era of tweeting and sensational journalism. The art, however still remains.

As a Native woman, I appreciated his courage; that he came from immense privilege and had the heart, resources and tenacity to tell stories in a way that only he could tell, and that he loved our community. He was a man who could write about nature and nuance of description perhaps better than any other. He wrote 33 books, and is the only writer to have won the National Book Award three times.

I remember Peter from 1980, when he had come to Indian Country, to the Navajo nation, where I was working on opposing uranium mining expansion proposals in an arid land already suffering from groundwater contamination. Here he saw a way of life challenged by health issues brought on by indiscriminate radiation contamination and an economic poverty forced upon an otherwise self-sufficient people.

He drove a rental car, and we talked as we traveled from house to sacred mountain, and from elder to elder. He was an apt listener, a genius at crystallizing the essence and chronicling the stories he heard.

It was later that he came to South Dakota, a place which would move him in profound ways, and where he found a story which would catapult this environmental writer into a national controversy.

Peter's *Indian Country*—a travel journal of sorts through the heart of Native communities—would be published in 1980, but it was his 1983 book *In the Spirit of Crazy Horse* that would draw the most controversy.

In this book, he wrote the story of the corruption, the so-called "Reign of Terror" on the Pine Ridge Reservation that led to the US political and military invasion of Pine Ridge, and of the Leonard Peltier case. The trials were held in Fargo, North Dakota.

"Whatever the nature and degree of his participation at Oglala, the ruthless persecution of Leonard Peltier had less to do with his own actions than with underlying issues of history, racism, and economics, in particular Indian sovereignty claims and growing opposition to massive energy development on treaty lands and dwindling reservations."
--Peter Matthiessen, *In the Spirit of Crazy Horse*

That book won him great respect in Native communities, and earned him a ten-year legal battle that reached both the South Dakota and U.S. Supreme Courts.

In the Spirit of Crazy Horse is perhaps the most complete story (told in Matthiesson's style) of the political and social history of Lakota people in the COINTELPRO era; of the conflict between Lakota resistance and the state's institutions; of the FBI working in league with armed paramilitary groups; and, of what was to become an all-out battle for survival for these Native people.

COINTELPRO was the acronym for the FBI's 1960s Counterintelligence Program, which was a secret operation used "to monitor, manipulate and disrupt social and political movements in the United States. Dr. Martin Luther King, Jr., the Black Panthers, anti-Vietnam War activists, and the American Indian Movement were among the program's targets," *Democracy Now* reported.

In the Spirit of Crazy Horse is a masterful chronicle, written by someone who initially knew very little (or what dribbles an American education can provide you) on Native history and current events.

The book's social and political weight—having been written by such a renowned author—brought immense legal wrath upon Peter, and he withstood it for nearly a decade.

Shortly after the publication of *In the Spirit of Crazy Horse,* Matthiessen and his publisher, Viking Penguin, were sued for libel by a former FBI agent named David Price, who thought he had been treated $49 million dollars' worth of unfairly.

William Janklow—the former governor of South Dakota and a man renowned for his dislike of Indian people—took exception to the book's illumination of that particular character flaw and also filed suit, demanding that all copies of the book be withdrawn from bookstores.

Eventually, in 1990, the South Dakota Supreme court dismissed the Janklow case and federal District Judge Diana Murphy dismissed Price's lawsuit, upholding Peter's right "to publish an entirely one-sided view of people and events." In other words, *In the Spirit of Crazy Horse* was protected by Peter's 1st Amendment right of free speech.

With the lawsuits killed off, the paperback edition of the book came out in 1992, almost a decade after its initial publication.

There are very few writers who could either withstand the pressures of such legal challenges to 1st Amendment rights, or stay loyal to a People and a Land for so long, and—through his books—speak forever.

"We belong to this Earth, it does not belong to us; it cares for us, and we must care for it. If our time on earth is to endure, we must love the Earth in the strong, unsentimental way of traditional peoples, not seeking to exploit but to live in balance with the natural world.

"When modern man has regained his reverence for land and life, then the lost Paradise, the Golden Age in the race memories of all peoples will come again, and all men will be 'in Dios,' people of God." –Peter Matthiesson, *Indian Country*

Photo © Keri Pickett

RUSSELL MEANS: A HERO MOVES ON

He was a hero. Make no mistake about it. His death is a great loss to America, not just American Indians. Russell Means challenged us all to be better people.

In 1973, life was not good on the Pine Ridge reservation in South Dakota, the reservation from which he came. That is to say, life expectancy was around 44 years of age, the reservation had a murder rate about eight times higher than the most violent American metropolis, and repression reigned.

Off the reservation, things were often worse. In 1972, Oglala Raymond Yellow Thunder was beaten, stripped naked and then paraded in the American Legion hall in Gordon, Nebraska. He was stuffed into a car trunk, and a few days later died of injuries sustained in his beating.

South Dakota and Nebraska were perhaps the most racist states in the country, barring perhaps Mississippi. However, that depends on if you were a Native or a Black person. People had to stand up to that.

Oglala Lakota elders asked for help and American Indians, from the Twin Cities, from urban areas or reservations came. Russell Means came. He was one of many.

That was the beginning of the American Indian Movement (AIM).

The passing of Oglala Lakota activist Russell Means to the Spirit World marked the end of an era, and hopefully it marks the beginning of a new one.

Means was a leader and an *Ogichidaa*, one who stood for the People. He joined with hundreds of other Native people in the occupation of Wounded Knee in 1973, a seventy-one-day takeover, which came to symbolize the renaissance of the dignity of Native people.

It was a time when a people said, "This is enough." The Native occupation of our own lands was met with the largest military force response of the federal government against U.S. citizens. According to Pentagon documents uncovered later, the government deployed 17 armored personnel carriers, 130,000 rounds of M-16 ammunition, 41,000 rounds of M-40 high explosives for grenade launchers as well as helicopters and other aircraft.

For those of us who were raised in the time following Wounded Knee II (named after the notorious massacre in 1890 at the same site), we were grateful for the commitment of individuals like Russell Means, and in awe of them as far-larger-than-life icons.

The media was fixated on Russell Means, Dennis Banks and the Bellecourts as the warriors they imagined we were. The American imagery needed new Indians for the Cowboys and Indians era, and in some ways the media set a bar that the rest of us could not meet.

We were raised in their shadow, yet we followed their direction. While I received a very good American education, I also received a very good Indigenous education, and some of it was at the direction of Russell Means and other leaders of the American Indian Movement.

I am indebted to him and his contemporaries, like Pat Bellanger, Clyde Bellecourt, Dennis Banks, Lorelei DeCora, and Madonna Thunderhawk for that.

Russell Means became an icon: one of a few images painted by Andy Warhol; an actor in *Last of the Mohicans*, *Natural Born Killers* and in many television series; the voice of Pocahontas' father in the movie of the same name.

Through it all, he continued his political critique of America and expressed his passion for Indigenous peoples. He was one of few Native people who could command the cover of a magazine, or a headline with just his name. This is a small group, unfortunately, and one that should be expanded in this new era.

He was large in his life, and in his passing we acknowledge his presence in our lives.

This writing is not about debt, it is about gratitude and it is about the future. Since the time when Native people stood up in the 1970s and said that we have a right to exist, we have been to the United Nations; and, in 2007, the UN finally affirmed the Rights of Indigenous Peoples.

Many state, federal and tribal programs have emerged (including our own schools, tribal colleges and radio stations), and Native people are not only mascots, but we are on television, featured in major motion pictures, and sometimes on the national news. Perhaps most importantly, this past summer the Iroquois National Lacrosse Team defeated the United States in the World Championships. Yet we still have a long way to go.

Pine Ridge remains one of the four poorest counties in the United States, and Native religious freedom, sacred sites, languages, and ways of living remain under assault.

White Clay, Nebraska, just south of the reservation, has some fourteen residents and yet its four liquor stores manages to sell 4.4 million cans of beer a year to a largely Oglala population. Despite several lawsuits and many protests, the (town) continues to hold its head high.

There are fewer Raymond Yellow Thunders now, but there are still Native people being killed for their land in the western hemisphere, particularly on the front lines of hydro-electric dams, mining and oil projects in the Amazon. And there is still an absolute need for people to be treated with dignity.

Russell Means lived a life proudly as an Oglala man. He lived fully and left us much to be thankful for. We honor him by continuing this work.

MUSHKOOUB AUBID: THE PASSING OF A GREAT LEADER

"They just can't go to a hospital and take a body from the ER and put it back into the station wagon and drive away. Pretty soon, everybody will be doing it."
—AITKEN COUNTY DEPUTY CORONER CHUCK BRENNY,
AUGUST 1990, REGARDING THE RECOVERY OF
GEORGE AUBID BY MUSHKOOUB AUBID.

Mushkooub took his father's body from the coroner's office in a station wagon to bring him home, to send him on his path to the Spirit World.

Some things change, but many stay the same. This month's passing of Mushkooub Aubid, son of George Aubid, followed the same story line.

Mushkooub Aubid, 65, was involved in a serious car accident on February 7 and was pronounced dead at Cloquet Memorial Hospital. His body was taken to the medical school at UMD, where an autopsy was set for Tuesday, long after the traditional practice would allow.

"We just want to prepare his body for his journey to the next world," his widow, Winnie LaPrairie, said. "This is the way it's been done for thousands of years."

It took a lot of pressure and 25 tribal members to bring their Chief home. Tribal attorneys said a forced autopsy would violate the American Indian Religious Freedom Act.

"We're trying to do this peacefully and according to the law," Dan LaPrairie, Aubid's son said. "But our beliefs supercede those laws. Our father gave us explicit instructions for what to do when he passed, and that's what we're trying to do here."

Representatives from most of the Anishinaabeg communities in the region and the traditional Midewin and Big Drum Societies were present. The funeral was held in East Lake, or *Minisinaakwaang,* home of the Rice Lake Band of Mississippi Anishinaabe or *Manoominikeshiins-ininiwag.*

Mushkooub's life, like that of his father Egiwaateshkang and the name Mushkooub received—*He that is Firmly Affixed*—was marked with defense of the land and way of life of the Anishinaabeg. At the center of their lives given by the Creator was the political autonomy of *Mini-sinaakwaang,* as well as *mino bimaatisiiwin.*

Mushkooub, who refused to fight in the Vietnam War because "that was not his war," was remembered for his courage and tenacity. He was among the American Indians who took over the Bureau of Indian Affairs building in Washington, D.C. in 1972; a year later he was part of the liberation of Wounded Knee; and he also joined his father in protesting dumping of military and toxic waste on the shores of *Gichi Gummi* (Lake Superior).

His accolades include: Mille Lacs Band Education Director; championship ricer, bringing in 650 pounds in one day; defender of land, of water, and of a way of life.

We Therefore Conclude

In some ways, it is not surprising that two days after Mushkooub's passing, the 8th Circuit Court of Appeals reaffirmed Anishinaabeg rights.

In reviewing a case called "Operation Square Hook," the 8th Circuit Court of Appeals found: "The United States suggests no reason why the right to net and sell fish would not be part of the usufructuary rights reserved by the establishment of the Leech Lake Reservation in the 1855 treaty...The context of the 1855 treaty establishing the

Leech Lake Reservation indicates that this 'general rule' applies. As the Supreme Court noted in Minnesota v. Mille Lacs Band, the silence regarding usufructuary rights in the 1855 treaty and the negotiations leading up to it suggest that the Chippewa Indians did not believe they were relinquishing such rights."

"Historical sources indicate that the Chippewa practiced such activities during the time period when the reservation was established. Even if the 1837 treaty does not apply, the rights it protects are relevant because in this particular case the Chippewa would have understood similar broad rights to apply on the Leech Lake Reservation. We therefore conclude that the exclusive on reservation fishing rights of the Chippewa Indians protect the rights to fish and to sell fish...."

"For people to negotiate a treaty that would stand 160 years later and protect present-day Anishinaabe is remarkable. That treaty was in a foreign language, and for our ancestors to do that, that was a great gift to this generation," Attorney Frank Bibeau, long time friend of Mushkooub explains.

Bibeau adds, "It is apparent the state was more interested in spending three years and hundreds of thousands prosecuting Native people for exercising treaty rights by taking fish by gillnet and then selling the fish, than working with Anishinaabe in protecting the watershed of those fish in the long run," referring to recent efforts to prevent the Sandpiper crude oil pipeline and Square Hook decisions.

"Our off-reservation treaty harvesting rights include a natural, pre-emptive right to protect our environment because we plan on our future generations living here, as we always have, forever," Bibeau said.

A major concern of Mushkooub was the mining proposals. The Tamarack Mine Project is in the same watershed as the *Minisiwaaning*, or Rice Lake/East Lake Band of Anishinaabeg. Mining interests have leased 35,000 acres of land not far from Big Sandy and Round Lakes, Savanna Portage State Park, and the Grayling Wildlife Management Area.

A venture of Talon Mining (based in one of the world's largest mining empires—the British Virgin Islands) and Rio Tinto Zinc/Kennecott (the largest copper mining company in the world), the Tamarack proposal has resulted in some 124,700 feet—or 23.7 miles—of drill core samples taken from the area.

Geologists estimate that more than 10 million tons of mineable ore is buried below, as copper mining has relatively low returns per amount of earth disturbed to extract it. The recovery ratio for copper is 0.16 percent, much smaller than the average for other metals (4.5 percent).

Talon officials say the copper and other valuable minerals are roughly 1,000 to 1,500 feet below the surface and that the mine "will be an underground mine, if it is able to get through Minnesota's exacting permitting process," or, essentially, to get past the strict regulations which protect wild rice, sacred to the Anishinaabeg, and the state grain.

The mining proposal would create sulfuric acid discharge into the very rice beds from which Mushkooub harvested his legendary 650 pounds.

This February, several Minnesota legislators (Senators David Tomassoni, Tom Saxhaug, Tom Bakk and Bill Ingebrigtsen) introduced S.F. No. 868. The bill would override state regulations regarding sulfuric acid, *"prohibiting the application of wild rice water quality standards..."*

Minnesota's water quality rule limiting sulfates to 10 milligrams per liter (mg/L) in wild rice waters was enacted in 1973 in order to protect natural stands of wild rice. The proposed legislative change seems focused on benefiting the proposed Tamarack and Polymet mines, both within wild rice areas.

Separately, the Enbridge Sandpiper line (now with a second line proposed to adjoin it, adding 1.4 million barrels a day of oil) goes through the same watershed.

What Mushkooub stood for is to be Anishinaabeg, and perhaps his father's words of 30 years ago remind us all of what that means:

"We do not have thousands upon thousands of dollars. We do not have great mansions of beauty. We do not have priceless objects of art. We do not lead a life of ease, nor do we live in luxury. We do not own the land upon which we live. We do not have the basic things of life which we are told are necessary to better ourselves.

"But I want to tell you now that we do not need these things. What we need, however, is what we already have. What we need has been provided to us by the Great Spirit. We need to realize who we are and what we stand for.

"We are the keepers of that which the Great Spirit has given to us: that is our language, our culture, our drum societies, our religion, and most of all our traditional way of life. We need to be Anishinaabeg again."
– George Aubid, Egiwaateshkang

In terms of the law, it seems that burial according to your traditional way of life should be possible. And, to be honest, it seems like twenty five years is long enough to figure out how to regulate tribal autopsies. It's not like this dying is a new thing.

Dr. Tadd Johnson of the University of Minnesota at Duluth explains: "Under current Minnesota law, the Medical Examiners have a great deal of authority. Even after a court order was granted which ordered the Medical Examiner to return the body of Mushkooub Aubid to his family, the Medical Examiner refused to return the bodies until the county attorney intervened. In states such as New York, laws exist wherein if the family of the decedent requests that an autopsy not be performed because of religious reasons, the Medical Examiner complies."

There is, in the end, a conflict between worldviews and ways of life. Some call it the White Man Paperwork, autopsy reports on deceased Indians, and the permitting of projects known to damage the ecosystem.

What Mushkooub stood for is living and dying with dignity.

Postscript: In the spring of 2015, the Mille Lacs and Fond du Lac bands, led a successful legislative change, allowing for customary autopsy and death proceedings, absent a controversy over the cause of death.

A SONG FOR HUGO CHAVEZ

"...And the devil came here yesterday. Yesterday, the devil came here. Right here. Right here. And it smells of sulfur still today, this table that I am now standing in front of."
—HUGO CHAVEZ, PRESIDENT OF VENEZUELA

Venezuelan President Hugo Chavez stood before the General Assembly of the United Nations in 2006 with the devil on his mind. George W. Bush had stood in that very spot the day before.

"The devil came here yesterday" is perhaps the most famous contemporary quote of a politician opposed to US policies, and one reason that Hugo Chavez was disliked by the US government so intensely.

The Owner of the World

As he was speaking, President Chávez made the sign of the cross, brought his hands together as if in prayer and glanced toward the ceiling. The video of the moment will live forever on the Web.

Chavez continued: "Yesterday, ladies and gentlemen, from this rostrum, the president of the United States, the gentleman to whom I refer as the devil, came here, talking as if he owned the world. Truly. As the Owner of the World," Chavez said.

To Chavez, the Devil was George W. Bush, and he said that eight times in his speech. That's what you get to say about the leader of the world's most powerful military force when you are a Third World leader who supplies maybe a million gallons of crude oil to an oil-addicted country every day, and you have no fear. You are ready for whatever they want to throw at you. You can say anything that you want to say.

Chavez held up a book by Noam Chomsky on imperialism and said: "The American empire is doing all it can to consolidate its hegemonistic system of domination, and we cannot allow him to do that. *We cannot allow world dictatorship to be consolidated.*"

An Indigenous Commitment

I was a great admirer of Hugo Chavez, thankful for his generosity, his courage, his leadership, and his commitment to Indigenous peoples.

My first memory of Venezuela, being an American-educated child, was dim. But I do remember seeing pictures of Native people in the Venezuelan jungle being gunned down and hanging like deer from trees, the result of lawless gold prospecting in their territories. The year was 1977. That is a stark image, one where humans are treated like game animals, and I have never forgotten it.

So, when the first Indigenous president in the history of the nation (Hugo Chavez' mother was a *Wayuu* Indian) came to lead Venezuela, I—like many other Native people—celebrated our relative's ascension to power and recognition.

At age 44, Hugo Chavez became the country's youngest president, winning with 56 percent of the vote. For the first time, we felt that we had gained some basic dignity, and subsequently a vote that would count and bring inclusion in the constitution and opportunities to effect reforms through a host of cabinet positions.

Chavez's politic was populist, and that ran counter to the history of several hundred years of entrenched, colonial political structures that have so dominated Central and South America. I cannot speak to all of that in this writing, but I can say that when Chavez became President, our people here in the North began to feel his generosity very directly, and very warmly.

CITGO: *Heart to Hearth*

At a 2005 Congressional hearing, oil executives were being chastised because their gargantuan corporate earnings were being contrasted with dire conditions in many communities. Exxon Mobil, Chevron, Conoco Phillips, BP and Royal Dutch Shell had reported total earnings last quarter of nearly $33 billion.

In the meantime, millions of Americans were facing fuel poverty, coping with absolute hardship about keeping their houses and their families warm, struggling to stay alive in the wealthiest nation in the history of the world.

Twelve U.S. senators asked these oil companies to donate some of their record-setting profits to people in need, Americans desperate for heating and cooking fuel.

Citgo was the only company to respond. Citgo Petroleum—Venezuela's national oil company—joined with Citizens Energy under the leadership of Joseph Kennedy and began emergency distribution of fuel oil from the Bronx and Brooklyn to the Alaskan Sub Arctic.

The White Earth reservation was included in the rescue effort. Our first year, we received roughly $1.7 million in fuel assistance, and this relief continued for six years since.

Each year, tribes in northern Minnesota, North Dakota and elsewhere have benefited from the generosity and humanity of the Venezuelan government-owned Citgo Petroleum Corporation. Some 240 tribal communities have received hundreds of millions of dollars of fuel assistance as rural fuel prices skyrocketed out of reach for many.

To Freeze or Not to Freeze

Some politicians encouraged our tribes to turn down the money, but Wayne Bonne of the Fond du Lac tribe commented: "To us, it would be a foolish move. We're not a wealthy tribe. We could make a political statement, but making a political statement while your people freeze is not very wise."

"The program is not a political program, it is an assistance program," the Venezuelan Minister of Petroleum explained. "You don't have to be politically loyal to us to be part of this program."

In his own country, Chavez's social programs won him enduring support: Poverty rates declined from 50 percent at the beginning of his term in 1999 to 32 percent in the second half of 2011. But he also charmed his audience with charisma and a flair for drama.

He was a king of the stage, and he put a lasting mark on the terrain of the Latin and South American politic, where in the past several years, another Indigenous president, Evo Morales of Bolivia, has come to office and where Michelle Bachalet rose from experiencing imprisonment and torture by the US-backed Pinochet regime to become the first woman President of Chile.

Venezuela's oil is still flowing into America, although in part it's rumored that the push for the Canadian Tar Sands is based on political disinterest in getting oil from any Latin American leftwing political leaders.

In his life and in his passing, I remember Hugo Chavez as a brave and generous man to Native and poor people. I never had a chance to meet President Chavez, but I certainly benefited from his life and his example; many others have also.

WHAT WOULD INGRID DO?

"We must recognize that we have hit bottom, that the war became inhuman, and it dehumanized us,"
—Juan Manuel Santos,
President of Columbia, July 26, 2013

"The roots of war and violence go deep, into the earth herself. As an indigenous woman, I wish to simply state that until we make peace with earth, there will be no peace in the human community."
—Ingrid Washinawatok El Issa

This turning of the month of March marks the fifteenth anniversary of the kidnapping and assassination of Menominee Ingrid Washinawatok El Issa, who was murdered while helping the U'wa People of Arauca set up a school and defend their lands and culture from oil exploitation by Occidental Petroleum.

Ingrid—along with Hawaiian activist Lahe'ena'e Gay and environmental activist Terence Freitas—was kidnapped by the Revolutionary Armed Forces of Colombia (FARC) on February 25, 1999 and all three were found bound, blindfolded and murdered on March 4 across the Arauca River in Venezuela.

These crimes took place long ago, but I remember Ingrid vividly and I often ask myself the question: "What would Ingrid do?" at times of conflict and danger.

I ask the question, *"What would Ingrid do?"* when I am vexed with our world. I also ask myself that because I believe that some of Ingrid's hopes are being actualized in the coming peace talks, scheduled for Cuba this spring, and set to address the longest-running war in the Western hemisphere.

Ingrid Washinawatok El Issa was a good friend and colleague of mine, a wise counselor, as we co-chaired the Indigenous Women's Network together for a decade.

In her life Ingrid led an exemplary role in the Indigenous community. Also known as *Peqtaw-Metamoh* (Flying Bird Woman), she served as the Chair of the NGO Committee on the United Nations International Decade of the World's Indigenous Peoples, and as the Executive Director of the New York-based Fund for Four Directions.

She is also known in her death. The FARC kidnapped Ingrid when she left the U'wa territory, on her way home. There she joined the U'wa, who were protecting their land from Occidental Petroleum and creating an Indigenous education system. She is missed always.

Ingrid and her companions understood well the dangers they were facing.

Columbia's National Centre of Historical Memory recently issued a report titled *Enough Already: Memories of War and Dignity,* investigating the nearly quarter-million deaths that have taken place there over some 54 years of deadly conflict.

"It's a war that has left most of the country mourning, but very unevenly. It's a war whose victims are, in the vast majority, non-combatant civilians. *It's a depraved war that has broken all humanitarian rules,*" said Gonzalo Sánchez, head of the investigation, which took six years to complete. The study also found that 4.7 million Columbians had been displaced since1996 and that 27,023 victims had been kidnapped since 1970.

The Huffington Post reports that "Colombia's internal conflict has claimed at least 220,000 lives since 1958, and more than four of every five victims have been civilian noncombatants."

From 1996 to 2005, on average, someone was kidnapped every eight hours in Colombia and every day someone fell victim to an anti-personnel mine, according to the *Memories of War and Dignity* report, which documents 1,982 massacres occurring between 1980 and 2012, attributing 1,166 to paramilitaries, 343 to rebels, 295 to government security forces and the remainder to unknown armed criminal groups.

Just as a reference, we US tax payers have an interest in this: The US has for many years financed a significant amount of the Colombian military budget and has provided many weapons as a part of the famously unsuccessful War on Drugs.

The report was produced by the National Center of Historical Memory, which was created under a 2011 law designed to indemnify victims of the conflict and return stolen land. The law prefaced peace talks now being held in Cuba with the Revolutionary Armed Forces, or FARC, the country's main leftist rebel group.

I live in a country which spends a third of my tax dollars on the military, so I do not know actually how peace is found. So say that you wanted peace. How would that work out?

"As Native peoples of the hemisphere, we have historically been the victims of violence and continue to be plagued by injustice and inequality. In our history we have had to go to war to protect our lands, as peace would simply mean our enslavement and extermination. And every course of action we sought--whether accommodation or resistance--had only one outcome, the theft of our lands. All this is well known." –Ingrid Washinawatok El Issa

The US Institute for Peace scholar Virginia Bouvier discussed the significance of this set of peace negotiations. She first pointed out a very big problem: "The distribution of wealth in Colombia is one of the worst in the world and has become more pronounced in the last decade...The parties have agreed on a limited, five-point agenda that will include land policies, political participation, the end of the conflict (this would include among other things questions of ceasefires and cessation of hostilities, security guarantees, and addressing paramilitary violence), drug production and trafficking, and truth and reparations for victims."

Who Owns the Land

Agrarian policy is the first item on the agenda for the meetings, co-sponsored by Norway, Venezuela and Cuba. The order of the agenda is important. Often parties choose to begin with the easier items in order to build confidence and show early results. Here, the parties have agreed to begin with the issue that is perhaps the most difficult: *Who owns the land.*

"Land has been at the crux of the insurgents' agenda from the start, and there seems to already be at least some basic agreement between the sides on the need for structural change...Land reform or restitution of lands, victims' rights, and reparations have been front and center on the presidential agenda since Santos assumed office," Bouvier stated.

After fifty years, nothing is simple. As Bouvier notes: "Once the cessation of hostilities occurs and a final accord is reached, the real work of peace-building, recovery, and reconciliation will begin."

For the U'wa, their struggle to keep oil out of their land won an important victory: On February 24, the U'wa issued a statement announcing that "The Magallanes gas exploration block has been completely dismantled. Ecopetrol S.A. has removed all the machinery that had been found there in a demonstration of respect for our rights as an indigenous people."

The struggle of the U'wa and other tribes facing similar threats to protect their land from other oil, mining and pipeline interests continues. I hope there is peace in U'wa territory. I think Ingrid would echo that.

"Ingrid was known as a tireless defender of the rights of Indigenous peoples," Mary Robinson, then United Nations High Commissioner for Human Rights, said.

"Indigenous peoples have long understood sustainable development. The wilderness that we inhabit is wilderness only to those who cannot grasp the complexity of our agricultural systems, which regenerate and produce in ways that work in accordance to natural laws, not against them. For this reason, our agriculture has existed with only little impact on the earth, for hundreds if not thousands of years, all the while producing for the needs of our people.

"Among the technologies we use to produce in harmony with this earth are products such as corn developed and cultivated in this hemisphere. Corn is truly a product of our technology: it cannot live without people, just like our people could not live without corn. For this reason it was central in our spiritual and cultural existence. It was also developed in infinite varieties that were each adapted to the particular environment where it would have to exist, so that they would best fit in with the other life. And so it was designed to feed the maximum number of people with the minimum impact on the environment, and people lived close to their corn, their way of life." –Ingrid Washinawatok El Issa

Let us honor Ingrid in supporting the work, the struggle to bring peace to the People, and to the Earth.

Geronimo, Militarization
and the Indian Wars

THE MILITARIZATION
OF INDIAN COUNTRY

by Winona LaDuke
with Sean Cruz

GERONIMO: TIME TO CALL THE INDIAN WARS TO AN END

That the death of Osama bin Laden was relayed with the words "Geronimo EKIA [Enemy Killed in Action]" prompted a din of protest in the halls of Congress.

Harlan Geronimo, a great-grandson of Apache chief Geronimo and an Army veteran of two tours in Vietnam, asked for a formal apology. He called the Pentagon's decision to use the code name Geronimo a "grievous insult."

His call for an apology was joined by most major Native American organizations. The Onondaga nation stated, "This continues to personify the original peoples of North America as enemies and savages ... The U.S. military leadership should have known better."

It is an ironic moment in history. A hundred years after Geronimo's death at Fort Sill, Oklahoma, where he died after being held for 27 years as a prisoner of war—because he was Apache—this great patriot is accorded little peace.

The analogy, from a military perspective, is interesting. More than 5,500 military personnel were engaged in a 13-year pursuit of the Apache chief. He traveled with his community, including 35 men and 108 women and children, who in the end surrendered in exhaustion and were met with promises that were never fulfilled. It was one of the most expensive and shameful of the Indian Wars.

A hundred years later, similarly exorbitant amounts of both time and money have been spent finding Osama bin Laden, but that is where the analogy ends.

Geronimo was a true patriot, his battles were in defense of his land, and he was a hero. The coupling of his name with the most vilified enemy of America in this millennium is dangerous ground.

But to the military, it is familiar ground. Native nomenclature in U.S. military affairs is widespread. From Apache Longbow and Black Hawk helicopters to Tomahawk missiles, the machinery of war has many Native names.

In a war zone, to leave the base is to "go off the reservation." To move farther away, into enemy territory, is to go into "Indian Country."

Indeed, former Defense Secretary Donald Rumsfeld visited Fort Carson in 2008 (named after the infamous Indian killer, Kit Carson). There, he instructed the troops to "live up to the legend of Kit Carson ... fighting terrorists in the mountains of Afghanistan, hunting the remnants of the deadly regime in Iraq, working with local populations to help secure victory. *And every one of you is like Kit Carson.*"

It may be time to end the Indian Wars.

Many military bases have been carved out of reservations and Indian Country, and at least 19 reservations are named after forts themselves (Fort Berthold, Fort Peck and Fort McDermitt among them).

The U.S. military has had a huge ecological impact on Native Hawaiian lands, ranging from Kaho'olawe to Pohakuloa. The former is an entire island seized by the military in 1945, and the latter is being seized today, for the expansion of the Stryker base. The U.S. military has detonated more than a thousand atomic weapons in Western Shoshone territory and in the Pacific, and until recently, Schofield Barracks in Honolulu was riddled with deadly depleted uranium waste.

Despite these and other impacts, Native people enlist in the U.S. military in high numbers, and have the highest rate of living veterans of any community. These people deserve respect.

It's been 100 years since Geronimo passed to the next world. It would seem that it is time to rethink the military's use of terms like "Geronimo EKIA" and "going off the reservation."

It is indeed time to bring the Indian Wars to a close.

(Excerpted from)
THE MILITARIZATION OF INDIAN COUNTRY

Domestic Wars

The Department of Defense states that as part of carrying out its mission to defend America, "certain activities—such as weapons testing, practice bombing and field maneuvers—may have had effects on tribal environmental health and safety as well as tribal economic, social and cultural welfare." That would be an understatement.

The US military is one of the largest landowners in the United States, with some 30 million acres of land under its control. The US federal government is the largest landowner in the United States, with much of this land base annexed or otherwise stolen from Native peoples.

The states with the top two federal land holdings are Nevada with 84.5 percent of the state, and Alaska at 69.1 percent of the state being held by the federal government. These represent takings under the 1863 Ruby Valley Treaty with the Shoshone, and the Alaskan Native Claims Settlement Act of 1971. The military controls a large percentage of Hawaii as well, including some 25% of Oahu, valuable "submerged lands" (i.e. estuaries and bays), and until relatively recently, the island of Kaho'olawe. The Army seized the entire island of Kaho'olawe after the attack on Pearl Harbor. This island was the only National Historic site also used as a bombing range. The military reigns over more than 200,000 acres of Hawaii, with over 100 military installations, and at least 150,000 personnel.

Seizing Land in the Name of the Military

"As of 1916, the US Army owned approximately 1.5 million acres. Land ownership grew by 33 percent in the course of the World War I mobilization. As of 1940, the Army owned approximately 2 million acres. The scale of World War II mobilization was unprecedented: the Army (including the Army Air Force) acquired 8 million additional acres, thereby quintupling land ownership. Military agencies were given nearly unlimited spending authority to acquire land from private owners and had the option of foreclosing on lands it deemed necessary to national security." –Hooks and Smith. *The Treadmill of Destruction: National Sacrifice Areas and Native Americans*

Most of the new acreage cost the Army practically nothing. More than 6 million acres, more than three quarters of the land it acquired, came from the public domain.—Fine and Remington, quoted in *Treadmill of Destruction*, ibid.

What is clear is that "public domain" is often really, truthfully Native land. Some of these land transfers came early from Native people. The Army took some 10,000 acres from the Cheyenne and Arapaho people for Fort Reno in 1881 and until 1993 had use of Zuni and Navajo lands near Fort Wingate.

In fact, much of what is today US military land was at some time taken from Native peoples, sometimes at gunpoint, sometimes in the wake of massacres or forced marches, sometimes through starvation, and sometimes through pen and paper, broken treaty, acts of Congress or state legislatures, or by Presidential authority, by the "Great White Father" himself.

As weapons became more lethal–as harmful to those manufacturing, handling or storing these materials as they would be against an enemy–access to more isolated lands became a major military priority. With the massive increases of chemical, biological and nuclear weaponry that took place during the Cold War, it was clear that the military would need to take more land far from populated areas. That would mean the additional seizure of Indian land.

NATIVE LANDS IN THE CROSSHAIRS

Alaska: Occupied Territory

Alaska Natives have felt some of the most widespread and deepest impacts of the modern military. Alaska has over 200 Native villages and communities and almost as many military sites. The military holds over 1.7 million acres of Alaska, much of this within the traditional territories of Indigenous communities in the north. Then there is the military occupation of airspace over Native territories and traditional caribou hunting areas, where low-flying planes and sonic booms have a disruptive impact on herd animals.

Seven hundred active and abandoned military sites account for at least 1,900 toxic hot spots. Five out of seven Superfund sites in the state are a result of military contamination. The 700 formerly used defense sites in Alaska tell a history of the Cold War and every war since. The levels of radioactive and persistent organic pollutants remaining in the environment impact people who are dependent upon the land for their subsistence way of life.

Alaskan Native lands were occupied for military reasons, but in many cases were annexed for their oil and natural resources under the Alaskan Native Claims Settlement Act of 1971. The military remains dominant on the land, joined by multinational oil, mining and logging companies, with factory trawlers mining the oceans for the remaining species of commercial value.

Alaska's Project Chariot

In 1958, the Atomic Energy Commission proposed blasting a string of five atomic bombs to create an artificial harbor at Cape Thompson on the North Slope of Alaska. Named "Project Chariot," this endeavor was part of a larger concept called "Operation Plowshare," a reference to the Biblical phrase "beating swords into plowshares" or finding peaceful (!) uses for weaponry of catastrophic destructive power. The size of this explosion would be 100 times more powerful than the bomb that destroyed Hiroshima.

Project Chariot had the support of the political establishment, newspaper publishers, the military and many others. However, Alaska Natives organized to protest this desecration in 1961, beginning with the Inupiat village at Point Hope, which is located just 30 miles from the intended blast, and successfully stopped this crazy idea.

By now most are aware of Project Chariot, a project dating from the 1950s that envisioned the use of nuclear detonations to build a harbor at Cape Thompson, Alaska. This was part of the old Plowshare or

'Atoms for Peace' program. Although the nuclear detonations were never carried out, 26 millicuries of radioactive tracers left over from ecological experiments were deposed of at the site. When news of these disposed radioactive tracers broke, the headlines told of a nuclear waste 'dump.' The worst fears of the local people living near Cape Thompson were awakened.—U.S. Senator Ted Murkowski (Alaska)

Point Hope, Alaska: Secret Radiation Testing

With the creation of the Plowshare Program, the AEC took radioactive materials from the Nevada test site on Western Shoshone land and secretly placed them in a number of test plots near the Inupiat Eskimo Village of Point Hope.

The purpose of this 1962 experiment was to document and study the effects of radiation bioaccumulation in caribou, lichen and humans in the Arctic. Over 15,000 pounds of radioactive soil were secretly placed in a number of locations in the area.

The 450 residents of Point Hope had never been informed of the testing. The study was inadvertently discovered in a 1992 Freedom of Information request on radioactive experimentation spearheaded by the Department of Energy. The village, along with organizations nationally, including Honor the Earth, pressured the DOE for cleanup, and won.

Fort Greely, Alaska and the VX Lake

At Fort Greely, Alaska, the military operated a nuclear power plant that ran on highly enriched weapons grade uranium. Originally built to house six anti-ballistic missile silos, the Army also used the area for extensive, and one might say chaotic, testing of chemical and biological weaponry.

Although the base has been closed, the nuclear reactor remains entombed on-site and significant contamination is certain to persist for a very long time.

"In the summer of 1969 the Army drained a small lake in interior Alaska. Though this presumably is not something that occurs every day, the event would be unremarkable except for one thing: From the bottom of the lake the Army recovered about two hundred artillery shells and rockets filled with nerve gas.

"The lethal weapons had been left on the frozen surface of the lake at Fort Greely's Gerstle River test site during the winter some years earlier. According to the Army, the chemical-filled munitions were scheduled for destruction when they were placed on the ice, but somehow the order to destroy them was never given. Apparently forgotten, the deadly stockpile sank to the bottom when the ice melted under the bright May sun.

"The poison gas weapons sank in 1966 and remained in the lake for more than three years before they were retrieved. The Army has not explained why such dangerous material were handled so carelessly, nor why the loss of a large quantity of nerve gas went unnoticed for so long. After reports of missing nerve gas weapons finally came to the attention of Arctic Test Center authorities, the Army decided to drain the lake in order to remove the weapons.

"The lost chemical weapons were part of the secret CBW program conducted under the aegis of Fort Greely's Arctic Test Center. This bizarre incident is only part of the evidence showing that the protective blanket of national security that shrouds the CBW program elsewhere has concealed the Alaska CBW test activities from the public eye. The story of the lake was unraveled with the story of CBW in Alaska. Together they make a case study in the secrecy with which the CBW program has been managed—and mismanaged.

"After the mishap was discovered, the servicemen were instructed to refer to the lake as 'Blueberry Lake.' Though this pleasantly bucolic name is now the official one, it has never caught on among the GIs who knew it as VX Lake." – Richard A. Fineberg, *The Dragon Goes North: Chemical and Biological Warfare Testing in Alaska* (Santa Barbara, CA: McNally & Loftin, 1972)

PCB Contamination in Alaska

Although less long term in their impact, the persistence of organic pollutants in the Arctic is more pervasive. The Distant Early Warning (DEW) Line consisted of some 63 separate military radar sites along the 66th parallel in Alaska, Canada and Greenland. These sites, although no longer in use, are heavily contaminated with polychlorinated biphenyls (PCBs), which are toxic and carcinogenic. PCBs and other bio-accumulative pollutants in the Arctic have been a major threat to the health of people, polar bears and all life forms. Studies completed in many of the sites in the north indicate that "no consumption" should occur of fish downstream from these sites.

Western Shoshone: Nuclear Testing and Nuclear Waste

"The food that my people survived on is not here no more on account of this nuclear weapon that we have developed. . . . The pine nuts aren't here no more, the chokecherries aren't here, the antelope aren't here, the deer aren't here, the groundhog aren't here, the sage hen aren't here."
– Corbin Harney, Naraya Cultural Preservation Council website

In 1940, President Roosevelt created with a stroke of his pen the single largest gunnery range in the world; the 3.5 million acre Nellis Range. After World War II, this bombing range would be absorbed into the nuclear weapons complex concentrated in Nevada, which has been described as the largest peacetime militarized zone on earth . . . really wasn't good for anything but gunnery practice—you could bomb it into oblivion and never notice the difference. –Hooks and Smith. *The Treadmill of Destruction: National Sacrifice Areas and Native Americans*

The Western Shoshone would disagree.

In 1951, the Atomic Energy Commission created its Nevada Test Site within Western Shoshone Territory as proving grounds for nuclear weapons. Between 1951 and 1992, the United States and Great Britain exploded 1,054 nuclear devices both above and below ground there.

Radiation emanating from these experiments was fully measured for only 111 of the tests, about 10 percent of the total.

Within just the first three years, 220 above ground tests spewed fallout over a large area, to be carried by the prevailing winds. The government maintained that the maximum radiation exposure from the tests was equivalent to that of a single chest X-ray. However, in 1997 the

National Cancer Institute made public a study of radiation exposure from above ground nuclear tests showing that some 160 million people had suffered significant radiation exposure from the tests, on average 200 times more than the amount indicated by the government.

In some parts of the country, the exposure was found to be 2,000–3,000 times that amount. The institute estimated that as many as 75,000 cases of thyroid cancer may have been caused by atmospheric testing.

None of that is news to Virginia Sanchez, a Western Shoshone woman who grew up in the shadow of the Nevada test site. "When the nuclear tests were exploded, in school we would duck and cover under the desk, not really understanding what it was," she said.

Virginia's brother Joseph Sanchez died of leukemia at 36, and she has lost many relatives. The Western Shoshone communities were directly downwind of the site. Virginia recalls:

We weren't wealthy, you know our structures weren't airtight. Besides, our people spent major amounts of time outside, picking berries, hunting, gathering our traditional foods. . . . At that time, we still ate a lot of jackrabbits. . . . In Duckwater, which, as the crow flies, is 120 miles direct north of the test site, the people in that community didn't have running water or electricity as a whole community until the early 1970s, so they would gather water outside. So we received some major doses of radiation. . . . The scientists figured that a one-year-old child who ate a contaminated rabbit within a month's time after the test probably had six times the dose of what the DOE's figures were saying. . . . There was a county school about three miles from the reservation, and all the kids wore the film badges (issued by federal officials to document the gamma rays) and they were never told the results.— LaDuke, *All Our Relations,* Virginia Sanchez interview

The MX Missile site and the Yucca Mountain Nuclear Waste Repository were also proposed for Western Shoshone Territory. Both were defeated.

———————

Makua and Kaho'olawe

"They bombed the houses in the 1940s. And took over the entire valley," Sparky Rodrigues *explains, one of many Makua, Hawaii residents still waiting to move home. "The government moved all of the residents out and said after the war, you can move back. Then they used the houses for target practice. The families tell stories that the military came to the families with guns, and said, 'Here's $300, thank you' and 'you got to move.' Those people remain without their houses, and for years, many lived on the beaches in beautiful Makua Valley, watching their farms and land get bombed."*
—SPARKY RODRIGUES INTERVIEW, JANUARY 2001

Live ammunition occasionally washes up on the beaches at Makua.

Malu Aina, a military watchdog group from Hawaii, reports, "Live military ordnance in large quantities has been found off Hapuna Beach and in Hilo Bay. Additional ordnance, including grenades, artillery shells, rockets, mortars, armor piercing ordnance, bazooka rounds, napalm bombs, and hedgehog missiles have been found at Hilo airport, in Waimea town, Waikoloa Village, in North and South Kohala at Puako and Mahukona, in Kea'au and Maku'u Farm lots in Puna, at South Point in Ka'u, and on residential and school grounds. At least nine people have been killed or injured by exploding ordnance. Some unexploded ordnance can be set off even by cell phones. It's an ongoing problem of expanding military *opala* [garbage] locally and globally."

Since the end of World War II, Hawaii has been the center of the US military's Pacific Command (PACOM), from which all US forces in the region are directed. It serves as an outpost for Pacific expansionism, along with Guam, the Marshall Islands, Samoa and the Philippines. PACOM is the center of the US military activities over more than half the Earth, from the west coast of the United States to Africa's east coast, from the Arctic to Antarctica, covering 70 percent of the world's oceans.

The island of Kaho'olawe was the only National Historic site also used as a bombing range. Finally, after years of litigation and negotiations Congress placed a moratorium on the bombing, but after $400 million in cleanup money, much remains to be completed.

Among the largest military sites in Hawaii is the Pohakuloa Training Area (PTA), a 108,793 acre bombing range between the sacred mountains of Mauna Kea and Mauna Loa in the center of the big island, Hawaii. At least 7 million rounds of ammunition are fired annually at that base alone. The military proposes to expand the base by 23,000 acres, under the Military Transformation Proposal, and has a plan to bring in Stryker brigades to the area. The military is hoping to acquire up to 79,000 more acres in total—so far.

Military Impact on Hawaiian Endangered Species and Archaeological Sites

Pohakuloa has the "highest concentration of endangered species of any Army installation in the world" according to its former commander Lt. Col. Dennis Owen, and it has over 250 ancient Hawaiian archeological sites. Those species and archeological sites are pretty much "toast" under the expansion plans.

In one recent report, the military determined that there were over 236 former military sites in Hawaii at 46 separate installations, all of which were contaminated. These sites, identified under the Formerly Used Defense Sites Program (FUDS) may be condemned by the military to avoid cleanup and liability.

There is no way to avoid an observation. It is as a result of our nation's history of colonialism, its Doctrine of Manifest Destiny and the subsequent expansion of military interests to support American imperialism that Indian Country communities are located adjacent to more than our fair share of these military toxic sites.

This is because many of today's US military bases are the legacy of old US cavalry forts, places where the Army built strongholds to support their invasions of Indian Country, places that were used to subjugate and imprison Native people.

The impact of the US military on Indigenous populations extends far beyond the shores of the United States. Take, for example, Guam, where first European and currently American military might has been forced upon the islanders for more than 500 years.

Getting Your Homeland Back from the Military

Recovery of lands from the military/industrial complex is a bit complicated. As it is, under the Federal Land Policy and Management Act of 1976, if and when no further military need for property exists, then the land can be transferred between agencies.

For a tribe to recover land, this means that the land is first transferred from the Defense Department to the Secretary of Interior. The Secretary, in turn, has to agree that the lands are suitable for public domain.

However, historically, "the transfer of administrative control from one federal agency to another is categorically excluded from environmental review due to the fact that this type of action normally does not have an effect on an individual or the environment." This loophole means that if and when we get land back, it may very well be contaminated with whatever the military left behind.

[Unexploded] ordnances on formerly used defense installations probably contaminated 20–25 million acres in the United States and the number could be as high as 50 million acres. Sadly, no one can give us an accurate appraisal of the problem. What we do know is at the current rate of spending it will take centuries, maybe even thousands of years or more, to return this land to safe and productive use. Some may be so damaged, we may not attempt to clean it up.—Blumenauer, quoted in *The Treadmill of Destruction*.

DoD's clean-up programs embrace relative framework and often do not consider tribal unique factors such as subsistence consumption, ceremonial use of certain plants and animals and the low population densities that exist on many reservations. As a consequence, DoD sites on Indian lands often receive low relative-risk scores, which means that clean up at these sites may be deferred for many years. –Hooks and Smith. *The Treadmill of Destruction: National Sacrifice Areas and Native Americans*

That's unfortunate, particularly if you live there.

Three Cases of Land Jurisdiction Transfers: Navajo, Lakota and Ho-Chunk

The toxicity of military lands has increasingly come into question, and the liability associated with these lands has resulted in some changes in policy. Cases of land jurisdiction transfers include: Fort Wingate on the Navajo reservation, Badger Munitions on the Ho-Chunk reservation and the Badlands Bombing Range on the Pine Ridge reservation. All three sites are in the process of "remediation" by the military or by the tribal community that must live with the damage.

The Navajo Nation and Ft. Wingate

Fort Wingate is located near Bear Springs and Horse Fenced in Canyon in the territory of the Diné and Zuni people on about 21,000 acres of land. There are, according to reports, thousands of archeological sites on this former military base.

The lands here had been occupied for thousands of years before the coming of the European colonizers, then the Americans, and with them the US Army.

The more recent history of Fort Wingate is associated with the military seizure of the land in 1850 from Indigenous peoples, the use of it as an interim prison camp and then, for almost 40 years, as a highly toxic military base.

Under the command of the infamous General James Carleton and his loathsome subordinate, Colonel Kit Carson, Fort Wingate became an interim prison camp when Carson's troops forced the Diné people on several death marches, known collectively as the Long Navajo Walk. The Army shot stragglers, and many died along the way.

Eighty years later, Fort Wingate became an important location for the testing of Pershing missiles and a storage facility prior to the shipping overseas of many of the weapons used in World War II, resulting in a wide array of toxic impacts.

The Navajo *Shush Bi Toh* Task Force worked for the return of aboriginal Navajo lands in the closed Fort Wingate Army Depot in the 1990s, although when the group leader Karl Katenay died, so did the task force.

Work continues, however, by the Navajo Nation, and researchers continue to assess the environmental health of the area.

The problems of Fort Wingate mirror those of other former military sites in terms of their toxicity. In the remediation and land discussion between the Department of Interior and the Navajo Nation, different categories of land are identified according to their toxicity.

The *Community Environmental Response Facilitation Act (CERFA)* was passed by Congress in 1992. Until recently, military lands were covered under CERFA. These include several categories of CERFA parcels: (1) those that are thought to have been fully remediated; (2) CERFA-qualified parcels with no evidence of storage of hazardous materials for the past year (but may contain radio nuclides, or unexploded ordnance); and (3) disqualified parcels that are heavily contaminated.

Around three-quarters of Fort Wingate is considered to be qualified to be transferred back to the Navajo Nation, but some 4,533 acres are too toxic to be returned. In all cases, however, groundwater contamination remains a problem.

The Navajo Nation began the process of recovering Fort Wingate from the military in 1993 and has been working on the remediation of this site ever since. Their hope is to return the land for residential use by the Navajo people

Fort Wingate Army Depot Activity Area (FWDA) demilitarized and test fired munitions from 1949 to 1993. Many improper waste handling practices such as the pumping of wash water containing explosive compounds which was pumped into storage and drying tanks, and allowed to overflow from tanks was drained onto leaching beds, thereby rendering the depot area and adjacent Navajo owned lands contaminated.

There are several chemicals that are not mentioned, in the characterization of contaminants present in soils, surface or groundwater that may have been test fired or stored at FWDA such as: white phosphorous, mustard gas, nerve gas, Agent Orange napalm and biological weapons. Further investigation of soil, ground and surface waters for chemicals commonly associated with periods of war and the manufacturing of ammunitions is of utmost importance to the impending decisions regarding remediation as well as to the health and welfare of the future residents of FWDA.—Rangel, *Base Realignment and Closure (BRAC) Cleanup Plan*

Fort Wingate cleanup and remediation is estimated to require 60–100 years before the area is rendered safe.

Until about 2005, Wingate Elementary School, a K-8 federally-funded boarding school for Indian children, was nestled among abandoned military buildings. Fences and barbed wire encircled some of the buildings to keep trespassers (and students) out. I taught middle school science there in 2001. Between the building in which I taught, and the Middle School office building was a boarded-up structure. It was off limits to anyone at the school, and presumably belonged to the U.S. military.

One morning, that structure caught fire. Brown smoke billowed from the windows of the shed, followed by smoke of varying colors. As I recall, no one on campus (including the Principal) knew what was stored there. The local fire department was called in, and school administrators frantically called to federal offices in Albuquerque and Washington D.C. Within a few hours federal officials arrived to survey the scene. It was just another reminder that we were teaching children on militarized land. —Micheal Baumrind, a former teacher at the Wingate Middle School, written statement on May 27, 2011.

The Lakota Nation and the Badlands Bombing Range

It is said that if the Great Sioux Nation were in control of its 1851 treaty area, it would be the third greatest nuclear weapons power on the face of the Earth.

This is due to the vast number of US Air Force, NORAD and other bases in the Lakota territories now called Nebraska, North and South

Dakota, Wyoming and Montana. Of particular concern to the Lakota Nation, however, is the gunnery range on the Pine Ridge reservation, which is part of a more recent seizure of land. "[T]he US Government seized 342,000 acres of the Pine Ridge reservation in South Dakota for a bombing range to train WW II pilots. The land seizure forced 15 Oglala Sioux families to sell their farms and ranches for three cents an acre."

The gunnery range, or Badlands Bombing Range, continues to be a source of concern for the Oglala Sioux Tribe, as both live and spent ordnance are found throughout the area.

In the summer of 2004, a "small bomb" was found and detonated in the Stronghold segment of the Badlands Bombing Range. The bomb was an M70, measuring 51 inches long, but was found to be largely innocuous—full of "photo flash powder." The bomb was likely 40 years old, a remnant of the military's use of the land for aerial gunnery and bombing practice. It is not known how many bombs remain in the area.

The Oglala Sioux Tribe is working on the cleanup of the Badlands Bombing Range, under an agreement with the military. The tribe determined that they wished to undertake this responsibility, stating:

The people of the Oglala Sioux tribe (1) are the rightful owners of the land (2) the bombing range land contains many historic and religious sites (3) the people agreed that they did not want outsiders digging up or removing cultural artifacts belonging to the tribe, selling and making profit from them.

Tribal members were trained by the DOD for ordnance remediation, but upon completion of the training, the funding was no longer available to continue the cleanup.

The Ho-Chunk Nation and Badger Munitions

The Badger Army Ammunitions Plant near Baraboo, Wisconsin, was established by the military in 1942 as a class II military propellant manufacturing installation. The plant produced propellants for small arms, rockets and a host of larger weapons.

Ammunition production ceased in 1975, but the plant occupied 7,400 acres of land, some of which became contaminated with a host of toxic chemicals including chloroform, carbon tetrachloride, trichloroethene and dinitrotoluene. Cleanup costs associated with the plant are upwards of $80 million. The plant now ranks as the 23rd most expensive cleanup project on the Pentagon's list, yet money for such mitigation trickles in slowly.

Over the past two decades, the Ho-Chunk Nation has been seeking return of the lands associated with the former Badger facility, with a focus on 1,520 acres of land considered the least contaminated. An attorney for the Ho-Chunk working on the case, Samantha Green Deer, reports that the tribe is cautious and awaiting more "remediation" of the toxic site as required under the law. The remediation is expensive, and the tribe would prefer that the military, which made the mess, clean it up.

Interestingly enough—and largely based on the expense of cleanup, it would appear—new regulations for transfer of military bases to tribal communities have come into effect in the past few years, pushing for a transfer into fee status as the BIA may be concerned about the liability of the former defense sites. In each case, an environmental assessment must be done for each parcel under consideration for return.

With this land the Ho-Chunk plan to create an organic bison operation to feed the tribal population. The land is currently toxic and the BIA oversees the transfer to ensure cleanup is performed by the military prior to transfer. The military is only required, at this time, to clean up the site to minimal standards. In doing this, the military cleans up the site, but does not remove intact dangers like asbestos—the military will not remove it unless it is exposed and poses a health threat.

The Price Tag of the US Military's Impact

Blowing things up is the military's strong suit, not cleaning up after itself. Of the whopping federal defense budget of $664 billion (2010) only a tiny fraction will be spent on cleanup and resolving its impacts on the environment either locally or globally.

An Associated Press story from 2004 read, "removing unexploded munitions and hazardous waste found so far on 15 million acres of shutdown U.S. military ranges could take more than 300 years, according to Congressional auditors."

This cost is now estimated at $35 billion and climbing rapidly. In one report, the military identifies some 17,482 potentially contaminated sites at 1,855 installations.

The military cleanup budget is not a reflection of the military's environmental impact. And, in reality, rather than clean up the toxins placed in the environment by the military, the Department of Defense has successfully limited all liability for much of their own contamination.

In this *Time of the Seventh Fire*

This book was intended to deepen a discussion on forces that surround us, permeate our cultural practices and determine some of our collective psychology, economic options and ecology of our land. The militarization of Indian Country surrounds us, and when we go off the reservation it controls our economy and worldview.

We are the people who have the opportunity to make a difference. In this book, we've provided some useful information on how and why it is incumbent upon us to look critically at the military—a daunting force in the world, and a daunting force in Native America—and consider our alternatives, consider our relationships and to reconsider how we might change our collective paths and transform the role of the US military on the Land and among the People.

It is vital to understand the differences between the use of the military in wars fought to sustain Empire, to maintain an iron grip on populations, land and resources taken as a continuation of the notion of Manifest Destiny, and the use of the military as *Ogichidaag*, to protect the People and the Land, to defend Mother Earth from those who would destroy her.

For those of military age, this book might prove useful in helping you plan out your future and that of your family, of your community and your people, for we are all related and it is never too early to consider the roles you might play at different stages of your lives as Ogichidaag.

For the community, it is important to prepare for those who will return to you from military service, to understand fully the scope of the problems that await you, recognizing that more than 20 percent of your veterans will need some form of intensive therapy, perhaps for the rest of their lives, and to meet them and their needs proactively.

For the nation, it is important to develop strategies where military resources are increasingly used for peaceful purposes, perhaps none more crucial as elements of true strategic long-term homeland security than achieving sustainable energy independence and food security, and in removing the toxins that already poison the land and the people, the water and the air we breathe.

> Water Spirit feelin'
> Springin' 'round my head
> Makes me feel glad
> That I'm not dead . . .
> *Witchi-Tai-To.* . . .
> —Jim Pepper, *Witchi Tai To,* 1971

Economics for the
Seventh Generation

Photo © Keri Pickett

EMMA: FROM A TIPI TO A TESLA

The End of an Era

I would like to drive a couple of cars in the next few years. I would like to drive a Jaguar—not own one, just drive one—across the Golden Gate Bridge. Maybe navy blue, or slate grey. And maybe a real old school car, too, like an old Chevy. A rounded-edges one. No sharp fins.

Why would I like to do this? Because—in their own way—they are works of art to me, perhaps to all of us, beautiful works of art created in a fossil fuel era. And that era will be over soon, because it is time. It is time to move on. I just want to see an elegant transition, not a crashing-my-way-out-of-the-fossil-fuel-era transition of climate change and poison.

The reason why I know that the fossil fuel era in cars will end is a simple energy inefficiency problem. Of the six gallons of gas you put into the car, only about one gallon actually moves the car forward. This is not smart, and it cannot be sustained.

Mara Prentiss is the Mallinckrodt Professor of Physics at Harvard University. Asked about her new book, *Energy Revolution: The Physics and the Promise of Efficient Technology,* Dr. Prentiss explained energy, Carnot cycles and efficiency to a Harvard Magazine reporter and why the combustion engine is outmoded.

The Harvard reporter wrote: "The most wasteful example is a gasoline-powered car driven in the city. The inefficiency begins with the engine itself, subject to the Carnot limit (the thermal engine loss exceeds 65 percent of the energy in the fuel burned), and it mounts from there: drive train loss 4 percent, parasitic (frictional) losses 6 percent, and other engine losses, 11 percent. In the final analysis, says Prentiss, just 16 percent of the energy actually moves the wheels. "

So, put it this way: you put in six gallons of gas, and only one moves the car. That is inefficient.

I had to impart this sad story to some American car dealers. It was a funny day in June, and an unusual request for an after dinner speech on the green economy. That was the day I spoke to the Minority Chrysler Dealers Association of America, all 90 of them or so.

The group had gathered at the swanky Broadmoor Hotel in Colorado Springs, all affable, hard working family men and women, who had earned their way into their Chrysler dealerships.

This is what you call an awkward moment. Me and 90+ car dealers, to whom I have to impart that the combustion engine is a thing of the past. Needless to say, dinner went well until I explained that the cars they were selling were—well, only 16% efficient, and not the future of the economy. Truth hurts, I guess.

This is not to say that the form of a Jaguar is not beautiful and could not be adapted to a Tesla. It is to say that an electric engine is 60% efficient, or four times as efficient as a combustion engine. And that is why we know the era will end, a matter of energy and physics.

That is, if our common sense and physics can overcome the stupidity of greed.

A Visit to Detroit: Land of Pontiac

If Detroit is an example of what is to come, the future does not look good. The place of the river, in *Anishinaabemowin* is called *Wawi-iatanong*, "Where the river goes round."

For our ancestors it was a great place of gathering. This is the land of Pontiac, the Odawa Chief who later led in a battle against British occupation and encroachment. To most Americans, lacking in a proper North American history, Pontiac became immortalized as a car.

As Bill Wylie-Kellermann would write in his beautiful historical essay: "The Europeans called the river d'Etroit, 'the Straight' and it was for them a channel for transport of firs, then timber, coal and ores. It was defended with forts and came to mark a border between nations. Eventually it washed their machines and carried off their petrochemical wastes."

This would mean the water would end up in the river, and then in the ocean. Over the long term, this will not work out for most of us.

So it is that I decided to go to Detroit. I wanted to go there because Marathon Oil is a third owner of a proposed Sandpiper pipeline which would cross our reservation and the watershed of our largest wild rice bed.

I wanted to see where the oil was to go and to understand "Need."

This "Need" is what I refer to, as the Minnesota Public Utilities Commission, on June 5, approved a Certificate of Need for the Sandpiper, to serve Marathon Oil as the largest client of the pipeline. Marathon is also an owner, and the public was not allowed to know if there were any more contracts for oil which needed to be fulfilled by this pipeline, the Enbridge/Marathon proposal. That would be a trade secret. So, I decided to go see where the oil would go that the big companies want to pump across my rice beds. And, I decided to see who Marathon was.

It was also my time to visit the Motor City, the great tribute to the fossil fuel era, and the car. Greeted by a water tower in Detroit that said *Free the Water*, it seems like things have not gone well here in the birthplace of the American automobile industry.

The glory days for Detroit were the post-war 1950s. A retooled America made cars the future including Pontiac. The Pontiac was first made in 1926 in Michigan.

Detroit—and in fact Michigan—represented the American dream in many ways, but it did not come easily. Certainly not to Native people, and African Americans.

The union movement had built a strong working class, one with security and the highest median income and the highest rate of home ownership in the 1950s. That working class was multi racial. Not that this was an easy path. Racism existed in the working class, culminating in the 1943 race riots. In the industry, Kellermann would write:

"Black folk were consigned to the foundry and the most dangerous or back breaking work, and at the lowest pay. (At a Packard plant), three Black workers were promoted on the basis of seniority and 25,000 white defense workers walked out. Outside, circling the factory, were vehicles with loudspeakers blaring, 'Better for Hitler and Hirohito to win the war than to work next to a nigger.'"

Things got worse, and it was like dynamite. In the riots which followed, thirty five people died. Of the 17 killed by police, all were black, some 1,900 people were arrested and 675 had serious injuries. It is said that change does not come without struggle. Yet through this, a working class, a multi racial working class which was unionized was born.

Once the wealthiest city in America, known as the "arsenal of democracy," in 1960 Detroit was the fourth largest city in the US, with a population of two million.

Corporate greed and accommodating federal legislative policies began the process of transformation, and the dismantling of Michigan's American Dream. During the 1960s and '70s, Japanese cars began entering American markets. Japan had a plan: put American auto companies out of business. Congress seemed to welcome this new foreign competition with open arms. Many of these same government and anti-union policies pushed American auto giants like Ford, GM and Chrysler out of the country.

NAFTA put the final nail in the coffin, making it too expensive for American auto companies to manufacture cars in the United States. Knowing they could no longer produce competitively, American automakers shipped their jobs to Canada and Mexico. Not to oversimplify the stupidity of American economic planning, but—twenty years after NAFTA's passage—on July 18, 2013, the city of Detroit filed for Chapter 9 bankruptcy.

As my family drives into Detroit in 2015, it is hard to imagine the Motor City's glory days. Abandoned and burned out, tagged houses are in abundance, and, as one reporter would write, "Detroit has become nothing more than a devastated landscape of urban decay with a current population of 714,000 whose unemployment rate at the height of the recession was as high as 29 percent, and has only decreased due to the rapidly decreasing population."

No Water, No Life

In March of 2014, the Detroit Water and Sewerage Department (DWSD) announced that it would start cutting off the services of homes, schools and businesses that were at least 60 days overdue or more than $150 behind. This was to effect 30,000 households, the vast majority of whom were African American, low income and unemployed. They live in a city which declared bankruptcy in the middle of one of the wealthiest countries in the history of the world.

The Blue Planet Project, an organization promoting access to clean water, submitted a critical report to the UN's Special Rapporteur on its resolution for the right to safe drinking water and sanitation. Water is a basic human right. City of Detroit officials say that the cash is needed to pay for aging pipes and infrastructure. "We have 90 water main breaks that are running in the city right now that we're trying to fix," said Bill Nowling, spokesperson for the state-appointed Detroit Emergency Manager, Kevyn Orr.

Nowling says there are lots of examples of neglected infrastructure. "We have stations that are 80 years old that can't even fit the fire trucks. They have to park the fire trucks outside the station when they're not on a call because they won't fit into the fire station."

The problem was not new. In a statement issued in 2003, Congressman John Conyers noted: "Immediate action must be taken to ensure the health and well-being of Detroit residents who are being deprived of these basic services. No citizen should have to endure what people are facing day after day during the coldest winter months. It is critical to impose a moratorium on the cut-offs. Human rights must come first."

By 2014, things were a lot worse. The Michigan Welfare Rights Coalition estimated that 30,000 households will be subject to closures in the austerity measures of this city without infrastructure and cash. Some folks, however, can pay for infrastructure. Those folks are corporate.

Enter Marathon "Blood Oil" and Emma Lockridge

"A reporter asked me what tar sands smell like, and it smells like death. And that's what it is." –Emma Lockridge

In 2012, Marathon Oil completed a $2.2 billion upgrade on their 81-year-old Detroit facility to process tar sands bitumen into oil. Marathon's expansion promises to create 135 jobs and generate millions of dollars in tax revenues, the company says. Even more important, Marathon says, it will help ensure that Michigan's only oil refinery will operate well into the future.

The upgrade also retooled the facility to enable the company to process tar sands oil. Company data confirms that processing tar sands bitumen into oil, because of its' composition, will increase discharges.

The Marathon oil refinery is in Boynton, Michigan, zip code 48217. It is known as Michigan's most polluted zip code. This is where I met Emma Lockridge. Emma's a woman about my age, retired now from her administrative work. Her daughter just graduated from Harvard Business School and is working in South Africa. Emma lives in the house she was raised in, along with her mother in Boynton, Michigan, right in the shadow of the Marathon Oil refinery.

I first heard Emma speak in a Detroit church basement, where local citizens had gathered to talk about new challenges in their communities, including, no water, fossil fuel pipelines and big refineries. My son and I went to Detroit because we wanted to see what the Marathon refinery looked like, and what "need" according to Enbridge would be met, and how the PUC of Minnesota determined that this need over-rides the health of our community. So I sat and listened, and Emma stands up. She is wearing a shirt that says "Blood Oil "on it, with a picture of the Marathon Refinery.

"We have a Tar Sands refinery in our community and it is just hor-rific... We are (a) sick community. We have tried to get them to buy us out. They keep poisoning us. And we cannot get them to buy our houses." –Emma Lockridge

She is holding a sign that says: "Marathon Buy my House."

The next day our family drives to Emma's house. It's hard not to see the refinery, in all the black pipes, and the bursts of orange and black soot pumping into the air. We drive around a bit until we find her neighborhood, and wait. It's a clean neighborhood, every step is swept, every tree is trimmed, and Emma's house is on a corner. She join us and we talk for about an hour outside.

In the meantime, my son got sick from the fumes and had to go into an air-conditioned car. My traveling companion, "Fractivist" Shane Davis, broke into hives from the chemical sensitivity he developed from exposure to the fracking industry. I persevere.

"I can't hardly breathe here," Emma says to me. "Look at this stuff on my house." True to form, there's an orange and black soot on her white house, looking something like the Marathon Refinery discharge. Emma continues to speak, we laugh a lot, share common interests about working on issues, and a love of Bonnie Raitt.

"I have had kidney failure. Neighbor died of dialysis. Neighbor next door with dialysis. Neighbor across the street has kidney failure. The chemicals in our pipelines and are in our water will be the same chemi-cals that come through your land and can break and contaminate. We have cancer, we have autoimmune illnesses, we have MS, we have chemicals that have come up into our home through the sewer. Those are from the companies, they end up in the public water and sewer system... They are poisoning us." –Emma Lockridge

Pointing to Marathon, she says: "In 2011, when Marathon had almost completed its upgrade, it did buy out over 275 homes in Oakwood

Heights, another neighborhood on its fence line, to create a green buffer zone. Marathon moved people from Oakwood Heights, and left us at the refinery. The people who they bought out were primarily white. The black people are left to die.... We want them to buy out our houses, so we can live."

The state of Michigan maintains that each industrial plant in and around the area emits no more of the chemicals and soot particles than allowed in their self-reporting monitoring. And, that there is far less pollution there now than there was decades ago, before many plants installed modern pollution controls.

Emma and University of Michigan scientists point out the lack of cumulative impact assessment, and the disproportionate impact on children. "There are no minimum requirements in Michigan for how far away from homes and schools industry must be," said Paul Mohai, one of the professors who did the University of Michigan study explains. "Kids are most at risk, because pound for pound, they breathe in more air," he said. "Yet, they don't have a say in where they live or go to school."

At least 14 states, including California, Georgia and Washington, prohibit or limit how close schools can be to sources of pollution, highways, contaminated sites or pipelines, according to a 50-state survey done for the Environmental Protection Agency in 2006.

California and Oregon take into account the cumulative impact of pollution in decisions on permits for industry. Michigan does not yet. Michigan's regulatory avoidance is particularly problematic in terms of environmental justice. Studies are far from complete, but it turns out it's hard to get a study done.

"We have asked the EPA for air monitors for the past five years," Emma tells me. "We finally got one air monitor." As we are standing there watching, a low-flying helicopter comes over the neighborhood. The next day, a group of men wearing EPA vests comes and looks at the sewers. "It was an accidental discharge", they told us. That would be a discharge into a public sewer system by the Marathon refinery.

Our family visits with Emma a bit more, and I ask her to come to the White Earth and Mille Lacs reservation for formal hearings sponsored by the tribal government on the Enbridge proposed lines. When I get her to northern Minnesota, she says to me, "I can breathe now. I can really breathe. You don't know what it's like to not be able to breathe."

At the tribal hearings, a smartly dressed Black woman goes to the front of the hearing to testify. She is far from home, but acknowledges that her life is now linked to the Anishinaabe people through a pipeline, a permit, and a company or two: Enbridge and Marathon.

"When you step outside now, it feels as if you strike a match the air will explode. The chemicals come into our homes, come into our basements and we smell it all the time. Don't let them put that pipeline here. I mean, it has always been bad, but not this bad...The air is just unbearable. It's like living inside a refinery." –Emma Lockridge

From a Tipi to a Tesla

So there is my story. In light of my recent trip to Detroit, I am wondering about the end of the fossil fuel industry. I am wondering because if this is what success looks like, and fifty years later it is Detroit, it is not what I want.

I would like to see an elegant society, not a city of decay, and sorrow. I would not like to contribute to Emma Lockridge's misfortune, and I would like to not be driving the last car. What to do? Mara Prentiss is full of hope. From her ivory tower, she is sure that an energy transition is underway, but needs a push. Prentiss argues that the inefficiencies will need to be phased out, and since transportation is only 20% efficient, and consumes the most energy after electric power generation, we will need to enlighten that sector and motivate it to move past the poisoning of Emma.

What is a sensible path forward? Mara Prentiss says she wrote *Energy Revolution* out of a conviction that information is a powerful way to help people make decisions about energy use, whether as citizens or consumers. I believe in our intelligence and our humanity.

I am for solar, I am for wind, hemp, efficiency and I am for the future. This past week, some daring guys did a solar flight part way around the world, and that Tesla guy Evon Musk has released a new battery for houses. Last year, I went to Washington DC, rode a horse to oppose the Keystone XL pipeline, and hung out in my tipi on the Washington mall. A gentleman came over to the tipi, stuck his head in the door, and asked if I would like to go for a ride in his car. He said it was a Tesla.

After negotiating with my 15-year-old sons, I followed the guy to his car. That car was a red four-door Tesla. No combustion engine, no six gallons of gas for one gallon of movement. I walked out of my tipi into a Tesla. That's what I want me and Emma to do. We want to go from a tipi to a Tesla.

— *Winona LaDuke, (Manominike Giizis, Wild Rice Making Moon 2015, Round Lake)*